"Jesus told them,
'This is what I kept telling you while I was still with you:
Everything must be fulfilled that is written about me
in the Law of Moses, the Prophets and the Psalms.'"
Luke 24:44

THE LINE

Finding God's BIG story
and your place in it

by
Henry Brooks

PRAVDA PRESS

REVOLUTIONARY BOOKS

REVOLUTIONARY BOOKS

First Published in English by Pravda Press in 2011.
PRAVDA PRESS – *Revolutionary Media*
Latterhead House, CA13 0RR, UK.

ISBN

Typesetting by A. Muggins & Co.
Cover design by ab@alexboustead.com

This book is dedicated to my church family at
Cockermouth Christian Centre

(for it is by travelling with them that I
discovered what I now share with you.)

Special Thanks
to Colin and Carol for all that
you've been to Ruth and I

also
many thanks to Derek, Helen,
Phillippa, Rob, Ian and my amazing wife,
for your hours of editing and theological balance.
(And for introducing me to the semi colon!)

Contents

General Notes on using this devotional guide to 'THE LINE'

If you want to receive the maximum benefit from this devotional aid, you will need to 'Journal' your own journey with the Lord as you travel with the characters in this book. As with almost anything; the more you put in, the more you'll get out of it.

You might also find it helpful to write out the questions first and then record any immediate answers, but also leaving space in case the answers come later. We feel this is particularly important as it will relieve pressure from you in feeling that you must somehow force an instant response.

Having said all this, do be prepared to sit before the Lord with your pen ready and record those 'almost' unconscious trains of thought that come in response to your requests. (For more on this subject the author recommends 'Dialogue with God' by Mark Virkler)

Remember to record the date too, for to dignify the story that God is writing with your life is in itself an act of faith. In so doing you are a witness against the inherent despair and meaninglessness of this post-modern era; you are declaring before angels and men that God has a purpose for your life, something unique and beautiful. Praise His name.

Bible references are generally in standard King James, if not they will be the author's paraphrase or translation using Strong's analytical concordance.

Introduction

The Master Plan

'The women of Genesis all got into THE LINE at the risk of their own lives.'

As he spoke the words my friend Colin leant far forward from the edge of the tuffet, glasses poised on the brink of his nose. I don't know where or in what era he had purchased these spectacles but, as far as any of us knew, their arms had never actually been able to reach the back of his ears and were therefore permanently threatening to fall. And if they had, it would have surprised none of the fifteen or so gathered at our midweek Bible study. 'Every single one,' he repeated, now snatching the spectacles and pointing them towards his Hebrew text.
It was only then that the words hit me like a juggernaut.

Was that true? Was there a story here?

I liked stories, who doesn't, but was this *the* story? The story behind all stories? I'd been reading and preaching from the Bible for nearly fifteen years. I knew a thing or two – so I thought – but that night things were to change. We were to spend over a year studying the book of Genesis with Dr Colin Slater, verse by verse, story by story and by the end of that time I was hooked, utterly and completely. It was not so much Colin's grasp of Hebrew, or physics, or archaeology, biology, chemistry, anthropology, though any one of these was treat enough for the hungry listener. No, for me – as a 'narrative junkie' – it was primarily the human story, the epic scale, the beauty, the heroism, even the pain and personal tragedy.
The story of the line is God's story, God's unlikely solutions to his biggest problem; quite literally, 'What do you do with a renegade creation who don't want to know you?' It is God sharing his dream with us, his dream for a family of people who love righteousness. It didn't really start with Abraham, but with

the lines of Seth and Cain, one going one way, one the other, though for the purposes of our story we will start with God's dream for the world and how he involved a childless couple. It was a dream he had a hard time sharing with most others and I know how that feels to a small degree.

You see, my proper job is trying to be the Orson Welles of landscape architecture. Very often I arrived at a client meeting with my designs and big dreams only to watch the client or the planners tapping their pencils. I wanted glass frontages, LED floor lighting, outdoor exhibition spaces under tensile structures and state of the art street furniture, they wanted a steel-clad shed and gravel car park. I once designed a prime forty acre wetland site into a marshy 'map of the world', complete with chalet village, restaurant, shops, garden centre and working industrial museum, all of which could be viewed from above on one of the world's longest bridges. We would have floating chalets, the latest eco-technology and everything would be a new bench mark in sustainable development. I was already dusting down the mantelpiece for my Nobel prize, or hoping at least to have my name up there with some of the landscape design greats of all time. The dream was reduced to one gravel car park, one building with museum and café around an existing pond, in fact even the ornamental shrub beds on the plan were eventually replaced with grass by the time the scheme could pass through planning!
So like I say, trying to realize a big dream can be a frustrating exercise. I do not believe God reduced the scale of his vision as I had to, but I do think he was forced to look in what we'd consider unexpected places for his materials. As one missionary put it, 'I wasn't God's first choice for what I've done for China … I don't know who it was … It must have been a man … a well-educated man. I don't know what happened. Perhaps he died. Perhaps he wasn't willing … and God looked down … and saw Gladys Aylward … And God said – "Well, she's willing." I don't think it was any different for THE LINE, I think here again the great and the good were simply too busy to be involved, and where did that leave him?

Exactly.

And this is the story of the Old Testament; a gripping epic written through the flesh and blood lives of the most contemporary and often shocking people you could ever meet. And I do want you to really *meet* them, whether pioneer or prostitute, adulterer or asylum seeker, murderer or child killer, that they become familiar enough for you to laugh and cry with them. And as you truly see them more fully, maybe just maybe, you will also catch a glimpse of yourself again as God sees you.

I spent a lot of hours in 2008–09 doing just that myself; studying, preaching, writing songs and then another twenty-five days in the winter of 2009 writing this book. With all of it my aim was simple enough, to bring these men and women out from between the leather bindings and into your front room. I didn't pore over commentaries however, not from arrogance but rather a naïve belief that the Lord wanted to use my eyes, my perspective and the experience of my friends and church family to be his avenue for communicating this story to a new generation.

The Lord called me to this ministry late one night on a mountainside shortly after my conversion. There I was, sleeping out under the stars by a good camp fire reading the little red 'Good News Bible' that my mother had bought me earlier that morning. I had come away to the wilderness to seek God, it was the first time I had ever really read a Bible myself and then – bam! – there it was, I was in Ephesians 4:11 and I turned the page right after the word 'pastors' and there, staring at me with lightning force was also the word 'teachers'. And then and there I knew how God had gifted me and what he wanted of me. The catalyst that saw this happen in earnest was probably the diagnosis of cancer back in 2009 and although it was the 'Will Houston Mysteries' that came first, I believe it is this book more than any other I have written to date is a discharging of that original commission. At the time of publication (July 2011) a CT Scan has shown up some unknown spots on my lungs and it has reminded me yet again how urgent the hour is; how precious each day. I do ask the reader to exercise some grace in overlooking my shortcomings as a writer and to approach each chapter carefully *and prayerfully*. God is not beyond speaking through asses still and they are wise who still listen when asses speak! This is very much a book for disciples; for those that already know the book; for fellow 'Voyageurs' and not mere Voyeurs – for it might be renamed: '10 Steps to the Crucified Life'. If you are still a seeker or even a new disciple, please remember this, and if you find some bits hard going don't get bogged down, just move on to another section, marking those difficult bits for later – for this story is important.

And why is this story so crucial to you and me?

Because there are certain people through whom the will of God is done – not in spite of but *because* of them – I want to be that kind of person and I want it for you too. I want God to write something beautiful and authentic with my life and your life. I want to live and die around people like that, people that aren't content with 'Sunday and Wednesday' religion. He's shown us something so big, how can we live for flash cars and suburban dreams any more?

'The world has yet to see what God can do with a man fully consecrated to him. By God's help, I aim to be that man.'

These immortal words were put in the mouth of D. L. Moody by an Englishman called Henry Varley. And so too today, another Henry not only wishes to own these words but also, by the spirit of the living God, to write them into your mind and heart as well. More than that, my prayer is that you and I would live them and prove God true at his word. Who knows, perhaps one of us could even prove the first line of the quote wrong?

Henry Brooks

Author's Note:

References: There are some statistics in this book which I regret having not referenced. They were sourced ad hoc from books, articles, academic papers or on the internet over the last three years rather like one would gather flotsam on a beach; grateful for the finding but not *so* grateful as to mark the exact spot! I now realise in hindsight that this was a mistake and I beg pardon for it.

Film References: I have used quotes and references to films; but this is not to say that in every instance I am suggesting that the film itself is suitable for all Christians to watch (in some cases I have not seen the film myself).

Search the Scriptures: In matters of history or theology I speak very much as a layman coming across many things for the first time, and as such tend to have all the zeal of a 'new convert'! If you feel that I have spoken out of turn or too dogmatically on occasions please bear this in mind and exercise the necessary grace, for Jesus is far from finished with me yet. As it says in 1 Corinthians 13 'we' – that is all of us – 'see in part' and I almost daily pray for greater understanding and revelation regarding these things. I would appreciate your prayers, even as I have prayed and do pray for you as you read it. God bless you.

Sarah ——●—— **Abraham**
Isaac
Jacob
Judah
Perez
Hezron
Ram
Amminadab
Nahshon
Salmon
Boaz
Obed
King David
Solomon
Rehoboam
Abijah
Asa
Jehoshaphat
Jehoram
Ahaziah
Joash
Amaziah
Uzziah
Jotham
Ahaz
Hezekiah
Manasseh
Amon
Josiah
Jehoahaz
Jeconiah
Jehoiachin
Shealtiel
Zerubbabel
Abihud
Eliakim
Azor
Zadok
Akim
Elihud
Eleazar
Matthan
Jacob
Joseph; *the husband of Mary; the mother of Jesus; who is called the Messiah.* (Matt 1:16)

Chapter 1

Into The West <small>(Read Gen 11-23)</small>

Tom and Heather *weren't* pregnant, yet again.

Of course they'd married later than average and at her age the clock was definitely ticking anyway. But that wasn't the worst of it, no, for now the medics confirmed a new double whammy; it was not just a problem with Tom, for the doctor said Heather was also deficient in an area that made any further medical intervention unviable. 'Just face it,' the doctor said to Tom while Heather was next to him, 'you're flogging a dead horse.' She fought back the tears and clutched her stomach. A dead horse, thanks. Then through that wound in their hearts rushed the torrent of despair, it was all over.

When I saw them at the weekend I don't know whose face expressed the anguish more. For Heather, the uber-efficient, primary school teacher who knew everyone else's schedules as well as her own, it was the lack of eye contact and the odd moments when I saw those ghosts in her eyes. Heather was anything but the stereotypical 'emotional woman' but during this time she would break off conversations in mid-sentence and leave the room, eyes streaming.

And Tom, the friendly local farmer and serial cycling enthusiast? That hollow, wide-eyed expression was to me - as a husband - more terrible by half. It reminded me of pictures of Jewish fathers when the Nazis separated them from their families, desperate, helpless. He'd have done anything financially or medically possible to give Heather what her heart craved but at the last to have had that love thwarted, bound, made impotent by a cruel twist of nature, or God, it was just unspeakable. And here they both were, at the end of themselves with those all encompassing and impenetrable walls of despair growing higher by the day. For Heather the weekdays weren't so bad, work wasn't the place for displaying family photos anyway and the distraction helped, but the weekends were crushing, church particularly, to see the other young families, to take yet another Sunday school class with that yearning, empty womb that could now never be filled. Ruth and I had just conceived our fourth child but dared not tell them for fear of causing more pain. They were two of our most treasured friends and we, like they, could do nothing now but pray. I will tell you how it ended for them at the end of this chapter. It was right in the middle of Tom and Heather's struggles that I came to study the life of Abraham and Sarah for this series. I believe the Holy Spirit used the emotional struggle of my friends to show me who Abraham and Sarah really were. It is hard to explain other than to say, when I saw Tom and Heather, I just saw it, the hinge on which Abraham's story turned. I suppose I knew it before but now I felt it too and that is a whole different thing. I have already said that THE LINE was *God's answer to God's problem* but it was also the answer to Abram's problem too. J.B. Phillips gave a great truism in *'Man's extremity is God's opportunity'* and Abram's extremity proved to be his greatest asset. For the American Novelist William Burroughs it was this desperation was always the material of drastic change, and he said that only those who had the ability to leave the old places and old ways of thinking could come through such times. I often wondered whether he had Abraham and Sarah in mind.

The Modern Iron Age Family

The old idea of a toothless Bedouin just won't do at all.

The Sumerian civilization from which Abram came was the birthplace of arithmetic, geometry, astronomy, agriculture, the wheel, the arch, the plough, irrigation, the first legal code, writing and literature. Familiar to him as to us was the lunisolar calendar, bronze sculpture and delicate jewellery, leather, saws, chisels, hammers, braces, nails, pins, rings, hoes, axes, knives, arrowheads, swords, glue, boots, sandals, harpoons and even beer. Some houses excavated in Ur were seven bedroom villas with running water and central heating. When they excavated one ziggurat they found it was the tax office and yes, there were thousands of tax receipts still stored, so no surprises there. For Abram, his dad and two brothers life in the city was good, they were part of something significant, something modern and progressive. The land of Shinar – or 'the land of the lords of brightness' – would extend a burning torch to ignite every other western civilization right down to our own. If they were the seed, we are the full grown fruit. And is the Sumerian outlook any different than our '18th century enlightenment' view of things; man bringing about the endless perfection of society and himself? No, it is the same myth of Nimrod and Babel, what we now call *Modernity* – with a faint shudder – for we have seen all too clearly that when men did come of age they were anything but well adjusted adults. 'Modernity' can be broadly defined as that 200 year span of human history between approximately 1750 to 1950 (some have placed it between the fall of two walls; those of the Bastille and Berlin - again curiously exactly 200 years apart.) The great humanist and atheist narratives for human origin and future society were proved to be barren, if not down right oppressive. After the world wars, the gas chambers and Gulags the west experienced a crisis of confidence in these grandiose stories (metanarratives) and with something akin to cultural repentance there now appeared the more modest declarations summed up well by Oz Guinness,

> *'Where modernism was a manifesto of human self–confidence and self–congratulation, postmodernism is a confession of modesty if not despair. There is no truth; only truths. There is no grand reason; only reasons. There is no privileged civilisation (or culture, belief, norm and style); only a multiplicity of cultures, beliefs, norms and styles. There is no universal justice; only interests and the competition of interest groups. There is no grand narrative; only countless stories of where people and their cultures are now. There is no simple reality or any grand objectivity of universal, detached knowledge; only a ceaseless representation of everything in terms of everything else.'*

But let us not deprive Abraham and his brothers of their glowing sense of pride at the possibilities, we cannot put old heads on young shoulders. What we have learned from bitter experience was still 4000 years in the future for them. Stretching their feet before the inglenook fireside and pouring over some lunar chart or mathematical conundrum, those three brothers may have sensed the very same twinge of pride felt by other enlightened men down the ages, the satisfaction that science, technology and the cult of order would gradually evolve to eradicate the evils of mankind, spreading in its wake the glad tidings of multiculturalism, commerce and above all peace. But any such thoughts were soon dashed by events beyond the control of their ordered existence. Life in a fallen world does that sometimes, it would do it now to Abram in two devastating ways, one fast, one grindingly slow.

Living With Grief

The first was a family bereavement. It must have been harsh beyond words as an oldest son, to watch your youngest brother's life ebb away. Haran, the one he cuddled and taught to walk, the cheeky one who got away with everything he hadn't. In the film *Legends of the Fall* it is precisely this that forms the crucible of the narrative. The innocence of family life seared by the death of the youngest of three brothers and the carnage that followed. 'When Samuel died I cursed God,' says Tristan to his father (played by Brad Pitt and Anthony Hopkins). I wonder how Abram dealt with his brother's death? Did it change his view of religion? Did it bust apart the family's complacency and priorities in life? These things tend to.

In *Legends of the Fall* the film's narrator is an old Indian who had lived with the Ludlow family. Sitting round the camp fire and musing over the character played by Brad Pitt he gives that classic line which opens the trailer, 'Some people hear their own voices with great clearness and they live by what they hear. Such people become crazy or they become legend.' In a limited sense we may speculate that this dichotomy appears in the lives of Abram and his father. For it is clear from the accounts in Genesis, Joshua and Acts that both men were following some sort of voice when they set out for Canaan. In Abram's case we know it was the voice of God. In the case of his father it is less clear. Perhaps he wanted to escape the sights and sounds that reminded him of his deceased son, perhaps there were opportunities out west for men who weren't afraid to dream big and dig deep? Perhaps he too had been met by God at his point of grief and been given the same call his son had been given, who knows?

Whatever it was, Abram's dad and middle brother settled halfway to Canaan in a town called Haran. Part of me wonders whether Terah actually named the town as a memorial to his son, a memorial to grief that he just couldn't go beyond. Or perhaps when he passed through this town (the name means burning light, or to burn dry) and he was reminded again of his youngest and perhaps favourite son, and maybe then it hit Terah afresh that the *light of his life had been quenched* and, he too was *burnt dry* by the bereavement. Perhaps he felt the moon-god Terah, after whom he was doubtless named, could not protect him beyond the limits of this dusty frontier town. Maybe it was there that Terah decided to just give up and be moulded by grief rather than the unseen god, he wouldn't be the first.

And Abraham, the eldest son? What can we say of him, here in Haran so far from Ur? I think he was a city slicker, a long way from home with a lot on his mind, particularly what he would have regarded - and certainly would have been regarded by others - as failure in his private life. The overland trail to the west lay in front and civilization and human progress lay behind. If he had thoughts of quitting, he didn't let it show, but then again he was desperate and desperate people do extreme things.

Living With Disappointment

My friend Matthew had a bunch of secondary school teachers with wild names, a woodwork teacher called Mr Carpenter, a ceramics teacher called Mr Potter, a music teacher called Miss C. Sharp and a zealous R.E. teacher called Mr Virgin. Now maybe it's nice when your name fits you, I named my own children that way. Abigail means 'that which makes a father dance for joy' and this is what she has been to us and to the Lord. For my oldest son we chose Edward for a middle name, it is old English for 'generous benefactor' and that is what we see and encourage in him. This week he did a stack of 'two-penny' jobs around the house and when it turned out we'd not be able to get to the sweet shop, he slipped the money under my pillow as a surprise gift. Our second son William is as feisty and determined as they come. William is old Germanic for 'resolute defender' and you try to get a toy off him when he wants it!

But what if your name doesn't fit? What if your name is a cruel mockery of something about you that you cannot change? Like, say a Mr Lean who has a serious weight problem? Well Abram is a name like that, only worse. Think back to my friend Tom at the beginning of the chapter, supposing his name was 'exalted father', how would he like that? In a culture that idolized reproductive prowess and where sterility was a curse from the gods, that was a major problem. In a society where having children, particularly male heirs, was the sole marker, even beyond the accumulation of wealth, that gave validity and significance to your manhood, you can see what a crusher it is. Now picture Abram, the man who has succeeded with the six figure salary but was cut short by the gods in being denied the one thing outside his control, the one thing that would make his life significant. Listen to his peers and neighbours, those perhaps who had been envious of his wealth, 'Hah, exalted father, what a joke!'

To live with this year after year was a grinding trial. To have fallen so very short of the expectation of his family, particularly his father who had named him and had such aspirations. To see the fuss Grandpa made of his younger brothers' children only made it worse. His name became his reproach, a joke, a cruel irony and constant reminder that his life had come to nothing and would come to nothing. All was pointless, futile. The most he could hope to achieve was to leave a thriving business to his manager; big deal, what's the point of that? I can't help think Abram might have been glad to leave the city with its harsh whispers, insinuations, the memory of so many of Sarah's tears and of so many arguments about 'their problem'.

And Are We So Different?

As you read this can't you empathize with them? Perhaps you have had the thick black words 'failure' written large across a section of your life? You compare yourself to others and you know you have missed the mark. You had dreams, life goals, aspirations that were crushed by cruel circumstance, by your own or other people's sin even, and now there is a part of your life that is quarantined and hidden even from those closest to you. This dark cellar has the most unusual doors behind which dreams and potential are all locked tightly away. The doors are patched affairs and need regular maintenance, but help is always at hand and most of us have become adept joiners. Distraction and day to day business make up the basic door frame but the rest must be variously filled with soap operas, film idols, sports, vacations and ad hoc religious sentiment, even Freudian psychoanalysis has helped some, whilst others have found straight medication or all out drug and alcohol addiction made an effective membrane.

British children have a head start in this department, we rank just behind Japan as the most secular nation on earth and our education system is so 'effective' now that over half the children leave with no sense of purpose whatever for their lives. I don't trust the statistic, I suspect at least another 49% are blagging or haven't fully considered the question. (I have written more about a Christian response to secular education in my book 'First Contact'.) Of course it is obvious that a purely materialist world view allows for no meaning or purpose, 'just blind pitiless indifference', but even so it is staggering that we can anaesthetize half a generation in one swoop from even dreaming that their life could be something lasting and significant. It is not new, it was the same monumental conclusion Picasso made after 1909; human life in an atheistic world has no meaning, it is absurd. It was a sonic boom that reverberates in our own ears a century later. First the artists laughed at 'all those serious little men who thought their lives really had any significance' and then later they wept for all humanism had cost us. What the writer Tolstoy called the 'quest for meaning' or what Ernest Becker called 'cosmic significance' has been swept away if there is no God, no absolute, no *universal* truth to give meaning to the *particulars* of a human life. The atheist Stephen Jay Gould admits that we do yearn for a higher meaning but, he assures us, none exists. Neitzsche insists that all future truth claims are just power plays; Freud, that all religious claims are just guilt projections, though in both cases Jesus Christ was annoyingly impossible to deconstruct according to their paradigms – but that is another story and I mustn't get sidetracked. What concerns us here is the gaping loss of meaning forced on us and our children by modernity and post-modernity. Now I'm not saying we can't blag our way through life, we can. We can all cobble some narrative together to reel off at parties, something that makes us sound important – I know I can – but there usually comes that crisis moment (sometimes in midlife) when all those patched up doors look inadequate.

In effect we might say, 'Oh sure, I dreamed great things when I was younger but that seems an age ago now, I grew up, it's a tough world, I'm *more realistic* now. I've been handed these cards and hey, it's not a great hand but it's better than Jo Blogs down the road. I'll play 'em the best I can and find fulfilment vicariously through my TV soaps, movie heroes and my kids, it'll be a better world for them, you know. Hey, did I tell you, Johnny got top of the class? I'm gonna get him that new iPhone I promised.'

The cry of Ecclesiastes echoes throughout every news bulletin and TV programme we watch, 'all is meaningless without God'. But the question for us is, can God do for me what he did for Abram? And of course, will I have the 'faith and patience' to be shaped by his plan and not by this culture or my circumstances? And, if he's such a specialist in salvage operations, what can he do for me anyway?

The Call

> *Now the LORD had said unto Abram, 'get thee out of <u>thy country</u>'* (Literally that which is firm, i.e. familiar, comfortable, stable, essentially your culture) *'and from <u>thy kindred</u> and from thy <u>father's house</u>',* (i.e. leave behind the benefits of your family name, connections and protection) *'unto a land that I will shew thee.'*
> Genesis 12:1

Whatever apprehension Abram might have felt, we can be sure that for Sarai the leaving of all those things mentioned above would be felt ten times over. Most men are internally wired for adventure, most women are not. In the days of the early American pioneers that triumph of testosterone over serotonin led many men to seek a better life beyond the frontier, but there again it was women who made the greater sacrifice, not just the burying of children along the overland trails but the isolation of the backwoods cabin or prairie farm. One woman remarked affectionately that the chickens were her only companions for months on end. I realize Sarah had servants but we should not overlook the enormity of all her exodus from Haran would mean. To risk all they had inherited and worked for by going to live in the ganglands is an extraordinary gamble. And remember, she had to trust that her husband had heard right, the call did not come to her direct. I mean, suppose I said to my wife that God wanted us to liquidate our assets, sell our house, pay off our mortgage, buy a motor–home and move to Mosside in Manchester, or the Bronx or Gaza because, 'God's going to give it to us someday'. Would she phone the estate agent or the doctor? Sarah risked her life and everything she had, to do the will of God. Her motivation is spelled out in 1 Peter 3, where Peter encourages Christian women to copy Sarah in showing their faith to God by getting behind their husbands, 'whose daughters you are too by accepting this duty and not giving up when it scares you.'

So Sarah's motivation was faith in God's ability to solve their problem. Her desperation led her face to face with God. And it is always just us and this unseen God too; always has been, always will be, just sometimes it can appear more that way than others. Sometimes our veil of control is shown for what it is. For Tom, Heather, Abram and Sarai it was fertility; for you it will be something similar or different; a brick wall, insurmountable, impenetrable – unemployment, relational crises, financial cliff hangers, medical impossibilities. But in other ways, this dark alley can be one of liberation for it exposes the impotence of all our technology and progress; these little gods of which we have become as much the subjects as the possessors. For once in our lives our impotence is left naked before his omnipotence and, as Alexander Solzhenitsyn reminds us, 'when you've robbed a man of everything, he's no longer in your power – he's free again.' Free indeed, for it is only here in the dead–end alley that most men will ever think of looking up.

And for those who do look up there is the call 'out' of where they have settled. Always out, always away from their 'comfort zone'. For Israel it was Egypt, for Peter it was the boat, for Elisha it was his career, for Abram it was what men call 'civilization'. And this is the call for us too; as Peter said to the Jews, 'save yourselves from this perverse and corrupt generation'. The Message renders it 'get out of this sick and stupid culture' and when I use the word 'culture' in this book (or 'civilisation') it will unavoidably have a negative connotation because I wish – in part at least – to fill those words with what is usually called 'the world' in other parts of the New Testament. This is not to say that every facet of collective human behaviour is inherently evil for in many ways men can still reflect their Creator's image, even now. (Revelation 21v26 says that the 'glory and honour' of each nation (literally ethnic group) will be brought into to the New Jerusalem.) But neither let us fall into the opposite error, for it seems to me that the great, unspoken lie is that God will somehow reform western culture or some religious denomination. He will not, he transforms yielded individuals. 'The west is just a place on the map, not a way to live,' says the mountain man Jedediah Smith in the 2005 film, *Into the West*. How very apt. To be salt and light may impact the culture well enough but the objective must be 'that they may ... glorify your father who is in heaven.'

The culture itself is always in decay, it cannot be reused, only displaced by a stronger one. I'm not suggesting we all join monasteries; to be in the world but not of it, is a delicate business. Paul's advice to 'use the things of this world as if not absorbed in them' takes abundant grace, but such grace is freely on offer. I don't want to appear austere or load anyone under a wave of condemnation; I believe the Lord is fully sympathetic to the cultural pressures we face that seek to suffocate obedience to him. But nor can we use that as an excuse. Secular humanism is a dry river bed waiting to be filled and no other world view or religion has a credible alternative to what we have been shown. The Globalists may struggle on to unite the world for the sake of peace but they will fail. In the meantime Jeremiah's words to the oppressed Jews at the time of the captivity, 'to seek the welfare of the city' is still sound advice; we don't need to 'tare pull' or attack the culture, but merely model the new citizenship as fully as we can.

> ' ... *Your fathers dwelt of old time beyond the River, even Terah, the father of Abraham, and the father of Nahor: and they served other gods. And I took your father Abraham from beyond the River...*' Josh. 24:2,3

Notice God had to bring Abram across a river of separation. The Euphrates for him was like the Rubicon was for Caesar, or the Mississippi was for the early pioneers; beyond those waters lay the dangers but also the great possibilities. We shall also see this when we come to study Salmon (who married Rahab), part of that new generation who crossed the Jordan with Joshua. The river here, like the Red Sea and baptism, also comes to be a powerful symbol of death and rebirth. To walk with a walking God is to travel light, old baggage must be ditched. On one side of the river Abram was part of a multicultural pagan society. On the other side he would be establishing another type of culture, one whose builder and maker is God. The idols were left at the water's edge and perhaps also the old ways of thinking, particularly 'that civilization, technology, progress and education were the answer to the human problem.' The answer lay somewhere entirely different and unexpected – in Sarah's barren womb.

I want you to ask yourself, what might need to die in your life before God can really use you? Don't say it must be a bad thing either, usually it is not. Friend, if I may be blunt with you I will say this; your major sin right now will almost certainly be that you have made 'good things into ultimate things'. Its called idolatry and it ranks at the top of the ten commandments. If you are willing to at least signal to God that you are prepared to have your career, leisure time and middle class aspirations pruned, it is a substantive start. One of my best friends was pulled from the worship rota at our church; he submitted that to

God and before he knew it he was gushing with songs which were later greatly used and recorded. My own ministry came forth through a similar baptism. My life was being threatened by a highly charged psychopath, my business by a hungry claims solicitor (not sure which was worse). At the same time I was unjustly slandered in public by a senior Christian minister to whom I'd submitted my gifting and then on top of that came the diagnosis of cancer. I'd like to report that under this – and a raft of crushing financial pressures – that my faith was always that 'Wow, God must be doing something wonderful', but my wife might get to read this someday!

The seeds of what we want must fall to the ground and die before what he wants can grow. Most people do want to serve God but only in an advisory capacity. That was once the case with a young woman who lived a just a few miles from us in the little village of Broughton. It was a hundred plus years ago and Amy lived in a big house that overlooked the broad lower reaches of the Derwent River. As a girl she felt God had not answered her very simple prayer, to change her eyes from brown to blue. It was such a small thing, why would God possibly not grant her request? Years later she got her answer after becoming a missionary to India where part of her ministry was smuggling young girls out of forced temple prostitution. She went unnoticed because her eyes were brown, like all other Indians. She later wrote,

> Give me the love that leads the way,
> The faith that nothing can dismay,
> The hope no disappointments tire,
> The passion that will burn like fire,
> Let me not sink to be a clod:
> Make me Thy fuel, Flame of God.

The woman's name was Amy Carmichael and her epic God–story is now part of history. I want to encourage you, friend, if you are struggling through weakness and disability, you are not abandoned. Part of showing your heavenly father that you trust him for the future is living with gratitude now. Check out Nick Vujicic on the web; he was born without arms or legs and is now an inspirational evangelist. If you can use that poem as a prayer with a sincere heart, then you cannot be far from the centre of God's plan for your life. In the end, this is all that matters.

But I also think it is well worth stressing that the path to the meaningful or significant life is more than just the clean break and good start that we saw with Abraham. The Bible knows no meaning of the word *faith* as most Christians understand it today, for we have cut away at least 90% of its meat.

Perhaps we need to use the old English word *fidelity* again, for it is much closer to what is meant. To have *fidelity* in Christ encompasses not just the altar call but also the life of obedience that follows. I am not saying the first response is unimportant, just that it does not in itself fulfil the Bible meaning. 'Oh, but now I'm worried,' you say, 'where would I get this faith from, mine is so wavering and fickle?' D.L. Moody had that same question;

> 'I prayed for Faith, and thought that some day Faith would come down and strike me like lightning. But Faith did not seem to come. One day I read in the tenth chapter of Romans, *"Now Faith cometh by hearing, and hearing by the Word of God."* I had closed my Bible, and prayed for Faith. I now opened my Bible, and began to study, and Faith has been growing ever since.'

But reading is only part of the answer, for what we read we must prove to be true in everyday life. It is called the walk of faith and it always involves the pruning of our flesh. Abram would find that the pruning work of this unseen God was an entirely ongoing and relentless process. First came the long wait, twenty-five years, that he should learn to hope beyond hope. That's a long time by any measure. Then came further pruning; *'Oh that Ishmael might live before you'* (Gen 17:18). But God doesn't need our best efforts, our DIY mentality, either the work is supernatural and eternal, or else it is wood, hay and straw, destined to perish. Next came the fulfilment in Isaac and the greatest shock of all; *'Take your Son, your only Son whom you love'* (Gen 22:2). God even asks Abraham to give up the fulfilment of the promise. It's a shock that many believers have felt since, for even at a time when we think we have it all together and finally can chart God's plan for 'our gifting and ministry', we hear the sound of those shears once again. Everything must be put on the altar and I do not think any of us are yet aware how much we may be asked to give up in the future. Perhaps that is a good thing, for he is very gracious and knows we are like grass. And then again, doesn't it say in Hebrews 11:8 *'By faith Abraham ... went out, not knowing whither he went.'* As Oswald Chambers once remarked, *'Faith never knows where it is being led, but it loves and knows the One who is leading.'*

For Abram it would mean three things in particular; **a new name, seven promises** for the future and also **a new revelation of God**. They are worth looking at in some detail for what they contain for you and me too.

A New Name

> 'And when Abram was ninety years old and nine, the LORD appeared
> to Abram , and said unto him, I am the Almighty God; walk before me,
> and be thou perfect (can also mean, sincere or have an open face).
> And I will make my covenant between me and thee, and will multiply
> thee exceedingly. And Abram fell on his face: and God talked with him,
> saying, As for me, behold, my covenant is with thee, and thou shalt be a
> father of many nations. Neither shall thy name any more be called
> Abram, but thy name shall be Abraham; for a father of many nations
> have I made thee. And I will make thee exceeding fruitful, and I will
> make nations of thee, and kings shall come out of thee. And I will
> establish my covenant between me and thee and thy seed (seed
> singular, i.e. Christ according to Paul in Gal 3:16) after thee in
> their generations for an everlasting covenant, to be a God unto thee,
> and to thy seed after thee. And I will give unto thee, and to thy seed
> after thee, the land wherein thou art a stranger, all the land of Canaan,
> for an everlasting possession; and I will be their God.' Genesis 17

From just Exalted Father to Father of many nations: there is an expansion
from the blessing Abram would be to his own family circle to what he would
be internationally, far beyond even the highest aspirations of his earthly
parents. We see the same pattern in the renaming of Sarai also.

> 'And God said unto Abraham, As for Sarai (My Princess) thy wife,
> thou shalt not call her name Sarai, but Sarah (Princess).' Genesis 17:15

Again, her ministry and ability to be a blessing moves from the personal to the
international. In like manner, none of us knows the level of blessing we may
impart to others in the future, but we can be sure that those who make it their
prayer will see it increase. But there is more to renaming, for with it God also
imparts his nature to the renamed. We will see this in the life of Jacob and
then again Peter; God literally 'calls the things that are not (don't exist) as if
they already are'. In Peter's case it was possibly the fickleness and instability
seen in his original name Simeon (or reed, weedy). It is a character weakness
we can all claim, and therefore take courage from, as Jesus replaces it with
Petros, something solid and suitable for building. His new name was in line,
not with what he was at that moment but what God would make him. And
what about us? In Jesus' only recorded letters, we find some startling
revelations about Christians who overcome as Abraham did.

> 'To him that overcometh will I give ... give him a white stone, and in
> the stone _a new name_ written, which no man knoweth saving he that
> receiveth it'. Revelation 2:17

And also later on,

> 'Him that overcometh will I make a pillar in the temple of my God, and
> he shall go no more out: and I will write upon him the _name of my God,_
> (Who you belong to) and the _name of the city of my God,_ (Where
> you belong) which is new Jerusalem, which cometh down out of heaven
> from my God: and I will write upon him _my new name _(Who you
> have become)'. Revelation 3:12

So take heart, you may never have been able to measure up to the expectation
of your family or peers, or church even, but God promises he can surpass it all
by the new names and character he imparts when you trust in him.

The Seven Promises

If you find it hard to claim some of the following promises from Genesis 12
for your own life then please remember the following passage. You are linked
to Abraham in more ways than you know.

> 'So get your head round this; it's only those who show Abraham's fidelity
> that are his spiritual descendants. The scriptures foretold that God had
> a similar "faith–journey" to freedom for other people outside Abraham's
> family, hence the great news he was given way back, "In you all ethnic
> groups will be blessed." But remember, it's only those which model
> Abraham's fidelity that get blessed like he did.' Galatians 3:7–16

1. 'I will make of you a great nation' – Of course, the 'nation' bit not only
refers to the overturning of their fertility problem but the transforming of it
into something beyond Abraham's wildest dreams. God is in the business of
making beautiful things out of broken situations and people; it is worth asking
him what he has in mind for you. My dyslexia was a major issue for my
English teacher. He asked my dad to get me out of his class, my essays were
'unmarkable'. My father pointed out that the word 'unmarkable' itself was
very bad grammar but nonetheless left me there to sweat it out. In hindsight it
would appear now that my unmarkable essays were the very things that made
me eligible for grace and for the Lord to give me the ministry that I now have.
I wonder what he will overturn and transform in your life?

2. 'I will bless you–' 'Ah, bless you' we say but this word bless (barak) does not mean a pat on the head and a few words of comfort. The Hebrew word conveys the transferral of spiritual life, power and intention. Barak literally means 'abundance and wholeness' and when you connect that meaning between a giving God and your spiritual life and gift, you can see it is an explosive combination.

3. 'I will make your name great' – Reputation and Significance run deep in all of us, particularly in men – to be known, noticed or famous. I was in the Welsh town of Llangollen for the first time in twelve years this autumn. Ruth and I took the children to the little jewellery shop where I bought her wedding ring. The woman recognized me straight away! Another time we invited a bagpiper down from Glasgow to help us on the stage at the turning on of the Christmas lights. We were going to pipe, 'Oh come all ye faithful' for the crowd but by the time he arrived he had forgotten my phone number, address and even my surname. It was a town of fourteen thousand people and we'd only been there a few years, but when he asked the first person he met whether they knew where Henry lived, they pointed him straight to my house. I seem to be the sort of person that people easily remember, but here I am talking about something deeper, something expressed in a famous musical. Remember the time when women and men wore leg warmers and sang, 'Remember my name. Fame! I'm gonna live forever, I'm gonna learn how to fly–high'; well, the cry has not changed since the fall. For Abraham's countrymen it was expressed in architecture, *'let us build a name for ourselves'.* For David's son Absalom it was a pillar for *'I have no son'.* Alexander the Great named a heap of cities after himself; the Americans did that a lot too. Julius Caesar named a month after himself. Biologists get to name insects and fungi. Some men will commit mass murder just so they will be remembered; some will be happy just to show a crumpled newspaper cutting with their name on it. The question I ask is, what's your limit? Would you be happy with a city, a university named after you? Or how about an eight-page spread in *Hello!* magazine? Okay a bit brash, well, what about an extended Wikipedia listing, would that do it for you? Michael Pritchard wryly remarked, 'No matter how rich you become, how famous or powerful, when you die the size of your funeral will still pretty much depend on the weather.' And the more we consider this the more we shout, 'No, no, it is not enough for me, I want to live on, I don't want to be forgotten.' God can meet these desires in ways that this world cannot begin to imagine or ask. The world offers stardom and the 'X factor' for a chosen few, a pattern unfortunately reflected in the Christian media also. But in the kingdom nothing is lost, for there our names and those deeds fuelled by love are remembered for all time. Noah, Daniel and Job were renowned in this way, *'Oh Daniel, man greatly beloved.'* Oh Lord God, give us hearts that yearn to be known there instead.

4. 'You will be a blessing' – The word here is 'berakah'; it means 'a gift, or a pool'. The 'Bless me' mentality that pervades the Christian consumer subculture is a horrid aberration of what life in the spirit should be. The divine principle 'it is more blessed to give than receive' is one of the central disputes in the spiritual world. God did not crush Satan the moment wickedness was found in him, but has waited down the ages to prove his way, the way of love, the way of giving, is the only way that works. Economists, political conditioners and eugenicists have all tried to force society to adopt their theories of what the grain of the universe is but each in turn proved to be disastrous. The warp and woof of this whole creation is God's all-giving love and we are wise when we work with that grain and no other. To be blessed is a given, we are sons and daughters of the most High God, but to be a blessing is a whole different ball game. In an arid world, for God to make you an oasis, to make you the answer to someone else's prayer is a tremendous privilege. It has been my prayer for more years than I can remember, 'Lord make me a blessing to your precious people.' I knew it was a prayer he could not resist and I would encourage you to make it yours, and then open your eyes to what he shows you. He'll make your home, your office, your heart a harbour for battered ships. He'll take what little loaves and fishes you think you now have, these he will bless and break to feed a multitude and before you know it, every sterile and cold area of your life will be full too.

5. 'I will bless those that bless you' – If an unbeliever offers to help you out or bless you in some way, this can be a great way for them to find an open heaven. So let them do it!

6. 'I will curse those who curse you' – Anyone worried about witches now? Oh, I realize that we should not be 'unaware of his devices' but sometimes we give the dark side way too much credit. 99% of Satan's current power against the church is given him by us; our flesh and unconfessed sin. He has a legal jurisdiction over areas of darkness; that is any area of your life, whether you consider it good or bad, that is unyielded to the Holy Spirit, or darkened by habitual sin, or where your thoughts are full of despair and hopelessness, literally disagreeing with the words of God. Balaam could not curse Israel but by getting Balak to send the pretty girls in, Balaam managed to get God to curse them for their idolatry and immorality. The lesson is clear enough for us, 'submit to God, resist the devil and he will flee from you.'

7. 'and in you will all families of the earth be blessed.' This last one may be the hardest of all to us to apply to ourselves as it literally refers to the Messiah, but suffice for us to know that we may safely trust the level of fruit that may come from our lives to God. For those who will live open-faced and authentically before him, there is no limit to what may be achieved.

A New Revelation of God

Now a deeper experience of God's character might not seem like a big deal compared to what you just read above but really *it* is the deal. This morning, Ruth and I had such a laugh reading our nine-year-old daughter's Christmas wish list. We educate our children at home and we don't have TV so her requests are usually as individual as they are free of media or peer pressure. This year's list makes classic reading:

1.   a sewing needle with a big eye
2.   some yellow felt
3.   an Egyptian necklace (with Scarab beetles on it)
4.   a blank mug and some bath bombs
5.   a long nightie and hot water bottle
6.   a tartan dress
7.   a multicoloured bauble or a snowflake Christmas decoration
8.   a secret diary with padlock
9.   a chemistry set (with test tubes and chemicals etc.)
10.   a book of practical jokes and *a realistic toy rat* (they used to sell them at Trotters animal park)

Now before you get all spiritual, 'Ah, of course, this is an illustration about the revealing of Abigail's character.' The answer is no, though it's a fair observation. (And no, I haven't managed to find a realistic toy rat yet either!) Actually what struck me most was the smallness of her expectation, asking mainly for duplicates of things she had already seen in the house, the rat excluded! Her level of expectation was based solely on what she saw rather than what was on offer, or who offered it. It's cute in a child's Christmas list but not so cute when it comes to walking with God. We can give so much emphasis on getting our ticket to heaven, or conforming our experience to what other Christians have, or even just being 'labourers together with God' that we can miss the whole point of the journey.

When John writes *'I write to you fathers (i.e. mature Christians) for you have* **known him** *who is from the beginning'*(1 John 2:13), he highlights that though younger Christians mostly know God for *what he does*, it is *who God is* that makes the journey sweet for the more mature. And so it will be for us as we follow Abraham and Sarah on the overland trail away from civilization. It is good to seek his hands but his face holds the richest blessings of all, to know as we are fully known. God's original and selfless plan in creation was to have a family that could share the riches of his mind. The dedication he has to this dream – which has been the subject of a 7000 year salvage operation – is something that the angels cannot quite get over as they sing *'Holy, Holy, Holy is the Lord God Almighty'* (Rev 4:18).

> *'Don't be scared Abram for I am your shield and exceeding great reward'* Genesis 15:1

> *'And when Abram was ninety years old and nine, the LORD appeared to Abram , and said unto him, <u>I am the Almighty God;</u> walk before me, and be thou perfect'* Genesis 17

The revelation of God's names is to have the experiential encounter with that facet of his personality. It was not just God's almighty power, provision and protection that Abraham experienced first hand, for God also revealed himself as Abraham's *'exceeding great reward'* and this, to me, is the pinnacle, for it comes directly after Abraham gives another 'exceeding great reward' away, that of the Sodomite king's wealth. Get it, you hold one while God's trying to give you the other. For beyond every blessing promised to Abraham there was something more precious. Beyond the baby, beyond the land, beyond the descendants like stars in number, beyond the lineage of great kings, even beyond the promise that one of his seed would bring blessing to every other nation on earth, there was still something better and that is to *know* Him. He is the exceeding great reward, we are His inheritance as He is ours, to know Him and experience an intimate, all-cuddling love with Him is beyond anything that this world was designed to offer. In the language of men, Jesus has already 250 names recorded in scripture; those titles which denote his character; his conquest and authority will be added to in the future, but 250 is enough to go on with now. Here lies the promised land we should pioneer, the great uncharted depths of his internal beauty, to know and prove them, to become them yourself. This is the great 'Mystery of God' to have his glory (his image) revealed in you. Billy Graham said recently in a very rare interview that his one regret was that he had not spent more time in prayer and communion with God. It will be your great joy on the journey, please don't miss it.

And what of Tom and Heather? Well, before I sat down to write this chapter I was round their place holding in my arms the most beautiful baby girl you ever saw. Weighing 8lb 12oz and fresh out of hospital this baby was conceived naturally...or perhaps we could say supernaturally. It seemed God disagreed with the best medical opinion; he often does. I took her in my arms and kissed her forehead, 'Wow, Heather, no guessing where the blond hair is from.'
She stole a cheeky glance at Tom's balding patch and said, 'Just as well.'
'Settled on a name yet?'
'Hannah.'
'Ah *grace*,' I said, 'of course, what else.'

> *Even though a root grows old in the earth,*
> *and the stem can appear to have died in the ground;*
> *Yet through the scent of water it will bud,*
> *and bring forth boughs like a plant.*   Job 14:8-9

The Pioneer

(From 'THE LINE' album, words and music by Henry Brooks)

(Abraham's song the night before leaving Haran)

Hey, I'm a city boy, my princess, never felt like pioneer man,
It was Dad who sold up and Dad who took us West to this dusty frontier town
So soon after my kid brother died, and I saw the light go from Dad's eyes
But now my Daddy's gone, and we're left here, God's call has come and I can see clearly

For the first time in our lives we have a chance to change this rut we're living in ... (oh don't you long to)
Be free from the pain, to be done with this shame and the failure that they say is our sin
You know, it wasn't the promise of more land, darling, it's just I want to see you smile again
And if this God's I've heard can give my life back its meaning, if he can bring purpose from our pain and laughter from this grieving
So come pack up your bags, darling, and let's sound the horn and get out on the trail tonight. Trade what we
cannot keep for what we cannot earn, we've got nothing to lose but our pride
Don't know all that he wants from me and you, th'things we're offering seem so little and so few
Now come, my love, won't you kneel with me, let's pledge our lives to this God we cannot see ... and say that

I'll follow this God, will see what he's like and prove that every word he said to me was true
I'm going to follow him though my flesh is crying out to stop and the doubts in my heart say it doesn't look good
though the family say I'm crazy and the friends say we're cursed, I will follow him because I am sure
that one day on the trail with someone like you is better than a lifetime filled with fear ...

Cos when I was boxed in by failure, had nowhere to turn I looked up, Lord, and saw you were there

When the world wrote us off, say we didn't make their mark, your promise came to me and blew away the fear
Now I dare to believe in a living God, who wants to get involved with me
and if he can beautify my troubled life then I won't stand in the way ...

I'm not afraid to be homeless, I don't care what they say, they can stay where they are if they like
The only thing that I want is what the world can't give, its what you've promised me Lord, right here tonight
Now Sarah, I know you're tired of dashed hopes my love, but don't you cry tonight cos I am sure,
that somewhere on this road to the promised land, He'll give us more than we've been praying for

So lets follow this living God, who heard our cry, when we'd lost faith in ourselves
When failure was written large across our lives, he chose you & me darling not someone else
For the first time in years the light's back in your eyes and honey you don't look so sad
I think that somewhere on this road to the promised land we've already found more than we ever had

I'm going to follow you, Lord, going to see what you're like and prove that every word you said to me is true
I'm going to follow though my flesh is crying out to stop and when doubts say it doesn't look good
though the family say I'm crazy and the neighbours say we're cursed, I will follow you because I know
that one day on the road with someone like you is better than a lifetime filled with fear.

Life Application Devotional Guide
*Please read the general notes at the front of this book before using this.

Chapter 1 – One Step Back

1. Name an area in your life (i.e. your ambitions, hopes and desires) that you have let die, even though you once thought it was from God.
2. How did the 'death of this dream' affect you, your relationship with those around you, and with God?
3. Prayer: (Start with thanksgiving & praise.) 'Oh Lord, My Exceeding Great Reward, is it your will to resurrect any of these desires? If so, is there anything in my life; good or bad, that needs to die in order for this to happen? Is there anything else that you want me to do? Is there any part of your character that I have not accepted yet and which you wish to show me?

Abraham
Rebecca — **Isaac**
Jacob
Judah
Perez
Hezron
Ram
Amminadab
Nahshon
Salmon
Boaz
Obed
King David
Solomon
Rehoboam
Abijah
Asa
Jehoshaphat
Jehoram
Ahaziah
Joash
Amaziah
Uzziah
Jotham
Ahaz
Hezekiah
Manasseh
Amon
Josiah
Jehoahaz
Jeconiah
Jehoiachin
Shealtiel
Zerubbabel
Abihud
Eliakim
Azor
Zadok
Akim
Elihud
Eleazar
Matthan
Jacob
Joseph; *the husband of Mary; the mother of Jesus; who is called the Messiah.* (Matt 1:16)

Chapter 2

The Mighty Heart (Read Gen 24-28)

'It's always the quiet ones.'

Both women were middle class professionals, respectable churchgoers from good families, yet both ended up marrying the same man. They weren't the only ones either. It became a national scandal.

Ann was a teacher and Emily, a lot younger, was a successful writer. The one thing they had in common – apart from the man – was their assumption that their Christian experience would never go beyond conventional 'Sunday and Wednesday' Churchianity. It's not that they doubted there was more, or that there should be women who do extraordinary things, it was just they assumed it would never be them. After all they were happy with the way things were, their careers, their social lives, their things. But that was before they met him. Now Ann was a party girl, a bubbly brunette who lived to shop and was never happier than on the dance floor. And before you say it, no, she wasn't a bad girl or anything like that, in fact she was a pastor's kid. Just a regular twenty-something, loving life and having fun. But then Ads and his mates turned up, young dudes who were already the talk of the town. The proper grown-ups said they were dangerous, crazy even. They had dangerous ideas, ones that no one had ever voiced before and Ads was the ringleader.

Ann's dad invited the gang for dinner, people said that was his biggest mistake.

Ads had been a respectable young man himself not long back, a pastor's kid too, but then he'd gone off the rails as so many second generation believers do. Some blamed his new best friend, Jacob Eames. Jake was a regular wise guy, in fact he'd led Ads into atheism. But one night Ads turned up in a pub asking for a room. The landlord said,

'Well if you're sure, but I've got to tell you that there's a guy in the next room who's dying, probably won't make it through the night.'

Ads took the room anyway but didn't sleep a wink for all the shouts and groans that came through the wooden partition. The shrieks died down to gasps and finally silence as the dawn appeared, but it was only while giving back his room keys that Ads asked the landlord about the sick man. The landlord shook his head,

'As I said, he didn't make it.'

Almost as an afterthought Ads asked his name and the landlord, thumbing the register said, 'A Mr Jacob Eames, so he said.' And then seeing Ads' eyes, 'Why, did you know him?'

This brush with death turned Ads' world upside down. Of course he turned 180° from atheism but many said that in running the other way he just went too far, but then again, young people are prone to do that. For now he would not be content with the polite, middle class Christianity of his parents, no cosy parsonage for him. He'd come face to face with eternity and that urgency made him dangerous. Banded with other like-minded revolutionaries he told America that they were going to evangelize Burma – at that time, a whole nation without the gospel. Quite literally, these radicals wanted to be the first American foreign missionaries ever. Many were against the idea: it was against government foreign policy for one thing. Many more said it was impossible, there were too few of them, they were too young with no experience. But then again some people are too young to know that certain things cannot be done. Ann fell for Ads straight off and though she never imagined in a million years that she had it in her, she consented to forsake everything else she loved in this world to serve Jesus. To gain her father's consent Ads wrote one of the most extraordinary letters of its kind in history, asking;

> '... whether you can consent to part with your daughter early next Spring, to see her no more in this world; whether you can consent to her departure, and her subjection to the hardships and sufferings of missionary life; whether you can consent to her exposure to the dangers of the ocean; to the fatal influence of the climate of India; to every kind of want and distress; to degradation, insult, persecution, and perhaps a violent death. Can you consent to all this, for the sake of Him who left His heavenly home and died for her and for you; for the sake of perishing immortal souls, for the sake of Zion, and the glory of God?'

Her father said yes. They spent their honeymoon on the boat and before her death fourteen years later, Ann had laid down for posterity one of the most remarkable examples of Christ–like virtue ever witnessed. She also gave the people of Burma translations Matthew, Jonah, Daniel and a catechism in their own language. The adventures and trials of Ads, or Adoniram Judson as we should now call him, read like a boys' own adventure. They are too numerous to recount here but suffice to say everyone should get a book about him and his co-workers. Some years after Ann's death, Adoniram married the widow of his co-worker George Boardman. Now Sarah, instead of doing the respectable thing and returning to America when George died, had pushed deeper into the jungle to bring the gospel to the Karen tribes, many of whom are still Christian today. They had ten happy years and many children but Sarah died on the ship back to America. Now Adoniram, newly bereaved and one of the most famous men in America went looking for someone to write Sarah's biography.

And so, by the 'chance' acquaintance of friends Emily entered the story. She was a career girl with an earnest heart and a bright future in literature. Being younger than some of Judson's own children, Emily had actually grown up reading Ann Judson's stories about Burma and now here she was with the legendary Mr Judson herself. Together they worked on the biography but soon the news which shook pews across the nation was out, *their* saintly pin up Mr Judson was engaged to a pretty young authoress less than half his age. Sure it was quick but he couldn't afford to hang around basking in the limelight of the Christian media circus. God had called him to live in the real world and he knew the value of a 'suitable helpmate'. And also he knew well enough the qualities which he saw in Emily, after all, he'd picked well twice before. Like Ann before her, Emily may have been less sure of her spiritual mettle than her fiancé but she took the plunge all the same and within twelve months was married and on her way to Burma. Looking out at the stormy ocean and thinking of the last Mrs Judson, whose shoes she now filled, Emily penned these words,

Blow, blow, ye gales! wild billows roll!
Unfurl the canvas wide!
On! where she (Sarah) labored lies our goal;
Weak, timid, frail, yet would my soul
Fain be to hers allied.

Though Emily knew she didn't have it, she saw what she should be and trusted God for the rest. In effect her heart was, 'I ain't got what it takes, but I know what it takes and I need God to give it to me like he did for Sarah.' She and Adoniram had two children and she outlived him by enough years to collect the materials for his biography, which became an inspiration for generations to come.

Rebecca's Mighty Heart

I focused on Emily and Ann because it is essential that we see ourselves in Rebecca; that we struggle to achieve our own exodus from the culture, the worldly mindset, the desires for success, wealth, suburbia, easy street or maybe even just to fit in and be ordinary; what the Swedes call Lagom, 'nothing to excess, just fit in,' something they see as a national virtue (rather opposite to the British).

Rebecca grew up back east on the safe side of the river with the old culture, the old mindset, the old idols. Her father Nahor was the brother who stayed put when Abraham upped sticks and pushed west. Perhaps they even had some smug satisfaction since they had heard nothing from him for so many years. I wonder how many times she and Laban would have been scolded when they showed inclinations to dream beyond the banks of that river, 'Just like your mad uncle Abe; you know he chased some pipe dream of an invisible god across that river; probably got himself killed and lost most of the family inheritance in the process.'

My friend Deborah once came to church with me soon after I started to follow Jesus. She bawled her eyes out during the worship but never came back because another friend told her he'd seen a programme about Christian cults on TV. That kind of peer pressure works on the majority but every now and again an untamed spirit breaks ranks and crosses the river. Rebecca was such a spirit.

This girl is beautiful, strong and proactive. It takes up to five hundred gallons to water ten camels, enough said! We do not see all that strength straight away but it is implied in Rebecca's response to her parents' request to delay her journey by ten days. Abraham's steward won't wait but they leave the final decision to Rebecca. In what must have been the biggest shock to the family, she says, 'No, it's okay, I'll go now,' and that less than twelve hours after she had seen to the camels. It is an enduring principle in the Bible that obedience to God's call must be prompt on occasions, all out and stubborn even in the narrowest possible way. I am talking here of heart response, not necessarily selling all we have and giving it to the poor; though as bond slaves we cannot rule that out either. Perhaps you are reading this and have resisted the call of God on your life for five years: friend, five minutes is too long. Rebecca saw it and gambled all on it. The outcome of history has never belonged to the statistician or to the man who has based the future on current trends; no, history turns on unexpected hinges and by those who dare to try the handle.

And I think this is the way the Lord can work with us too, on occasions; not just gradual progression but sudden explosions of providence, the wave that rises above the surf which we must choose to ride or not as the case may be. But it does beg the question, what was going on in Rebecca's head the morning she went to the well?

We must assume she was a teenage girl as she was not already married and, as we know, teenagers can be very perceptive at seeing through the inconsistencies of their parents' generation. The latter half of the twentieth century was characterized by such teenage rebellion as the post-war generations reacted against their parents' limited creed of 'peace and affluence'. It was not enough for them to live for and they were of course right, although where they then looked for meaning – sex, drugs, rock'n'roll and eastern religion – they found no answers, only chilling examples of wasted lives. And so too Rebecca perhaps wondered why her granddad, dad and brother were so content to live for so little. Perhaps she had secretly dreamed of something bigger than suburbia and easy street, perhaps you have too. Perhaps she had longed for a grand destiny, a grand purpose for her life, another lifestyle beyond just getting and accumulating stuff. Perhaps every time they joked about her 'mad' uncle Abe, a tingle of destiny fluttered in her chest, but then maybe she caught herself, 'Stop kidding yourself, Becky, you've not got what it takes, you could never leave all this stuff behind, it's all too much part of you now.' It was the same struggle faced by Ann, Emily and anyone who has gone all out for God. You can't let the enemy use your lack of self confidence as a weapon against you. When that voice comes just agree, 'I know I've not got what it takes but I know God has and I've seen what he can do with an open heart. I've got one life and I'm not backing down any more.'

The Bible is a vast canvas onto which God paints the most important part of human history. But God's dealings with us have not been written down as systematic theology or catechism but in human stories, stories that we can almost touch. We've got to love these stories, tragedies, biographies, histories, epics, heroics on a canvas that spans all ages. And not just stories either, we have poetry, songs and other people's letters too. And it is not just good people that are the players, usually anything but. Finding our place in this story is the reason for this book, allowing God to write you an authentic part is the whole point to life. In the story of the line we see God stitching and hammering together the raw materials of open hearts and sin-traditioned lives into something that angels will wonder at for all time. The picture will not be complete until this great artist's vision of a large family free from sin is realized. Until then God is like Bruce Springsteen in the hit song 'Working on a dream', not there yet but working towards it.

Tried by Fire

> *It is only those who go down to the sea in ships, who find their duty among the great waters; who experience how God really operates, particularly his miraculous powers when they hit the troughs.* Psalms 107:23

This verse from the Psalms sums up the course of Rebecca's life following that momentous decision. But we should note that for her – and for us if we should choose to follow her – the 'desired haven' mentioned later in that psalm is only reached through great trials. Like us, Rebecca would experience God in life's great troughs – and not just the peaks – but eventually she would have to die in faith without seeing what she had lived for. Her trials, which might be shared with many modern women, can be neatly summarized into three categories: a deferred promise, an indifferent husband and a distressing teenager.

A Deferred Promise

Rebecca knew the promises made to her Uncle Abraham and now she stakes her very life on them. To be in the most important family on earth, to be at the centre of the most important events on the planet, not the emergence of civilization or democracy but the Line. But it became quickly apparent after a few months of marriage that her mother-in-law's shoes were not easy to fill. Month on month the periods kept coming, what was happening? She'd come all this way to do the will of God, where was the baby? Unfortunately Sarah was not alive to steer Rebecca through that same lesson she and Abraham had learned some fifty years earlier, simply that God has a strange insistence on not being glorified by our best efforts but by overturning the impossible.

My friend Chris is an international mountain guide, he and Ann waited fourteen years for God to fulfil his promise of a child. At the start of that fourteenth year all they had was a name, 'Samuel'; had they heard right? Was this whole thing make believe? And what about all the family and friends they had told? I am sure that many of you are in the middle of such trials with no end in sight. Maybe they're not dramatic but they are very long, like illnesses and disabilities that will possibly last for the rest of your earthly life. It is certainly easier to preach and write books about this than to go through it, but I would encourage you in this; long after Job's family, career and possessions were taken, Satan knew how to grind the best saint down, 'Ah, but touch him in his body and he'll eventually curse you.' We need to size up trials the way the Bible does and honour those brothers and sisters who persevere through physical disabilities and other long trials. The trial for Rebecca was infertility and all the stigma that we observed in the preceding chapter. For her it was not fourteen but *twenty years* before she had children, which incidentally may say more than we can speculate over regarding their prayer life and marriage.

> And Isaac interceded for his wife to the LORD, because she was infertile: and the LORD was entreated of him, so Rebekah his wife conceived. But the babies were fighting inside her womb, so she said, '<u>If this is supposed to be God's will, what's going on?</u>'

> And she diligently pursued the LORD very often about this until eventually the LORD answered, 'Two nations are in your womb, and two communities will be divided from your heart; and the one community shall be more courageous and steadfast than the other; <u>and the elder shall serve the younger.</u>' Gen 25:20-23

An Indifferent Husband

We will say much more about Isaac later for he is certainly a complex character and, though inspirational in other ways, there are also major shortcomings that are hard to overlook when dealing with Rebecca's prophecy and the raising of Esau.

Indifference to her prophecy

Those babies were literally bruising and crushing each other inside her womb (the Hebrew word means to 'crack in pieces') and for this first and so-long-awaited pregnancy I get the feeling Rebecca thought she might even be dying. Sometimes being in the centre of God's will can feel just like that. If you don't believe me then I just dare you to pray earnestly for patience! Pretty soon you'll be joining Rebecca in saying, 'If this is supposed to be God's will, what's going on?'

The first shock is that God answers a woman, which for the time and culture was extraordinary. Perhaps not so extraordinary was Isaac's reaction, for he shows over the years a wholesale disregard for his wife's 'word from God'. Following the cultural norm, he favours the oldest, the sporty one who brings him venison. But hers was a direct word of knowledge, *'the elder shall serve the younger'*; how very isolating it was not to be taken seriously. Being a beautiful woman possibly didn't help, 'I mean, everyone knows they don't have anything useful to say.' (The isolation and loneliness of beauty is well documented.) And it certainly is hard to hold on to a word from the Lord in a world of grown-up experts, friend, but you must, you really, really must, as God will hold you accountable for it. Read 1 Kings 23 about the prophet who ran on someone else's vision and got killed by the lion, it's all there. And if you like the Narnia books, you'll remember what Lucy says to Aslan in *Prince Caspian*, 'I couldn't have left the others and come up to you alone, how could I? Don't look at me like that ... oh well, I suppose I *could*. Yes, and it wouldn't have been alone, I know, not if I was with you.'

You cannot fuel a journey of faith and obedience on someone else's oil.

For years I subcontracted all decision making to 'the spiritual experts' until the Lord showed me that half of what I called submission was really laziness and idolatry. I thank God for the elders at my local church, of which I too am an elder. There is real safety in mutual subjection; in fact I can say that I submit to the so-called least of the saints and always have one ear to heaven in case any of them should be used to speak to me. That's the way it was meant to be; 'submit you one another out of your reverential awe for Christ' and I thank God for the many wonderful times he has encouraged me and preserved me by words of prophecy and exhortation from others, but there is a real balance to be struck here. Either Christ died for the priesthood of all believers or he said, 'Hey, you know what, I'm too busy to coordinate this whole living-body thing right now, you guys chose some executive managers, build a pyramidal organization like every other one in the world and hold stuff together until I can free my schedule a bit.' Friend, if you are born again and filled with the Holy Spirit then *you are the anointed of God*, end of story. You might be the only anointed one some people will ever meet, don't trade that kingly privilege for a cosy back seat and a Sunday hymn sandwich, the adventure is always with Jesus 'at the wheel'.

In order for James Hudson Taylor to fulfil his calling to reach inland China with the gospel, he had to leave the mission organisation to which he originally belonged, to disobey the advice of doctors, pastors, every other missionary and – as if you couldn't have guessed – the cultural laws of respectable Victorian Britain. Even more tellingly he had to flout the laws of the great god of the British empire, trade. He was even denounced in the Houses of Parliament for jeopardising British interests in the Orient by his reckless insistence on spreading the fame of Jesus to 200 million souls who had never heard his name before. I know it sounds fanatical but there may come a time in your life when to obey God's voice is to close your ears to every other and none more so than in actually making disciples.

But back to our story. For the next forty years Rebecca looked on as her husband overruled all that she knew God had told her so clearly, possibly the only time she ever did hear his voice. It is very distressing when you feel that what God has given you is rejected by those you love. Rebecca would not be the last, though it was seen supremely in the life and ministry of our Lord, whose rejection and loneliness is also prefigured in the lives of Joseph and Samson. In Samson's case the whole nation – filled with unbelief – chose to reject his ministry at Lehi choosing, rather, betrayal and an impoverished servitude under the Philistines. And Delilah is the perfect foreshadowing of Judas; the Jewess who sold Israel's deliverer for money, even after witnessing his supernatural ministry so directly. I would hazard a guess that she regrets it bitterly from where she suffers today.

When Isaiah says Jesus was 'despised and rejected', he means Jesus would not be taken seriously and therefore dismissed out of hand. In 2004 God used a visiting preacher with a prophetic gift to speak powerfully into my life; 'I know many have not taken you seriously, they've misunderstood and thought you were playing around but I say this; I have anointed you to wield the sword of truth with the left hand and the right, only avoid distractions.' It was water to my thirsty soul and also armour for what lay ahead. From that time on the trials increased but so did the increase of grace for the teaching gift he had given me. I interpret the 'left and right hand' as the twin blades of music and writing through which I bring the word. You may feel taken for granted or despised but I would encourage you – and I know how hard this is, believe me – to find your ultimate identity and validity in what God says about you, not your parents, or spouse or society, or church even.

Indifference to disciplining Esau

Isaac was not indifferent to the effects of this neglect as we shall see but we cannot escape the fact that his penchant for *'Esau's venison'* was symptomatic of a wider issue between them and I cannot help think that this must have been a cause of friction.

'Isaac, you indulge that boy, you're going to ruin his character.'
'Nonsense, woman, boys are boys, let him enjoy himself while he's young, you've got Jacob tied to your apron strings, so let Esau live a little, won't you.'
I'm sure you have heard fathers you know say similar things, particularly about sons who the neighbours say – with a raised eyebrow – are 'lively'. The amount of energy needed to maintain a consistent standard of discipline cannot be underestimated, I have four lively boys myself and would never hold myself up as an example by any means. You can write books about it but nothing can quite prepare you for the slog, day in day out. Laziness in yourself is the number one enemy here. 'You're watching the TV, having some dad time, let Rebecca deal with him if she's so bothered about it, besides he's only

being a bit cheeky, it shows character and he'll probably grow out of it anyway.'

But behind this 'discipline' situation lies the real crux of the issue, that of leading by example. For children will almost never imitate a father who preaches one thing and demonstrates another. Some lesson are caught not taught, character training is one of them. Hypocrisy is usually hideously obvious and always instils wholesale disgust. This is not clear cut in Isaac's case, as we shall see in the next chapter, but there is definitely an element of his flesh life that is first excused and later amplified in Esau's behaviour. It is very much the story of history too. As G. K. Chesterton said, 'Christianity has not been tried and found wanting but rather found difficult and left untried.' One of the atheist lies about British history is that the growth of secular humanism from the late Victorian period was the product of the progress in science, that Darwin's resurrection of Greek myth had disproved religion and we'd all grown out of it etc. But careful analysis shows that only four out of the one hundred and fifty leading intellectuals of the day cite 'scientific revelations' as their reason for ditching faith in God for faith in man. So what happened to the other 97%? Actually it was an *unlived and distracted* Christianity that caused them and nearly half the church goers in the England to drop out over a fifty year period. Most frightening of all it was the generation that had witnessed the fires of evangelical awakenings quenched under the deluge of cold moralism, where just being 'respectable and signing the pledge' was enough to be seen as 'a good Christian'. People aren't stupid, if the church shows them an achievable holiness without God's power, they say, 'Why bother; I can do that myself without having to sit through your boring sermons.' The writer and intellectual, George Eliot, is a very good example of this, though in fact its seems later she still held to a form of Deist belief. The battle for the mythic 'Christian Britain' was not lost over 'Sunday trading' or any such triviality, it was lost a century and a half ago when Christians settled on the wrong side of the Jordan, the side of man–centred religiosity rather than spirit filled holiness. It is quite a lesson for us too. Does my changed life demonstrate a power that cannot be attributed to anything other than miraculous means? (Another interesting statistic on this point is that in 1917 and 1997, a survey of scientists was taken asking this same question, *'Do you believe in a prayer answering God who interacts in this world today'*. In both cases the ratio's were the same 40% said Yes, 40% said No and 20% were not sure. So much for progress!)

The same is true of the modern New Age movement; we have repackaged Hindu and overtly occult practices in our hospitals and schools at tax payers' expense but where did this acceptance of a pantheistic spirituality start? The answer again is the revulsion of thinking men against a complacent institutionalized Christianity; not firstly in the 1900s but in the 1700! This upper-class complacency was expressed succinctly by Alexander Pope in his *Essays on Man*; 'Whatever is, is right'. He meant the disparity between the rich and poor. By his words he eased the consciences of 'the rich men in their castles' by affirming that 'the poor men at their gates' were assigned that position by God; it was his divine will, they need not change it. The result of this 'unlived Christianity' was the poet William Blake's new mythology which tore into the fabric of eighteen-century complacency and would influence the Romantics into a more pantheistic view of nature. Again the battle was won or lost back then, not now when the government wants to give acupuncture on the NHS or teach yoga to young children in primary schools. And again, it's no use 'tare pulling', the onus is very much on us to let our light shine before society, and not to walk around with snuffers to extinguish their dead-end efforts.

A Distressing Teenager

To say Rebecca experienced family difficulties and disappointments is a mild understatement. Here she was in the centre of God's will for her life and gifting. She was a focal part of the most important thing God was doing on the earth. Her part was pivotal and would be written of and talked about for millennia to come, and yet, at the time, for the most part all she could see was a dysfunctional family that would make most of us wince. If there had been an accredited Christian counsellor at Beersheba, it might have been interesting.

Counsellor – 'Has Esau come back to church yet?'

Rebecca – 'No and not likely to either since he married the heavy-metal-pagan-witch sisters from hell.'

Counsellor – 'You mean there are two of them?'

Rebecca – 'Oh yeah and to see the way they corrupt him, well, it makes me suicidal.'

Counsellor – 'Oh well, I see. Hmm, let's be positive, after all he did marry them and with so many young people just co-habiting these days ...'

Rebecca – 'Very consoling, thanks.'

Counsellor – 'And your husband?'

Rebecca – 'What about him? Of course he's upset too.'

Counsellor – 'But I think you blame him?'

Rebecca – 'Of course I blame him, he shows more interest in Esau's sporting career than his church attendance, never disciplined him, it's no wonder.'

Counsellor – 'Don't you think that's a bit harsh?'

Rebecca – 'Well, I don't know, that's what I pay you to tell me.'
Counsellor – 'I see, well, er, have you … er …?'
Rebecca – 'Have I what?'
Counsellor – 'Tried praying about it?'
Rebecca – (Whack! … interview terminated.)
If your family looks anything like this, take courage, it is not too messy for God, he's had far worse.

But Was She Right to Make Jacob Lie?

You must have heard of Jennie Churchill; one magazine called her 'the most influential Anglo Saxon woman in the world'. A prime minister's wife said that Jennie 'could have ruled the world'. Give you a clue? You might know her but *not* because she was a director of theatre, an editor and publisher, an organizer of a hospital ship for the Boer War upon which she herself travelled, nor as a pianist of professional ability, playwright, author, reporter, political campaigner, no, you will know her because she was a *wife and mother* of the most extraordinary ability. She turned her playboy husband into one of the most important men in the British Empire, and was the primary influence in the life of her son, a boy that would grow to be one of the greatest in world history. She sent him books to mould his mind and speech, used her stamina and 'go-getting' American attitude to get him transferred from one war to another, acted as his agent to get him published, campaigned alongside him in his early elections and had him introduced to the right people. That man was Winston Churchill and his mother – though certainly no saint – passed on some tenacious element of her character or DNA to him, something that enabled God to use him, something that the western world could be thankful for. Winston would one day say something about necessity that might have come from Rebecca's mouth, 'A man does what he must – in spite of personal consequences, in spite of obstacles and dangers and pressures.'

There is no doubt in my mind that God would have overturned Isaac's decision if Rebecca had not intervened. It is unthinkable that the 'eldership-ness' would be transferred to the 'profane fornicator' – as Esau is called – who had turned his back on the family calling. Esau might have been killed or an angel would have restrained the blindness of Isaac. But Rebecca did intervene to save THE LINE and we should look at that briefly.

She had no Bible, no ten commandments, just the promise to her Uncle Abraham and God's words to her, *'The elder shall serve the younger'*. It might be fair to say that having come 'out of the world', unlike Isaac, she realized more fully the corrupting influence that Esau was now subject to. Behind the father and son bonhomie now lay the seeds of pollution that would poison the purposes of God. Quite simply, Rebecca was zealous for something she had given her life for. I do not think that it is sufficient merely to say that, *'ah well, Genesis 25:28 says that she loved Jacob'*, for that is never to ask 'why she loved him?' – what her root motivation was. If Esau got the blessing, it would have all been for nothing – her whole life for nothing. Like Jennie Churchill, she had ploughed her hopes and dreams into the life of her son, what else could she do? For the second time in her life, she saw what must happen and made it so. It won't be the last time when a wife steps in to undo her husband's compromise; remember Jael in Judges 4 – who can forget the tent-peg-in-the-skull story? Her husband Heber was General Sisera's local informant against the Hebrews, imagine the conversation when he got home that night, 'Hi Honey, what's that you say, Sisera is inside the tent, good, he must have some money for me, is he staying for dinner?' 'Urhh well, not exactly!'

Rebecca is just like that; she sees the opportunity 'and strikes'. We have a tendency to moralize with New Testament hindsight but we should beware lest we miss the point. Of course we cannot condone deception, but can you blame this woman for being so zealous for God's plan, his righteousness? The intention and motivation was right, the method was not, but considering the enormity of what's at stake are you going to cast the first stone? Particularly as neither her husband, nor her God are recorded reprimanding her for it. Let us be frank, friends, we simply cannot, or at least certainly not until we are as passionate about God's interests as she was.

Jealous for God

Paul says there are few people who mind God's interests above their own; he cites Timothy as one. We know Elijah to be another who was 'jealous for the Lord' his God, careful Bible study reveals Jonah as another. (Kings 14) Jonah had seen Jeroboam II – a man who was undeservedly used by God to rescue the northern kingdom from its pitiful condition – later run roughshod over God's grace (Read the prophets Hosea and Amos). This explains Jonah's mysterious reference, 'Is this not what I said to you while I was in my own country...' It is the linchpin in his decision to run away (nothing else can explain his actions); he knew that people were apt to tread under foot the grace of God. And then, of course, there is Jeremiah;

> *'... his word was in mine heart as a burning fire shut up in my bones, and I was weary with forbearing, and I could not hold it in.'* Jeremiah 20:9

Rom Heuben was trapped inside a coma following a car crash in 1983. The doctors thought he was brain dead but it was only recently, with new scanning equipment, that they realized he had been fully awake for twenty-three years but unable to communicate.

Twenty-three years hearing everything, imagine that.

He has now recovered enough to type messages and tell of his frustration for all those years of isolation. Rebecca was alone with her prophecy and frustrated with her marriage for a lot longer than that. Psalm 105 talks of Joseph being *'tried by the word of the Lord'*. What we see in the life of Rebecca is no less real than Joseph's rejection and trials. She was tried for forty long years before she saw the rightful heir receive the blessing, though – it is also worth noting – that she died before Jacob achieved his *own* 'exodus' from Haran. Rebecca was very much a 'Hebrews 11' woma, who 'died believing' for her children. As it does others, it nearly cost Jacob his life to get away, but Rebecca's part in the story was over, her 'mighty' heart had won through. Like Ann and Emily Judson and so many more, Rebecca could say with Job,

> *'But he knoweth the way that I take: when he hath tried me, I shall come forth as gold. My foot hath held his steps, his way have I kept, and not declined. Neither have I gone back from the commandment of his lips; I have esteemed the words of his mouth more than my necessary food.'* Job 23:10-12

'Mighty Heart'
the duet of Eliezer and Rebecca – *Rebecca's words in italics*

(From 'THE LINE' album, words and music by Henry Brooks)

(Oh Becky, I've) seen a lot of things in my life, but nothing like you
and I've known some answers to prayer, but you stretched my faith with that water you drew
But my mind was well and truly blown, when you left all you'd ever known
To find the will of God, that takes a mighty heart

We'd always raised a glass to mad Uncle Abe and his promised land
But when we laughed at him, I yearned inside to live for something more than the family had
But suburbia and easy street, seemed so much more a part of me ... who was I kidding
That I would be the one to shake myself free ... but that's where you were wrong

It took a Mighty Heart to say 'yes', like that, my dear
and in that mighty heart, he put mighty desires for more than this world is
living for
and it doesn't get much bigger than this, God only had one name on his list
and that day when destiny rang it was faith that took the call –
yes, you've got a mighty heart,
oh, you've got a mighty God

Now, I watched you weep twenty years for the child that was promised to you
... I saw you
hope beyond hope, year after year as you pressed in deep, till the promise
came true
Oh I remember when I started to show, for weeks you supernaturally glowed, *Oh*
cos I proved God true how could I doubt his word again

It took a Mighty Heart to cling on like that, my dear ... and he's a
Mighty faithful, Almighty God that's clear ...*and some days I*
thought he had forgotten me, but his time was perfect now I see ... oh but to last out
twenty years, that takes a mighty heart
yes, you've got a mighty heart,
you've got an almighty God

(Hey, now did) those boys run you ragged, d'ya feel you fetched 'em up on
your own ... did it
worry you sick when Zak did not heed your word from the Lord when they
were grown ... *Now I know*
I shouldn't't'a made Jacob lie, but for years I'd been so churned up inside
Oh, but to be jealous for God, that takes a mighty heart

It takes a Mighty Heart, to care that much, my dear ... Most people just
live for this world but your heart was for him, that's clear ... oh but you
should not have worried, my friend, God usually gets what he wants in the
end
... and he never spoke against you, Becky, for your part ...
No, cos he has an almighty heart and he stuck by you to see you through
because he has an almighty heart for those who care for his plans like you do

Now I heard some people said that as a man of God, Zak was not all that he
could've been

*Oh, but he was faithful to me those dry twenty years and he never gave up on the
promise he'd seen
and though his flesh said quit and go home, he set his face like a flint and pressed on
by faith he blessed our boys, believing that God could use them too*

It took a mighty heart just to stick to his guns and stay here ... when
temptation says
Cut and run, it takes faith to push through the fear
*Yeah, we clung to that destiny, that our dysfunctional family
would be used by God ... to set the whole world free*
that takes a mighty heart ... and one almighty God

Life Application Devotional Guide

Chapter 2 – Positive and Negative Peer pressure

- Name three Christians whose spiritual experience and ministry you particularly admire.
- Why these three, is there any correlation?
- Rebecca faced strong and prolonged opposition. Can you identify any similar opposition to what God wishes to accomplish in your life?
- 'People are as spiritual as they want to be.' Would you agree with this? If so, in what areas would you wish God to change your heart to make you more like He wants you to be.
- Prayer: (Start with thanksgiving & praise for God's faithfulness to you.) 'Oh Lord My Provider, show me where you are wanting to change my heart, and what you want me to do. Is there any area where I need to repent? Is there any area in my life and service to you where I have given up too soon?

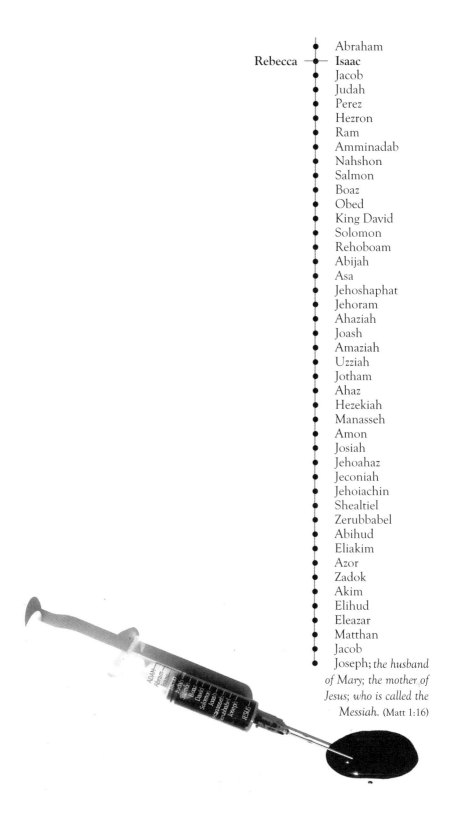

Abraham
Rebecca —— **Isaac**
Jacob
Judah
Perez
Hezron
Ram
Amminadab
Nahshon
Salmon
Boaz
Obed
King David
Solomon
Rehoboam
Abijah
Asa
Jehoshaphat
Jehoram
Ahaziah
Joash
Amaziah
Uzziah
Jotham
Ahaz
Hezekiah
Manasseh
Amon
Josiah
Jehoahaz
Jeconiah
Jehoiachin
Shealtiel
Zerubbabel
Abihud
Eliakim
Azor
Zadok
Akim
Elihud
Eleazar
Matthan
Jacob
Joseph; *the husband of Mary; the mother of Jesus; who is called the Messiah.* (Matt 1:16)

Chapter 3

The Quiet Man (Read Gen 24-28)

'Diana's no longer a member of the Royal Family. She's not an HRH. This is a private matter!' This line expresses the hinge on which the most critically acclaimed film of 2006 turns.

In *The Queen* the monolith of royal protocol collides with the public hysteria after Diana's death. The plot is suspended between the daily growing gulf in public expectations about 'the people's princess' and a stoic grief from another age; an age incomprehensible to an increasingly existential age. Shouldn't the Queen dance to the media tune: every other public figure must? Why shouldn't monarchy be 'subject to the breath of every fool' as Shakespeare put it? Or should she remain what she is, something other? That 'ever-fixed point' for her family, her grandchildren, her people, even the ones who might prefer something more 'Barbara Cartland'. It's a masterful piece of script writing complemented by Academy Award winning performances. And, in the end, republican zeal dissipates as 'monarchy' herself arrives back at Buckingham Palace.

What I wanted to highlight here is that we too may foster very different expectations about what makes a 'worthy' Bible hero, or a great Christian leader, or a 'successful' church, a well lived life even. When we come to the life and ministry of Isaac, we need to read his life in the context of history and prophecy to make an objective assessment. In a word we need 'perspective'; not so much zooming out to get greater context as much as 'seeing through' to the heart of a situation or person. That is literally what the word means (think Perspex) and that is what we all need most of all; quite literally 'heaven's eyes.' In the last chapter we saw one side of Isaac's life, an area of failure, but in this chapter I want to balance that deficit with better news. 'Oh no, you're not going to make me rethink 'back–slidden' blind Isaac are you?'

Well yes, of course I am. Absolutely.

The world disdains such contradictions; it hates anything it cannot neatly fit into a box, anything that takes up too much time to chew over. We have increasingly become a generation who cannot process logical argument beyond the sound–bite. With simple cartoons and limited shades of colour we may well train our children to see the basics, but this will not do for adults, certainly not Christians. For the scriptures always cause us to look closer at others and, in consequence, also at ourselves. If our neat preconceptions struggle with a certain passage, we should change our theology rather than skip bits.

And in Isaac, if we see nothing else, at least we will learn how unfathomably gracious God is toward us and I list five things that have helped me; things I hope that will encourage you too.

Isaac's Life is a Remarkable Foreshadowing of Jesus

The First Image we see is the much loved, favoured son.

Isaac, the darling of his mother, the apple of his father's eye. It shows us what we can see so clearly in God's affirmation at Jesus' baptism, *'This is my beloved son in whom I am well pleased'*(Matt 3:17); perhaps not so much for what he has or will do - particularly in Isaac's case - but just for who he is. It is widely understood that a father's affirmation and loving input are crucial to a child's development. When 40% of children in the U.S. currently have no father on the birth certificate and many more have little or no paternal contact, it is more than just economic analysts that may fret about the long term results, for the cost will be felt in every area of society.

When someone says, 'you just take God's kindness for granted' there is part of me that says, 'yes, why shouldn't we?' My children take their father's care and provision for granted and I don't think it would be healthy for them to think otherwise. Suppose they grovelled every morning to the breakfast table, 'Oh, great and loving Father, we humbly beseech thee to look upon these thy wretched and unworthy offspring and give unto us cornflakes out of thy generous bounty.' We are cherished and spoilt by God, end of story, get used to it for it is the natural way of things. I understand what people mean when they say 'unworthy' but the prodigal's *worth* is never measured by his guilt but by a value set by another. For the prodigal son that value was his father's acceptance, his ring, a robe and a fattened calf, for us it is the life of God's most treasured son. Yes, I feel guilty but God says I am also *worth* every drop of Christ's blood according to the heaven's economy. You can't argue with that. We need to take some aspects of God's character for granted, pure and simple. I believe this is his will.

The second image is the Sin Bearer

See him; a man in his early thirties carrying a great wooden burden upon which he himself would be sacrificed. The father follows with heavy heart and at the last minute the ram with its head caught in thorns becomes the substitute. God himself provided a ram for Abraham and for us. Isaac as the 'sin bearer' is perhaps not the facet of his life that we can easily identify ourselves with, but we should not pass over it without considering what it shows and the mark it left on him. Isaac had grown up saturated in the story, 'Out of all families on earth God is going to bring an answer through ours. But not through your brother Ishmael, no, God has said it would come through you Isaac, you're the chosen one, it's your destiny.'
We should not be thrown by the word 'lad' used for Isaac, for it can also mean a young man and we must assume that he was somewhere under forty as this would be his age in the next chapter. I certainly have never seen a Sunday school picture showing a little boy carrying enough wood on his back to burn a human sacrifice. The implication is striking: when his aged father produced that rope Isaac knew exactly what was going on and yet did not resist. He chose in that moment to submit to binding, thus showing, even through the bewilderment and uncertainty, that he trusted his father beyond life itself. Of course, in that moment he also showed a willingness to let his dreams, destiny and future ministry die. If he had done no more in his life beyond this, he would have left us something very precious indeed. It is hard to imagine how this event would impact on his character but one thing is certain, it left him hungry to meet this God for himself.

Isaac Was Looking for the Same Face-to-face Relationship his Father Had

'For I know him, that he will instruct his children and household after him, that they should closely follow the journeys of Jehovah.' Genesis 18:19

Here is one powerful reason why God chose Abraham. He would be able to transmit the ways of God to the second generation.

'Second generation believer' has become a byword for vision-less and flaccid Christianity. Of course it doesn't have to be this way but it often is and which parent has not agonised over an indifferent child? I know I have, and I know that there are very few things that rank as more important than a man's ability to *'manage his own household well'*(1 Tim 3:4). No wonder Paul makes such a big deal about it when choosing deacons and overseers; a man is proven already in his patriarchal role at home, a happy wife and godly children make compelling evidence. (Big prayers and fine sermons certainly do not!) Abraham's strategy was simple, first 'gates', then 'windows'. First close the gates; Abraham minimised the cross-cultural impact that his son would experience, even if it looked a bit separatist (i.e. no going back to Haran, no settling in a town, no unequal yokes.) And then with that established he opened selective *windows* by which his son would come to understand the world and this unseen God who was leading them. To attempt one without the other is madness.

The church in the West has substantially failed to do either of these things at anything like the required level. Her swift decline in influence in the twentieth century is testimony to that. The cry of the Sunday school teacher, 'We just don't know how to keep the young ones at church when they hit that difficult age' is all too familiar. I've been a Sunday school teacher since the last century! I've tried everything – and I mean everything – but quickly came to the conclusion, 'peer pressure is only one small press in the larger factory of secularism.' Words like, 'saint, sin, devil and vicar' were taken out of the Oxford English Dictionary for children in 2008. (Brings to mind the 2005 Film, *The Usual Suspects*, 'The greatest trick the devil ever pulled was convincing the world he didn't exist.') Is one hour at Sunday school and the odd Bible story at bedtime going to overturn the secular state education, entertainment and media culture? It has not and will not.

Fathers and mothers, you are gatekeepers to your homes and it may be time to rethink where we place those gates before we start to train our children. Ruth and I decided to home educate and not to have a TV. Too extreme, perhaps? Not really, we've got the internet, and loads of DVDs and friends. Besides it is nowhere near as extreme as what some of my dearest, most godly friends face. Their children have been overtaken by the secular tide they were exposed to and swept away in it. The pain of a churched-teenage daughter clearing out her room to move in with another boy is *more extreme* than any father dare think about, though we thank God he is the God of the prodigals. (I know, I was one.) The lifeboat must be in the water – sure, it's a given – but how much water will any lifeboat take before it becomes overwhelmed? I'm not trying to be heavy with anyone but I do say we need to give more attention to our gates than has been previously thought 'normal'. Yes, even if everyone calls us 'Puritans'. When we break secular society's dominance over your home is a bit like getting Neo's first view of the reality outside the Matrix; it's a bit weird, a bit chilly, exposed, disorientating even, but equally exhilarating and above all real.

The size and positioning of gates are only ever a temporary measure before that next generation grow strong enough to achieve their own exodus, to prove all God is for themselves. This is the real test of all Abraham's 'gates and windows'; will Isaac seek a personal encounter with this unseen God? I believe he did and I'd like to show the stages of how this courtship happened.

- **Blessing:** First God blessed Isaac after the death of Abraham. At this unsettling time God makes the first move by giving him a general increase in his relationships and business affairs.

- **Posture:** Isaac pitches his tent at the well called Lahai-Roi – the *living God who sees me*! It was named when God had *seen* Hagar there some years before and it had become a marker stone in what the family had discovered about the character of God. The *living* and *me* bit are all important, Isaac was meditating at that very place the day Rebecca arrived long ago and now here he is again hanging around, perhaps looking for a one-to-one encounter with a living God. Perhaps his father's shoes are too big to fill, a cold semblance of ancestral religion is not what he wants, he needs a *living* God who *sees* and interacts with him as well.

- **Breakthrough:** I believe Isaac was still here at this place and in this searching position when God hears his prayer for Rebecca and gives him children. But, as we have seen before, to see God's hands in answered prayer is one thing, his face is quite another. And I believe this is the great triumph of Abraham's training; he modelled a relationship with God that his son would spend his early adult life trying to rediscover and authenticate. Here is our major key to winning the second generation; not a half lived Christianity, not a list of don'ts, that's hardly aspirational. I remember Spurgeon talking of a holiness that is little more than a corpse at the morgue; washed and clean but still cold and dead. As Our Lord said, 'white washed tombs', God help us. The next generation should look at us and see high adventure, deep intimacy and a demonstration that there is nothing more wonderful than 'journeying with Jehovah' themselves. And again, don't think everyone has to be like you, Oswald Chambers wisely said, 'never make a principal of your experience, let God be original in other people's lives as he is in yours.'

- **Revelation:** And then it comes, the personal affirmation and ratification of the covenant.

> '*And the LORD appeared unto him, and said, Go not down into Egypt; dwell in the land which I shall tell thee of: Sojourn in this land, and I will be with thee, and will bless thee; for unto thee, and unto thy seed, I will give all these countries, and I will perform the oath which I sware unto Abraham thy father; And I will make thy seed to multiply as the stars of heaven, and will give unto thy seed all these countries; and in thy seed shall all the nations of the earth be blessed; Because that Abraham obeyed my voice, and kept my charge, my commandments, my statutes, and my laws.*' Genesis 26:2-5

And so all that camping out at Lahai-Roi paid off, just like when Joshua hung round the tabernacle and got his personal affirmation after the death of Moses. Obed Edom was another one. When David took the ark from his house (2 Sam 6:10-12) Obed Edom moved his family to Jerusalem to become door keepers in the house of God (1 Chron 15:18). He'd had God living in his house and like Isaac he'd been blessed, but that wasn't enough for him, God was his '*exceeding great reward*' too and if it's the same family then we can find Obed Edom's descendants later on as members of the choir as well (1 Chron 15:21, 16:5). It seems very clear, when you've been near to God, or in Isaac and Joshua's case with someone who has been near, nothing else in life makes sense, nothing else will do for you. Question is; can I say in all honesty that this is my experience? If not there is not a moment to lose.

And for Isaac the breakthrough may have come not a moment too soon, '*Go not down into Egypt.*' (Gen 26:2) Was he about to throw the towel in and find something more respectable in Egypt? Whatever the reason, the command is clear enough, 'Forget the blessings of Egypt, Isaac, I'm going to bless you right here where you are.' God comes to authenticate and validate the covenant for Isaac. And I think if most Christians are honest, they will tell you that they have doubts about their relationship with God and whether he is using their lives significantly. Isaac's encouragement to us is that if we hang around the Lord, that is if we position our prayers and priorities to seek the journey that he has for us, pretty soon we'll look up and find him right there on the road saying, 'Don't be afraid, there's no need to run away, I'll be with you in it to prove my love for you and demonstrate before angels and men all that I am on your behalf.'

He Was Persecuted by Men
Because God Blessed Him

Isaac was not the first 'Quiet Man' to be persecuted because of his wealth. In the 1952 film *Quiet Man*, John Wayne plays the rich outsider come to find himself in a strange land – not unlike Isaac in some ways. The gossipers say, 'He's a nice, quiet, peace-loving man, come home to Ireland to forget his troubles. Sure, yes, yes, he's a millionaire, you know, like all the Yanks. But he's eccentric – ooh, he is eccentric! Wait till I show ya ... his bag to sleep in – a sleeping bag, he calls it!' Comic enough and well handled by the 'Duke' but the enmity Isaac aroused was a far more serious and dangerous matter.

> 'Isaac planted crops in that land and the same year reaped a hundredfold, because the LORD blessed him. The man became rich, and his wealth continued to grow until he became very wealthy. He had so many flocks and herds and servants that the Philistines envied him.'
> Genesis 26:12

A 5 or 6% increase is what we called blessed, 100% seems at little O.T.T., why such a huge increase? What's this guy up to? Surely that's asking for trouble. I surmise that God is showing Isaac off in a way that he wanted to do on a national scale if only Israel had cooperated (see Ezekiel 5:5-7 where God lets us in on his secret plan for Israel as a missionary nation at the great trade-crossroads of the ancient world – rather like Birmingham became for UK trade in 1810 when it became the centre of the new canal systems). With Isaac, the abundance of God brought problems. The Philistines could just have been jealous, that is, wanted what Isaac had and joined the people of God to have the same; that would not have been a problem, God is not picky about ethnicity as we will see when we come to Rahab and Ruth. But envy differs from jealousy in that the Philistines would rather deprive Isaac of his blessing than look to that blessing's source and change their lifestyles. British law outlaws Jesus' claims for himself as too exclusive, forgetting the obvious paradox that Christianity is of course totally inclusive too.

There is nothing your enemies hate more than when they see you enjoying the fruit of faith in Jesus Christ. To some we are *'the smell of death unto death'* because we demonstrate that their creed – be it communism, humanism or the personal peace and affluence of middle class respectability – is manifestly false, unworkable and unfulfilling. In fact, those who have decided to become adversaries to me have, to a man, been energized because of this very thing.

He Had to Contend With The Enemy
for What God Had Given Him

'Isaac reopened the wells that had been dug in the time of his father Abraham, which the Philistines had stopped up after Abraham died, and he gave them the same names his father had given them. Isaac's servants dug in the valley and discovered a well of fresh water there. But the herdsmen of Gerar quarrelled with Isaac's herdsmen and said, "The water is ours!" So he named the well "Esek", because they disputed with him. Then they dug another well, but they quarrelled over that one also; so he named it "Sitnah". He moved on from there and dug another well, and no one quarrelled over it. He named it Rehoboth, saying, "Now the LORD has given us room and we will flourish in the land." ' Genesis 26:18-22

Well Stealing

It is an old trick of the enemy to claim a heritage that is not his; for Isaac it was two wells, for us and our culture it is many other things. When I think of the sad history of humanism – particularly since the renaissance – I cannot help remember my third son Jonathan who when young could not put his own socks on and so – to his mind at least – did the next best thing he could; keep taking them off! This in a sense is the sorry tale of the modern history, not that these Titans create anything new but that they appropriate and corrupt what God has already given. In so doing it is not the sacred things the secular humanism spoils but the very secular things that they first had thought to emancipate; as Chesterton said of the Titans of Greek myth; they did not, 'scale the heavens but laid waste the earth.'

 Usually, as in the case of Marxism it will be one element separated from the rest and ridden to madness but we must not fall into the trap of laying this charge exclusively at the doors of atheism for the church led well in advance on this sin. Though there are some striking myths still rammed down our throats today, none gall me more than when the books and documentary people claim some great battle between faith and science. I realise these so called New Atheists have to make a living like anyone else, but really it is maddening to see such obvious falsehoods peddled so brazenly, when all along anyone of any reading could tell us that the scientific revolution came from monotheists – precisely because they were! What atheist would have a worldview that would cause him to search for unifying laws in the universe? The Christians looks firstly because they believed in a reliable creation (as spoken by a reliable creator) and second; that we were made in his image and so were capable, as Newton put it, to *think God's thoughts after him*.

In a similar way the same optimistic humanists try to manufacture a total lineage of 'liberty and social reform' out of the enlightenment tradition. But as Chesterton said in his excellent book 'Orthodoxy', *the modern world is full of the Christian virtues gone mad.* The impetus and original practice of social service, voluntarism, education, trade unions and healthcare came straight out of the church, or more accurately from the teaching of Jesus Christ.. (Some very readable histories are *Christianity and Social Service in Modern Britain* by the American historian, Frank Prochaska, also *Atheist Delusions* by David Bentley Hart, *Modern art and the death of culture* by H. Rookmaaker and *How Then Should We Live?* by Francis Schaeffer) The Philistine herdsmen of Gerar and Esek are themselves impotent to give their society water, therefore these 'immaculate' conceptions of their modern counterparts perhaps should not surprise us. I was interested to hear N.T. Wright comment that whereas at one time Christians were once despised for telling a different story to the modern world, now they are ridiculed for having any story to tell at all. Humanism – that system of thinking that exalts men without reference to God – cut free from God is like everything else (including the new society it fashioned); devoid of meaning or purpose. Their great dream of an endlessly perfecting society died a death during the World Wars and for half a century the west has tried to struggle as best it can to readjust to the reality of an impenetrable pessimism. But remember this, in the final analysis history is always written by the conqueror, and in that regard the real books aren't even opened yet.

New Wells

And I think we should do as Isaac did and not stay too long to bicker over the old wells; we'll never get them back anyway. It's no use whining, 'The government won't let my children learn about the alternatives to or the problems with evolution.' Start a Christian School or home educate. We Brits are no strangers to this; what do you think all our dissenting academies were for? An NHS nurse might say, 'It breaks my heart, I can't pray with my dying patients even when they ask for it because I'd lose my job. All I'm allowed to do is pump them high with drugs to the point where they cannot think straight to seek him.' It might be the burden there is from the Lord. Why not ask him if he wants you to start a Christian hospice? Sounds far out, I know, but if you read about the Ranyard Bible nurses and others like them – who basically invented modern nursing in the nineteenth century – you'd soon see it's a well trodden path.

And even on a personal level I have found this to be true. Being very laid back and easy going, I saw a lot of myself in Isaac. I'd been given a lot and I assumed that being an 'inheritor' rather than a 'grabber' like Jacob, was my calling in life. To some extent this may be true but the Lord has also taught me the necessity of having the fight to possess what he had given. For the Jews it was the land, for Isaac it was the wells. The struggle brought him into a 'broad place', he called it Rehoboth which means just that. In 2002 the Lord gave me a building development opportunity, something he'd been training me for in tandem to my main occupation as a landscape architect. In a series of miraculous 'coincidences' my company won the barn complex at public auction and we developed the fourteen acre rural site where we now live. It was a gruelling and traumatic few years when I was extended emotionally, mentally, physically and financially beyond any limits I previously thought existed. Through it all I experienced the solid-ness of God and from it there also appeared a Rehoboth-like space for my family to spread their wings in.

Isaac Showed His Faith
in Two Very Startling Ways

I have tried to show a different side of Isaac's life than usually preached, for, as I said earlier, our basic worth and that of our lives and ministries is calibrated by the Holy Ghost and not by men. This is nowhere more clearly seen in what is written about Isaac in Hebrews 11. Having said that Abraham had looked for 'a city which has foundations, whose builder and maker is God, the writer goes on to say a few verses later,

> *'And truly, if they had constantly been looking back to where they'd come from, they might also have then wished for a convenient occasion to go back.'* Heb 11:15

The 'they' of course includes Isaac and when I understood this I began to see Isaac's great act of faith was not to go anywhere but to stay where he was and to continue day by day, choosing to go on believing what God has promised and resist the temptation to go back to his family in Haran. Part of Isaac's faith résumé, as mentioned in Heb 11 was what he *did not do* rather than what he did; he did not cave into temptation and leg it back to where things would be easier on his flesh. It is a major mistake to underestimate the pull of our flesh for Egypt. It is something we must guard against, not necessarily just by great fastings and austerity, I found moving the mail order catalogue or car magazines away from the toilet worked wonders! We cannot say how many times the temptation to quit tried to overwhelm Isaac, or indeed how deep he had to dig in those times just to hold his conviction that he wasn't mad or making the whole 'destiny' thing up. James 1:12 puts it well, *'Blessed is the man that goes on enduring trials: for when he is proved, he shall receive the crown of life, which the Lord has promised to them that love him.'*

Of course I don't know what trial you are facing right now but I would encourage you to pray for this sort of 'stickability', this faithfulness. Sure it isn't glamorous like, say, raising the dead or healing the sick but those can be the fruit of faithfulness so keep on keeping on. When Richard Wurmbrand was jailed and tortured by he Communists his whole energy for a season was taken up with *not* informing on his Christian brothers and sisters under torture. He never did and it may be a strange illustration but I want to highlight this; none of us can tell what everyone else's ministries are by just looking with critical eyes. God gives to each his gifts *and trials* according to our abilities, let's not be swift to judge our brothers and sisters.

In 1865 there were no doubt people who tut-tutted when Robert Thomas took employment on board an American trading ship bound for Pyongyang. He had a burning desire to be the first Protestant missionary to the Korean people but instead got himself decapitated before he could witness to anyone. At that moment for all anyone knew, especially Robert, was that his ministry had been wasted. All, that is except the man who killed him, for shortly after the deed this Korean thought it strange that this man was unarmed apart from a small book which he waved while shouting 'Jesus, I love you Jesus' in his the Korean language. He then wondered whether his victim might be a good man and so retrieved that little book, dried its pages and took it home where – because he could not read – he covered the outside of his house with its pages. One day he was surprised to return from the fields and see a group of wise men reading the Chinese script. One man became a Christian and it was his nephew that became the first pastor and the first man to translate the Bible into the Korean tongue. So it turned out that Robert Thomas' obedience was amply repaid, despite what the critics might have said and so was Isaac. It might not seem heroic to us to stay faithful to a barren wife or stick at camping for all your life but that was the battle he had to fight. What Isaac faced was real enough to him and as far as God is concerned he passed the test.

The other particular verdict we have on Isaac comes a few verses later and is possibly even more revealing of his and Rebecca's trials.

'By faith Isaac blessed Jacob and Esau concerning things to come.'

Heb 11:20

This is a remarkable twist for the verse states that Isaac spoke those words over his sons believing God would really use his dysfunctional family to bless the entire earth, not once but twice. I was praying with my friend Amanda last weekend; her husband died a few years back and she was left to raise her two sons alone. The Lord gave her a promise that he would be their father and even though they may wander, he would bring them back eventually. As the boys pass through their teen years into adulthood, she now clings to that promise against all the outward evidence. Like Isaac, Amanda is a hero of faith, showing the same belligerent contempt towards what her eyes see in favour of what God says. It takes great perseverance and faith to speak what God says over our situations and our families. He says that I am a beloved son in training to rule in Christ's coming government; the world says that I'm an ugly failure who'll amount to nothing; which opinion should I base my self esteem and life goals on? Obvious really, but it's easier said than done.

So stay with it, God has not left you, forget Egypt, stay in the land with the Lord and see what he will do for you too.

Life Application Devotional Guide

Chapter 3 – First Things First

- On a scale of 1–10 how would you rate the closeness of your relationship with God? (10 = Jesus, 0 = haven't had a personal encounter yet.)
- How many minutes of an average day do you spend developing this relationship? (i.e. reading the bible and prayer.)
- List any 'gaps' in your schedule that you could use to double or triple the figure given above.
- Prayer: (Start with thanksgiving & praise, particularly for his many faceted love for you) 'Oh Living God who see *me*, I acknowledge that the answer to my feelings of loneliness and deepest desires for wholeness can only be met in you. Lord please teach me how to walk with you. Change my heart and align my priorities with yours. Send me whatever help is necessary for us to have the communion you intended. Is there anything in my life; good or bad, that needs to change in order for this to happen? Is there anything else that you want me to do?

Leah ——●—— **Jacob**

● Abraham
● Isaac
● Judah
● Perez
● Hezron
● Ram
● Amminadab
● Nahshon
● Salmon
● Boaz
● Obed
● King David
● Solomon
● Rehoboam
● Abijah
● Asa
● Jehoshaphat
● Jehoram
● Ahaziah
● Joash
● Amaziah
● Uzziah
● Jotham
● Ahaz
● Hezekiah
● Manasseh
● Amon
● Josiah
● Jehoahaz
● Jeconiah
● Jehoiachin
● Shealtiel
● Zerubbabel
● Abihud
● Eliakim
● Azor
● Zadok
● Akim
● Elihud
● Eleazar
● Matthan
● Jacob
● Joseph; *the husband of Mary; the mother of Jesus; who is called the Messiah.* (Matt 1:16)

Chapter 4

The Wrestlers (Read Gen 25-32)

'I just want to tell you, I'm the one who was supposed to take care of everything. I'm the one who was supposed to make everything okay for everybody. It just didn't work out like that. And I left. I left you. You never did anything wrong. I used to try to forget about you. I used to try to pretend that you didn't exist, but I can't. You're my girl.' The Wrestler, 2008 Film

Scooping over seventy-five international awards *The Wrestler* was one of the most critically acclaimed films of 2008. It was a story of broken relationships and missed opportunities. The quotation above is from a beaten up wrestler talking to his estranged daughter but it could equally have come from the mouth of an older Jacob to his unloved wife, Leah. He would not be the first man to realize too late the qualities of a good woman. Jacob and Leah were two of a kind, *bruised reeds* who wrestled with God and men for affirmation and blessing in a society that nearly always awarded such things only to the unworthy. They both won through in their own ways but it's a great tragedy that Jacob couldn't have seen it sooner. Looking at just how similar they were and what they foreshadowed in Jesus' life and ministry is the major theme of this chapter. The other will be dispelling the Sunday school myths about Jacob and, particularly Rachel, and possibly surprising a few readers that the line does not in fact go through her and Joseph but through Leah, mother of Judah. Did you ever stop to wonder why this is? It makes a compelling human story and we shall examine it in this and the next chapter.

So how were Jacob, Leah and Jesus so similar? The three major ways are listed below; they all grew up under varying weights of social disability, they all traded material things to gain spiritual power and they all pushed through to a fruitful (and fruit*filled*) lives by dealing directly with God.

Jacob, Leah and Jesus Grew Up Under
Varying Weights of Social Disability

'The world ... hates me because I testify that what it does is evil'

John 7:7

'If you were of this world system it would love you like its own but you don't belong to the system, (because I called you out of the culture) therefore it hates and persecutes you'

John 15:19

Jacob

I always feel sorry for the 'bait fish' when I watch wildlife documentaries. There they are in their vast shoals being cut up by tuna, but what could they expect? Their name says it all, it's all they're good for, bait. Men have a nasty habit of attaching labels to others and in many cases it can say more about the 'labeller' than the one labelled. Jacob was called 'grabber' – understood to be 'deceitful' within the context of the culture – and why was that? Because he was trying to do the will of God from the womb. Not very fair is it?

This is why he grabs his brother's heel, he wants to be the first born, to have the 'eldership-ness', the spiritual heritage and promise pass through his line. Sounds far fetched? Not really, look at John the Baptist; by leaping in the womb he is already fulfilling his ministry in pointing to the Messiah. Now it is not just his father who, in a fashion, speaks against Jacob, there are many others. But when you examine the accusations of his profane brother Esau and deceitful Uncle Laban, you quickly see their lies say more about them than him. You may have been on the receiving end of this too, in which case you will also identify with Jacob's prophetic description of Joseph;

> *'Joseph is a fruitful son, a fruitful son in charge of a fountain; whose influence will transcend boundaries. The 'Master of arrows' laid in wait for him to wear him down with arrows. But his strength was established with permanence, and his forearms and hands were made strong by the hands of the mighty God of Jacob through whom he will shepherd, build and rule with God. Even the God of your father who will help you and shall bless you ... who was separate from his brothers.'* From Genesis 49:22-26

Joseph, like Jacob, received attention from the 'Master of arrows' when he did not join his brothers in sin. For as Joseph was separate from the sins of his brothers, so too Jacob was separate from the lifestyle and outlook of his profane brother, Esau. Of course Satan himself did not appear and speak directly to him, I doubt he would appear to you either, for his methods are usually to use the mouths of others close to you, the closer the better. In both cases Satan is aware of the spiritual anointing on both Joseph and of course Jacob. Satan also can see their ability to be fruitful to the point that their *'influence will transcend boundaries'*. This is a major problem for Satan but in trying to wear them down by a barrage of discouragement he only makes them eligible for more grace. Their 'forearms and hands' are strengthened, their ministry and gifting are *'established with permanence'*. The very same can be true for you, if you too overcome as they did, for remember; none of the blessings and rewards mentioned in Revelation are promised to believers, only to 'Overcomers' (Rev 2:10).

Unfortunately Christian preachers have joined the ranks of 'Jacob–bashers' too, perhaps historically inherited by an unconscious anti–Semitism. The simple matter is that we are often led more by what preachers and commentators say than what is actually written. The Holy Spirit records that Jacob was a *'perfect man living in tents'*. Somehow the King James translators couldn't quite translate the Hebrew word 'Tam' as being any more than *'plain'* in Jacob's case, even when they use *'perfect'* for Job a few books on. But it is the same word and means *complete, pious, gentle, dear, perfect, undefiled, upright*. Not the average pulpit view you've heard, I bet. The *'living in tents'* bit is also very important for that was the family calling, the 'be sojourners in the land of promise', not to settle down. My pet theory is that Esau had settled down in a house (like everyone else), for we see Rebecca go to a 'bayith' or house to borrow Esau's clothes to dress Jacob.

'Ah but this 'perfect man' stuff doesn't tally with the way he deceived his father,' you might say. But I'd say this: he was obeying *the 'law of his mother'* as all children are commanded to in Proverbs. *'Now obey me ... and let the guilt be upon me'* she says. Jacob would have enough time to learn that God can look after his own interests, but at that age, in that situation, he did as she said and once again the hand that rocked the cradle shaped history. It would not be the last time. A thousand years later when the exiled Roman general Marcus Coriolanus returned to smash Rome with an enemy army, it is his mother that turns him back, 'You have already repaid the Romans' she says referring to the towns he had already destroyed, 'but you have not yet repaid your debt to me.' In front of all his troops he obeys even though he knows it will cost him his life at their hands.

George Washington was another such great man whose path was irrevocably changed by a beseeching mother. In his mid teens he was about to board a war ship for the new career his brother had worked hard to procure for him. His trunk is loaded on the ship, everyone is watching, it's his big chance. But suddenly his mother – an exceptional woman – appears on the gang plank telling him to come home. Maybe jeers of 'Mummy's boy' or 'Sissy' followed him and his trunk back down the gangplank, who knows. But this we do know, this redirecting of his career from sailor to surveyor and then to soldier would have far reaching consequences for that continent and perhaps world history. (Some very readable histories of the various American Presidents – though being more hagiographies with a Christian leaning which needless to say I like – are done by William Thayer; 'From Log Cabin to Whitehouse' is about President Garfield but there are others about Washington and Lincoln.) The power of a tenacious mother has perhaps more mystery than any dare imagine, Kate Ogg gave birth to 27-week-old twins in March 2010. The doctor informed her that the male child, was already dead. She held the fragile bundle for a while, telling him that his name was James, that he had a sister and all about the things they would have done together if he had survived. But, perhaps where other distraught mothers would have given up she carried on, talking and warming him to her skin for over an hour. And then she noticed a little shock run through his body. The doctor apologised and said that was quite a natural reflex action. The shocks continued every now and again as Kate cuddled him and then finally after two hours she let some of her breast milk into his mouth on her finger. At that moment James came to life to the utter astonishment of parents and staff. I hope James will learn the wisdom of deferring to his mother as he gets older, this remarkable woman to whom even death yielded up its gains. If he does, he will follow a path trodden by some great men like Jacob, George, Coriolanus and many more besides.

Now regarding Esau, I think we may assume he was the favourite and that Jacob may have sought his father's affirmation with difficulty. Esau was sporty and hard in a way that matched the very culture his father was supposed to be separating them from. Jacob kept to the family calling to be counter culture, but it did not impress his father half as much as Esau's venison. The pain of *never being quite enough* to please the ones we love is acutely felt by many young people, I have felt it myself. At the growing loss of absolute values – moral or otherwise – our modern and post-modern society has increasingly retreated to the relative comforts of the Greek idea of virtue; what they called *'arete'*.

That is not so much being *'good'* as being *'good at'* something, hence their – and our – love of sports and propensity to deify human achievement and those 'superstars' that advance beyond the realms of us mortals. It's hard when what you're good at isn't what is cool; when only the loud mouths and trouble makers get noticed; where muscle equals kudos. I've heard sensible and educated women tell me that school is necessary for toughening up their little children: 'Well, it's a big bad world they'd better learn to survive while they're young.' Of course changing lambs into goats is no solution, though the temptation for Jacob must have been real, the hunger for his father's validation must have been heartbreaking at times.

Leah

If we are allowed to exercise our sanctified imaginations, we might well start to see Leah and Rachel as a mirror to Jacob and Esau. I have nothing against beautiful people, they can't help it, but it's no fun when you are the ugly duckling. We are told that Rachel has a beautiful face and is generally great; she's the all American girl, great student, cheerleader and athlete. No chips on her shoulder, she's Daddy's favourite, has been loved all her life, it's made her confident, optimistic. 'But' says the scripture, *'Leah had weak eyes'*, and she wasn't nearly so nice, a bit jealous and spiky actually, not like her sister; boy that Rachel really is quite a girl. In C.S.Lewis' seminal book 'Mere Christianity' he says that having a head start in life in some areas – like Rachel does here – can not be claimed by us as merit but rather as yet one more gift from God for which we must one day give account. (So if you're naturally confident and beautiful don't worry, its probable not your fault!)

I have an aunt called Dolores, which means grief or sorrow; not exactly aspirational and neither is Leah, for it is from the Hebrew *la'ah*: to be weary, or to grieve. Those 'tender' or 'weak' eyes are a bit of an enigma but I assume that she may have had some visual impairment. Now, if this is correct – and it must have been something of a disability to get a mention – then we need to think how this would affect her ability to work and, of course, how being disabled might affect her acceptance in the family and in the culture. It will have troubled Laban that his eldest daughter might never find a husband, be secure, bear him grandchildren. Perhaps this physical disability had shaped her character; it is hard to grow up or grow at all when you are surrounded by other people whose brilliance only highlights your own imperfection and failure. It can happen unintentionally; we can, out of jealousy, model our aspirations on a sibling or neighbour but still always end up disappointed and bitter.

Most of us are not beautiful in the world's eyes like the Beckhams, the Pitts or the Cruises. Perhaps you did not have perfect parents who rejoiced in your uniqueness but rather compared you to a younger sibling or a clever cousin. Each of us carries the weight of unfulfilled dreams and unrealized expectations. Leah wasn't pretty, Rachel was, it's there by implication. Like

Esau, Rachel was the favourite and another thing, she got to meet Jacob first. While beautiful, strong Rachel is at the well, where is Leah? Is she sitting in the shady half light doing some menial task, basket making, dreaming of a wide world which, for a large part she will never be able to fully enter? Does she perhaps live her life timidly through the eyes of her sister, always being interested in what Rachel has been up to, a bit like sickly Beth does later on in *Little Women*? It is an interesting nuance to ponder, though one thing is sure, whatever was under the surface of that family would soon come to the fore on the day Jacob arrived at their house.

If I understand the story right, I think Leah saw what no one else did, including Rachel. The old saying 'in the land of the blind the one-eyed man is king' could well be as true here as it was in the last recession for Michael Burry. As a one-eyed Aspergers sufferer, he seemed to see what no one else would admit to and in gambling against the market made a fortune. Leah saw what her family could not admit, that Jacob was way more than just a 'meal ticket', that all that stuff about Great Uncle Abe and the line really was true and here was her chance to be a part of the action. I believe it is for this that Leah risked her heart, her future, her life.

Of course on the night of the wedding she did as she was told by her father; that was the way things were for women back then. But for the wedding night deception to work, she had to have wanted it and that really makes us ask the interesting question: why? In Joseph Conrad's masterpiece *Nostromo*, we see a very similar love triangle again involving two sisters; the younger, more beautiful but spoilt Giselle and the older, more spiky and dutiful Linda. The dashing Jean Baptiste gets engaged to Linda through a misunderstanding with her father when all along he loves the younger, Giselle. But for Linda the engagement is the fulfilment of all her desires. I won't say more than that although I cannot imagine Conrad did not have Rachel and Leah in mind when writing that part of the novel.

I believe Leah wanted Jacob with all her heart. I think she not only saw him as a man far above any other she had seen in Haran but also as a way out of Haran, as Isaac had been for her aunt, Rebecca. After all it is usually those at the bottom of the pile that can see through the hypocrisy of the set up that serves up hope to everyone but them. Something like this is currently sweeping the Dhalit 'untouchable' classes in India as I write. It is no surprise that it is they and not the Brahmins that are seeing the Caste system for what it is. Leah went into that bedroom with her eyes well and truly open, she wanted to be part of this thing that the unseen God was doing beyond the river with the other branch of the family. Why couldn't it be one of her descendants that would bring this great blessing to humanity? She carried out her part and did not reveal herself until the marriage was consummated. She put up with his using the name 'Rachel, Rachel' as she imagined how over the years she would make him a great wife worthy of love herself. She would turn his now passionate 'Rachel, Rachel' into 'Leah, Leah'. The tragedy of Leah's story is that this does not happen, men are sometimes too dumb to see what's in front of them, though God compensates Leah in other ways.

Jesus

Psalm 69 v7-21 will crop up again and again as we go through the line; initially we see David being persecuted and ostracised by his family and fellow Bethlehemites but then as we look we can also see Our Saviour in the those hidden Nazareth years too.

> *Because for thy sake I have borne reproach; shame hath covered my face. I am become a stranger unto my brethren, and an alien unto my mother's children. For the zeal of thine house hath eaten me up; and the reproaches of them that reproached thee are fallen upon me. When I wept, and chastened my soul with fasting, that was to my reproach. I made sackcloth also my garment; and I became a proverb to them. They that sit in the gate speak against me; and I was the song of the drunkards. But as for me, my prayer is unto thee, O LORD, in an acceptable time: O God, in the multitude of thy mercy hear me, in the truth of thy salvation. Deliver me out of the mire, and let me not sink: let me be delivered from them that hate me, and out of the deep waters. Let not the waterflood overflow me, neither let the deep swallow me up, and let not the pit shut her mouth upon me. Hear me, O LORD; for thy lovingkindness is good: turn unto me according to the multitude of thy tender mercies. And hide not thy face from thy servant; for I am in trouble: hear me speedily. Draw nigh unto my soul, and redeem it: deliver me because of mine enemies. Thou hast known my reproach, and my shame, and my dishonour: mine adversaries are all before thee. Reproach hath broken my heart; and I am full of heaviness: and I looked for some to take pity, but there was none; and for comforters, but I found none. They gave me also gall for my meat; and in my thirst they gave me vinegar to drink.* Psalm 69:7-21

Through David's own persecution at home – we see Jesus started to seek God for his ministry and gifting. At the very point that he starts to fast and pray, opposition and persecution rise up on every side. He says he becomes a stranger to his brothers, the town drunkards make him the subject of their songs and even the town elders who sit in the city gate speak against him. It has never been easy for people when there is a question mark over their parentage and this would follow Jesus all his life, but we should realize what this did to him. Further down the psalm tells us that the reproach crushed his heart, that he was consumed by distress and, worst of all, that he searched diligently for someone to give him comfort but could not find a single person. He pushed against all this stigma for eighteen plus years, until he would emerge at Jordan with a fully developed spiritual ministry, ready to minister to people all screwed up like you and me.

For those who have come through bullying and social stigma we need look no further than this to find a saviour who has experienced and triumphed over it all. If you want to add your name to this list of people who triumphed over varying weights of social disability then you are in very good company.

Jacob, Leah and Jesus Traded Material Things to Gain Spiritual Power

Jacob

The right of the firstborn was sold legally by Esau to Jacob, no question. There is clearly 'consideration' (a legal term for payment) with the stew and then the contract is also bound by an oath. Esau will try to make out that Jacob 'stole' it; later on we are told in no uncertain terms that Esau couldn't give a flying fig about his family's spiritual heritage or anything beyond the gratification of his bodily desires. 'What good is all this 'Family Line' business? I'm living for now, not some mumbo jumbo religious quackery.' When the writer of Hebrews describes him as a 'profane' man, he means that Esau treated something very holy as if it were ordinary (common). For him there was no repentance even though there was clearly remorse and regret. He had the outward vestiges of a bona fide evangelical, the right religious language of repentance, even taking one of Ishmael's daughters as a wife just to please the 'old man'. But this surface religion doesn't cut it with God, for the *'living God who sees me'* also saw Esau's heart a long way off. God's verdict isn't like my teachers, who used to write on my school reports, 'could try harder'. It's worse than that, much worse, for God says, *'Jacob I have loved Esau I have hated.'* That is very scary and the implications are clear enough, as five out of six New Testament letter writers warn; there is a place where the faithless can be lost forever, no matter how orthodox their mental creed. All but two of Jesus' warnings about hell are given to so-called *believers*; simply put, we need to treat our spiritual calling as Jacob did and not follow Esau.

Leah

My friends Nestor and Kerry have some very film-star-like wedding photos of themselves on a beach in Cyprus. A few years down the line they now have six beautiful children and when we were over at their place the other day for lunch she pointed at the wedding photos and told us what a thoughtless teenage girl had said when she had seen them; 'oh, was that you!' Yes, exactly, 'ouch!'

Well, bear that in mind when we pick up the story with Leah some years later as things are looking pretty grim for her. Now she is a middle aged mother of four lively boys living with her younger sister Rachel who, at this time seems to have a total night time monopoly on Jacob. To be slightly blunt, Rachel – the 'younger woman' without child care responsibilities or stretch marks – controls the most important sperm bank on the planet at that time, for from Jacob's loins would come that one man, possibly in the next generation for all she knew, who would be a blessing to the entire human race.

Before this point God has seen that Leah was 'hated' or 'odious' to Jacob. She's been crying out in her distress (as we shall see in the next point) and God helps her get pregnant. How do we know she can't get a night with her husband? Simply because she has to trade mandrakes with her sister for the privilege. Yes, that's right, Rachel trades a night with the most important lover on earth at that time for a few pieces of fruit. What Esau trades for stew she trades for fruit; she despised – thought little or nothing of – the spiritual significance of her husband's seed. Rachel, the one whose heart clung to her father's idols was profane in a similar fashion to Esau, though perhaps nowhere near as bad. I think if the boot had been on the other foot Leah would not have given up a night with Jacob for the whole earth. God saw that and rewarded her with another son.

Jesus

The verses that we have studied in Psalm 69 show us a teenager who is already forgoing luxury to seek God for power on our behalf. Verse 10 says *'When I wept, and chastened my soul with fasting, that was to my reproach. I made sackcloth also my garment; and I became a proverb to them.'* This verse shows that – without succumbing to sin – Jesus conquered *'every weight that doth so easily encumber'* through the spiritual disciplines of fasting and prayer. How many good ministries have fallen or gone bad because men and women did not subjugate their physical and material appetites to their spiritual calling? The extent of the revival during the ministry of Jesus and John was all decided in these critical years.

You may feel that you are, as Jesus was, an 'arrow hidden away in God's quiver', but I must tell you now that it is at this very time that you must decide how deep you will dig in repentance, fasting and prayer. For it is here that the extent of your usefulness and fruitfulness will be settled. No amount of tooth brushing on the morning of the dentist appointment can make up for months of laziness. You don't need to blow your own trumpet about what God is doing with you, Nehemiah made sure he told no one until he had done his preparation work. The whole point of Jesus' *'house on the rock'* parable isn't about finding a bare rock to build on, but rather digging through the sand to locate the bedrock. Jesus blesses diggers.

'Oh but Henry, you don't understand, I'm so busy battling with temptation and worldly desires that I can never see myself ever being set free enough to have an impact in this world.' Maybe, but I remember a fishing lake restoration I managed a few years back where one of the problems was pond weed near the fishing platforms. We could do the paths, parking sign boards, furniture and drainage but if we couldn't shift this weed – the whole project was a disaster. We could spray the weed but we knew it would be back in two years, so what did we do? We got the biggest excavators we could and dug down as deep as we could around those fishing platforms. Those weeds grew in the shallows and by digging down deep we removed their habitat. So don't focus on sin but dig deep in repentance, fasting and prayer. Paul's antidote for carnality is to *'walk in the spirit'*, pure and simple (Gal.5v16).

John Wesley got his young men to fast every Wednesday, 'You get on fire,' he'd tell them, 'and men will come to watch you burn.' And they did, in their thousands and the world was never the same again. Jesus became the pioneer of faith during those years, he blazed a trail to show what could be done by anyone who trusted God. He endured the persecution of Nazareth, everyone against him, even his own brothers. It says he could not find one comforter even though he *eagerly and consistently* looked for it. (The inference from Psalm 69v8 & 20 is that this even includes his own mother and it is almost certain later that she was among the crowd of friends and family who came to take Jesus home because people were saying that he was schizophrenic, literally; 'beside himself' (Mark 3v21-32). But we should not think harshly of them for we can see now that this was the Father's plan so 'bruise him', and so that *'morning by morning'* as Isaiah 50 says, God would *'open his ear'*. But open his ear for what? Simple yet profoundly moving, *'to give him the tongue of the learned so that he would have a word in season for <u>him who is weary.</u>'* Like the parable of the guy banging on his neighbour's door for bread for his guest, Jesus' whole motivation and focus of those years was to get 'bread' for us. And this should be our inspiration too, not power and gifts for prestige's sake, but for bread for others, the 'bruised reeds' and 'smouldering candles'. We should allow God to show us the great needs he could meet through us, let it break our hearts just a little as it breaks his and then ask the simple question, 'Lord, what is getting in the way of you using me to make a difference here?'

Would you be willing to give up some leisure time to see God use your loaves and fishes to feed the multitude? Spend a few nights away from the TV in order to study and pray *or bring a word in season for them that are weary?* What about foregoing that second income, that foreign holiday, that bigger house, that newer car? The very meaning of the Greek word, 'soldier' in the New Testament is 'one who sleeps outside', i.e. foregoes luxury, presumably – as in Uriah's case – because of loyalty to the king and fellow soldiers. (2 Sam 11v9-11) The people who are called *'great in the kingdom'* are the people who will answer 'yes' to this question. If you struggle in all honesty to do this but the desire is there, then offer this to the Lord right now, it's a good start.

Jacob, Leah and Jesus Pushed Through to Fruitfulness by Dealing With God Direct

What I mean here is that they did not complain to men, like Esau and Rachel did, but dealt straight with God. This is an enormously important point for we all have a tendency, like the Jews at Horeb, to send the pastor up the mountain to talk to God. The real lesson here is not to settle for 'second hand' Christianity, we must live *'in front'* of him. We must live with an *'open face'* before him, not whine on about how the pastor said this or that; we must come to grips with God, literally wrestle with *him*.

Jacob

Jacob wrestled all his life; with his father for affirmation, with his brother for recognition and, of course, for the birthright which was his by prophecy and now with his uncle for basic justice. I disagree with the preachers who say, 'Ah well, you can see "tricky Dicky" is getting a taste of his own medicine at Uncle Laban's place.' It sort of assumes that Jacob's nature was in some way worse than everyone else's and 'certainly nothing like ours'. Frankly I think we need to cut the moralizing rhetoric and stick to the text because this sort of thinking flows very naturally from a misreading of all that had gone before. Jacob's dream at Bethel in Genesis 31 is yet more confirmation that God is on his side, to preserve him from the injustice and dishonesty of others. So it is not to punish or brow beat him into submission. Stealing and bullying is Satan's work and that is what we see in Haran. Jacob steps into a Mafioso and occult world from which Satan would scarce have let him escape if angels had not worked on Jacob's behalf.

I was caught up unwittingly in the Bosnian war when travelling as a student. The lorry driver I was with said I slept through a gun fight in Belgrade, but when I left him the next day I spent some time in the area, later travelling up the Adriatic coast and eventually escaping from Pula by boat across to Venice. As the archetypal budget traveller, I was sleeping rough on overnight buses or in public toilets and it is hard to describe the sense of exposure and vulnerability you feel being in a destabilised social environment. One night I narrowly escaped being mugged by a gang in Mostar and I always slept with an opened butterfly knife in my hand, stupid really when the baddies had guns! But it gives me a bit of empathy with Jacob, for some nights I would dream of home and particularly being back with my mum. Now I had spent the largest part of my childhood away from home at boarding schools but this was different, this wasn't just homesickness, this was 'I may never get out of this alive to see home again.' But of course this is nothing compared to Jacob's twenty year ordeal at the hand of 'Don' Laban. I wondered how many times on a freezing hillside had he dreamed of his mother too?

The enemy robbed Jacob of some prime years of his life; he can do that to us by various means of deception, even to Christians. But the Lord can also restore the years those cankers of distraction and locusts of deception have eaten away and indeed he did this for Jacob by giving him the strength of Laban's flocks. Jacob had the ability to 'make things work'; it's something we see in Jacob and the Jewish nation as a whole throughout the ages. But this innate sense of business acumen has been a great source of persecution too for, like Jacob's success with the flock, insecure and greedy eyes are never wanting.

I would never hail the virtues of capitalism but it is clear to me that socialism has never been able to handle the idea of entrepreneurial zeal. The old maxim, 'If it moves tax it, if it keeps on moving regulate it and if it stops moving subsidize it' is unfortunately all too true. It was the Muslims who first made the Jews (and the conquered Christians) wear the distinguishing clothes of slaves but it was later, under the reign of Edward I (seven hundred years before Hitler) that the English would insist on the infamous yellow star armband. To be able to 'make stuff happen' or be fruitful in the Mafioso badlands of Laban (or Red-tape land) is a difficult business, I know from bitter experience. I've had many clients who took advantage of my youth, or of my laid back relational approach to business. They're happy enough for me to design their golf course or holiday park, or even defend them at a public enquiry, but when it comes to writing cheques they are very quick to lie or delay or be 'out of the office'. Of course I have had great clients too, but it is very much Laban's world out there.

I only had my fees cut once or twice; Jacob's wages were changed ten times and Laban's daughters, who were later ostracized by their association with Jacob, rejoiced in God's righteous judgement against the sin of their father. Their lazy brothers and father can now have what they deserve. For he has used his provincial nephew worse than a slave, changing his wages on top of the harsh conditions of employment. He never intended Jacob to leave and, like Apollyon in *The Pilgrim's Progress*, Laban pursues Jacob to kill him and steal his wealth. Like I said before in a previous chapter, achieving your exodus from the god of this world is a life and death business. Jacob knew it, Leah knew it, they all did. But God kept his promise and Jacob lived to wrestle another day.

His wrestling at Peniel (Gen 32v24) is a supernatural extension and culmination of all that had gone before. Here we see that tenacity inherited from his mother on full display. How often have I given up praying too soon or have we ended a time of worship before we 'got through' to God? Jacob will not let go, pure and simple. He knew way before Paul ever wrote it that he needed to *'apprehend that for which he was apprehended in Christ Jesus'*(Phil 3:12). God may have a call on your life, friend, why wouldn't he? But if you do not take hold of it, of him and say, 'I'm not letting go Lord until you make me fruitful' then you will never see what he intended. Jacob not only got through to God but also got what God wanted to give him, nothing less than the affirmation he had craved since childhood from his own father. God vindicates his past actions *'You shall be called Israel* (meaning prince with God) *for as a prince you have wrestled with men and God and have prevailed'* (Gen 32:28) and sends him away with a *'thorn in the flesh'*. One preacher said 'never trust a man without a limp' and I'm sure you get the point. As Tozer put it, 'It is doubtful whether God can bless a man greatly until He's hurt him deeply.' Jacob had lived his life full-on to do God's will, even from the womb, but the level of blessing that he yearned to deliver could only ever be proportionate to the weakness of his flesh. In that he is just like the Apostle Paul and hopefully like you too. If you are struggling with medical or emotional weaknesses, remember how Peter sees it when he talks about the salvage operation under way in your life. He says,

'... though now for a little while it is necessary for you to endure distress through different types of adversity that the testing of your fidelity – which is far more precious and durable than gold even though it can survive fire – will obtain the commendation, honour and glory when Jesus Christ appears.' 1 Peter 1:6–7

Do not care overly much what men say about you, live for an audience of one for long after their opinions are proved false and long after the pain of that thorn or limp has passed from memory, you will see the fruit of your labour if you keep going.

Leah

There was once a woman in Guildford with crippled legs. She had prayed for healing year upon year but eventually came to the end of herself. It was a stormy night when, in her bedroom she attempted to stand and curse God, blaming him for all her misery and failed expectation. But in doing so she fell and knocked herself unconscious. The next time she opened her eyes she was surrounded by a blinding light and her first thought, 'Oh no, I'm dead and the last thing I did was curse God!' In fact she wasn't dead at all, it was the morning light streaming through her bedroom window. She was just thanking God for not taking her too seriously when she realized there was no longer pain in her legs. She stood up and cupped a hand over her mouth, 'I'm healed, it's a miracle, I don't believe it, God's healed me!'

Of course many women have sunk under their circumstances but just as many have risen with the waters. Anna Baubauld and Lucy Montgomery both had husbands who were ministers with depression. Life was not easy at all for those women – in fact, Anna's husband even tried to knife her before one day drowning himself – and yet they let the hardship drive them to prayer and writing. Anna's 18th century literary criticism, children's stories and hymns are now highly regarded. (Though previously ignored because – as a godly woman – she did not fit neatly into the accepted story that Feminists wanted to tell.) And Lucy? Well, who has not been blessed by the 'Anne of Green Gables' books?

Maybe they were similar to Leah in that, at the last she was only able to take her heartache, loneliness – and perhaps even just plain bitterness – to God. But that is better than nothing for even if we've only got hurts and complaints to share then let's at least take them, if we really believe God is a God of comfort. The pain of Leah's loveless marriage forms the core of her prayer life and can be seen through the names of her sons. With each name we see her journey as she wrestles with Jacob for affection and with God for an answer, which is in sharp contrast with Rachel who complains to Jacob that she is infertile. 'Am I in the place of God?' he says angrily, though even after this she would rather find a human solution (Bilhah) than face God herself.

Leah's first son Reuben was a major affirmation of God's approval, for she says *'The Lord has looked on my affliction'*, i.e. when she took the only thing she had – her aching heart – to God, he filled it with a child. She carries on calling to him in her loneliness and he hears, Simeon means 'heard' for she said *'God heard that I was hated'*. But nothing changes in her relationship with Jacob and so she presses on. Eventually she conceives Levi (*'attached'*) named because she hopes beyond hope that after three sons Jacob will be *attached* to her like he is to Rachel. It's really quite galling and demeaning to see her go through this humiliation but like the *'importunate widow'* of Jesus' parables and the Syrophonecian woman of Mark 7 who – in a sense – overcomes him with her persistence, so Leah makes her breakthrough with her fourth child.

Judah means 'praise' for she said *'Now I will praise the Lord'*. What I see here is a woman who has been looking up so long that her focus has started to stay heavenward. The situation doesn't actually change but her attitude does. Now the baby's name doesn't reflect her marriage problems but her relationship with God. Something literally breaks in her and, temporarily at least, this causes Leah to rejoice in what God had done for her; that this disabled daughter of an idolatrous farmer in a dusty Syrian town was building the foundations of a great nation. That perhaps even this child in her arms might be the one through whom the promise would come; it was major league and she knew it.

Jesus

We have already discussed the true conquest of Jesus' early years at Nazareth but it is necessary here to look at the bar mitzvah trip to the temple (Luke 4v21-51). So little is made of this extraordinary act of thoughtlessness on twelve-year-old Jesus' part that I wonder if anyone ever wondered why he would do such an extreme thing. I mean, what factor drove him so intensely that he could not go back to Nazareth until he had answers?

One answer might be given by Nathaniel in the form of a rhetorical question; 'Can anything good come out of Nazareth?' Does this mean it was a spiritual black hole? Yes, I would say this is the inference and it certainly tallies with Psalm 69 and Luke 4, when they try to throw him off a cliff. Simply put I believe Jesus could not get theological answers in Nazareth. The Rabbis there had become so hardened by nationalism and legal religion that they could not minister into Jesus' life, in fact, as we know from Psalm 69:12, they actually derided him.

Here we step into the realms of exactly what Jesus' humanity meant and, of course, how he 'awoke' to his divine identity. I know that the scholar N. T. Wright has tackled this boldly in *Simply Christian* but I find myself only able to go so far with him – perhaps you feel the same about what I am saying; after all we are in deep waters here. How can we speak of these things and still uphold the *full* humanity and *full* divinity of our beautiful Saviour? Conservative and Liberal theologians have usually emphasised one or other; not least to correct what they felt was the imbalance of their counterparts. In this chapter I am stressing Jesus' real humanity.

You see, there were no special 'Son of God' downloads that he would have that we could not. If he was to triumph and be sifted as the first Adam was, he must do it all as we do it and yet be without sin. His father started to visit him *'morning by morning'* with prophetic messages, perhaps visions too and as he prayed he became more hungry to know God. The level of this hunger and eventual desperation is seen in his disappearance at the temple. He knew, as you must also, that any ministry must be built on the word of God and not just prayer. Who would teach him if the Rabbis in Nazareth were so backslidden? Can you see it now? That trip to Jerusalem must have been like water to Jesus' soul and it shows us also his determination to dig deep into the word and to learn about who he should be. There was no easy road for him, he studied hard and saw himself, his destiny modelled in the lives of the Patriarchs, the prophets and kings, no wonder he was different from his contemporaries, his mind was immersed in a biblical world view at a time when others were all 'politics, current affairs and the tithing laws on herbs'. There was no desert retreat for him, he had to work the long days, pray and study at night after his younger brothers and sisters were asleep, or before they all woke up. He came out of Nazareth untouched by the moral filth and unbelief, not bitter towards his countless enemies, even his brothers who teased him (and must have witnessed or even been participators at the Luke 4 assassination attempt). Through all this he emerged aged thirty with a fully developed prophetic, healing and teaching ministry. How did he manage not to let the 'master of arrows' succeed in wearing him down into bitterness? He did the same thing he had read that Joseph, Jacob and Leah did, it's written in Psalm 69:13 that he *'made his prayer to thee, oh Lord.'* That's right, not to men, he dealt straight with God as we should, as we must.

And did Jesus get that vindication that Jacob and Leah got from heaven?

Yes, at his baptism when he appeared for public ministry, no matter what all the liars, gossips and bigots had said in Nazareth, God said, *'You are my Son, whom I love; with you I am well pleased'* (Mark 1:11) The psalms are full of this and many other people beside you have been strengthened down the ages in their trials by the knowledge that despite all that men say may about them and their situation, that in the final analysis their 'way is known to God', literally that he understands even if no one else can. Job 23v10 has been the mainstay of millions too 'For he knows the pilgrimage I'm on and after I've gone through this furnace I will emerge like pure gold.' Like I say, history is always written by the conquerors.

'Wrestling With God'
Duet for Jake and Leah – Leah's *words in italics*

(From 'THE LINE' album, words and music by Henry Brooks)

Leah I'd think, that we had nothing in common,
no common ground to start from, and we were falling apart
And you said, Rachel always came between us,
the family always came between us and that I just didn't care
But the longer I have travelled through this troubled life of mine,
The more I see you were just like me, and I had been so blind
And that it was you baby who was wrestling with God,
And that it was you darling that I should have loved

Now, I don't need to tell you about growing up in someone else's shadow, No
The pain of never being enough to please the ones you love, is something we
know,
(But I was) not so blind, I couldn't see how God was using you
And I prayed that I could have a part in the story too ... oh Jake,
When I said 'I do', I wasn't going in blind, no
Cos my dreams had come true, now I was in 'the Line'

Yeah, both you and me had to trade to get all that the Lord would give to us
two
I was just so desperate for one night alone with you, what else could I do
But God rewarded you cos you could see what it was worth
And Jake he's raised you too, so that your seed could bless the earth
It was me and you, darling, who were wrestling with God,
And we pushed through for the promise we knew would one day come

Life Application Devotional Guide

Chapter 4 – Wrestling with God

- In the lives of Rebecca, Isaac, Jacob, Leah and Jesus, we have seen that considerable effort was needed by each of them to push through to fruitful ministry. Which of the above do you identify with most? Why?
- Can you identify an area in your life where God is calling you to dig in and fight?
- Jacob and Leah both traded earthly things for spiritual blessing. Prayerfully ask the Lord if there is any area in your life where something similar is needed.

Prayer: (Start with thanksgiving & praise.) 'Oh Lord God of Jacob, My Defender and Shield, forgive me where I have been lazy and then knowingly re-labelled it 'faith' or 'quiet acceptance'. Lord please train 'my hands for war' in the things to which you are calling me. Fill me with your spirit of power and strengthen me against every person, every thought and ideology that does not agree with what you have given or what you say about me

(Tamar) — Abraham
Isaac
Jacob
Judah
Perez
Hezron
Ram
Amminadab
Nahshon
Salmon
Boaz
Obed
King David
Solomon
Rehoboam
Abijah
Asa
Jehoshaphat
Jehoram
Ahaziah
Joash
Amaziah
Uzziah
Jotham
Ahaz
Hezekiah
Manasseh
Amon
Josiah
Jehoahaz
Jeconiah
Jehoiachin
Shealtiel
Zerubbabel
Abihud
Eliakim
Azor
Zadok
Akim
Elihud
Eleazar
Matthan
Jacob
Joseph; *the husband*
of Mary; the mother of Jesus;
who is called the Messiah.
(Matt 1:16)

Chapter 5

The Palm Tree (Read Gen 33–45)

We all have family skeletons; my great uncle Francis married the scullery maid. There, I've said it and now you're all shocked!

'Of course, he had to move to Ireland,' my mum would occasionally warn us, a bit like other children might be told about the bogey man. Nobody spoke of it, though I believe the couple were very happy. I had another distant Victorian relation called Jane Digby who divorced her husband after one week and then travelled to Syria where she married a Sheikh who was twenty years her junior; it was a national scandal. On later occasions, when asked if he was related to her, Jane's estranged husband would always shake his head, 'Only by marriage.' But that's not really the worst; another of my grandmother's distant forbears was in charge of torching the Whitehouse and Senate buildings in 1814 – though we never mention it at the dinner table!

The epic of Judah and Tamar is one of Israel's family skeletons, it could be subtitled 'Prodigals, Prostitutes and Prevailing Prayer'. These two give us some of the most moving and gripping biographies found anywhere in history and yet I bet my boots you will never have heard a sermon let alone a song about them. Why not? Perhaps because it is not 'surface digging' but even so, I can assure you that if you are prepared to go a little deeper then the treasure will be worth every stroke of your pick. The other reason might be that we find it distasteful, for here we find lurid sexual detail and other matter unsuitable for the Sunday school stories and yet here it is slap bang in the middle of the Joseph story. How very inconvenient. Have you ever wondered what it is doing here? I bet there have been scores of Sunday school teachers who would gladly have taken it out so that their pupils could read the Joseph story straight through. Simply put, it is one of those stories that really makes you ask yourself, why am I reading the Bible in the first place?

If you have got this far I am guessing you don't read just to find mere sentiment or sensation, but we should still be aware of the danger. We are studying the most important family in history and the most important things that were happening on the earth at that time. Most people missed what God was doing, but some 'understood the times and knew what Israel should do' (1Chron 12v32) and these are the people we're interested in. So let us find out why God loved them and chose them. Maybe we'll learn to love them too and who knows, people say you become like the people you love so there's a good enough reason to read the Bible.

Judah

Early Influences

My mother had a craving for sherry when she was carrying me; apparently it showed in my blotchy red cheeks when I was born. Judah was carried by an anxious, unloved, but prayerful mother and born into a dysfunctional family where there was constant domestic friction. That sort of home life is the kind of thing that will affect you. But I believe there was one particular event that above all others shaped him as a youth: the genocide at Shechem. The Genesis account says that it was only Levi and Simeon who did the killing but that every other brother took part in the spoiling of the town, while the sisters, mothers, wives and grandmothers of the men of Shechem cried over the slain.

Bloodbath

When I was a student in Leeds, my flat mate and I had to restrain a man who was in the process of murdering his old father. I don't know what was worse; the gut wrenching tale of generational abuse or the sheer volume of blood that covered the pavement, the cars, the walls, our hands, faces and clothes. We were so shaken up it took a neighbour to come and help clean us up. I could barely sleep the rest of the night and hitch hiked back to Cumbria that weekend just to get away. It was a long time before I could shake off the images and I tell the story because when I saw images of the bronze age east gate of Shechem on the internet I knew I was probably looking at the bloodied gateway that Judah ran in and out on that fateful day, his initiation into violence and bloodshed. It must have affected him and the way he saw the family. 'Dad can talk all he wants to about our special family and the blessing one of us will be to the world. But if Shechem is anything to go by, I'm not so sure any more.'

The Favoured Son

Following this massacre and up until Rachel's first pregnancy, Judah must have thought he was first in line for the blessing. Reuben was out of the picture because he had been sleeping with his father's concubine. The 'Kray twins', Simeon and Levi, were out too, following their knifing spree in Shechem, that left Judah the next oldest. But he was already 'damaged goods' and I think Joseph's arrival became another nail in the coffin of Judah's faith. He was not stupid – he knew how his father viewed Rachel and what he now intended for Joseph, what else could the foreman's coat mean? It was just too easy for Jacob to forget all that the other sons had become and focus on this new baby. I read a book once that claimed *almost* all marriage and family problems stemmed from the father. A bit harsh I think but whatever the reason, it must have been too easy now for Judah to give up hope and sink into bitterness. Selling rather than killing Joseph was Judah's idea remember; perhaps he couldn't face any more innocent blood on his hands, perhaps he just wanted the cash. Either way it shows that Judah had sunk to some serious depths. Can you imagine facing your father after that and watching him grieve for years on end? This is why chapter 38 begins with Judah leaving 'after these things', what things? The selling of Joseph of course, the night and day crying of his father, the accusing conscience that wouldn't let him sleep while he was still in sound of all that grief that he had inflicted. Somehow the others stuck it out and carried on the hideous pretence but not Judah; I'm guessing it just got to him more than to the others, which perhaps is a good start; but where could he go?

Losing Faith

Roald Dahl's head master was a vicar and a man, who in Dahl's opinion seemed far more keen on justice than mercy. Apparently an offending boy would kneel on a sofa and be caned with intervals given between strokes to allow for moral lectures and the packing of the master's pipe. After the ten minute ordeal the boy would then use the sponge, water and towel provided to clean the blood away from his backside so as not to soil his pyjamas. Yes exactly, not very nice. I tell you because it was this – and the fact that the same clergyman went on to be archbishop of Canterbury – that caused Dahl to begin questioning the validity of Christianity. How sincere his questioning was I do not know but he was a lifelong atheist from what I can make out. Everyone has their story, Judah was no different. As Jacob retreats into his grief Judah goes further off the rails. He moves away from his home which, to me at least, signals that he has officially given up his faith. Maybe if you asked him whether he believed in God he would nod, but that is neither here nor there, most of your friends would say the same. I think he had become what I call a 'Practical Atheist'. Theologians call them Deists. A Deist believes in a God who has wound up the world like a clock, but now it is a closed system, he cannot interact or affect my life, answer my prayers. This is a real struggle for many believers who by some strange mix can even believe God can work through some people's lives (the pastor, the missionary and the big shots on the TV) but their own Christian lives must be lived out in coldness and impotence. Perhaps you have been like this at times, wanting desperately to believe God could have a special plan and destiny for your little life, your little gifting, your little church – but never getting through.

I'd like to report that Judah found his way back to God by going into the world, but he did not. I know many parents of back-slidden teenagers console themselves with similar thoughts but the world cannot do any other than its master's bidding: steal, kill and destroy. The grace of God often finds and binds up the prodigals there, but that is another matter entirely. I was found there by him aged twenty-one, but I wish with all my heart that I had heard the gospel sooner. A friend of mine, now deceased, did not accept the gospel until he was ninety-one. He would weep through the worship times for the life he had not lived for Jesus. 'What can these old limbs do for him now?' he'd say. I dare say he's busy enough now!

Dangerous Liaisons

One of my many jobs as demi-patriarch at our little ranch in the mountains is to de-tangle the hair of the two women in my life. My wife and daughter perhaps have the thickest hair known to mankind, women everywhere admire it but they don't have to take conditioner and comb to it when a morass of knots appear. I do; it is not a pleasant job for me, them or anyone within a two mile radius! But I do have a technique which works every time. I merely separate the 'clumplets' on the outside and savage them with the comb until they yield, nothing else will work, for you could not get a chainsaw through the main clump. This method of 'divide and conquer' is well known to the enemy when he comes to deal with us and now we will see Judah, already damaged and on the edge, being fully separated from the family and taken out.

> 'And it came to pass at that time, that Judah went down from his brethren, and turned in to a certain Adullamite, whose name was Hirah. And Judah saw there a daughter of a certain Canaanite, whose name was Shuah; and he took her, and went in unto her.' Gen 38:1-2

First Judah starts running with a new crowd down in Adullam. They say friends are like buttons on an elevator, they either take us up or down and Judah's new buddy, Hirah, was no angel. His name means 'splendour ' or 'riches' and that is roughly all they live for in Canaan; in fact it's all they really had. Judah's descent was the same as Samson's and perhaps some of us too, separation from family, new peers and then binding covenants that ensnare. Judah's friendship with Mr Splendid was one thing, but marrying the Canaanite pageant queen Miss Wealthy (as Shuah means) is quite another. What started as a simple friendship has now become a permanent lifestyle. Judah and Shuah raise three sons together and he marries the oldest to one of the most extraordinary women in the Bible, Tamar.

Crisis

But then comes the crisis: God hates Judah's oldest son and kills him. According to their culture the second son takes the place and marries the widow. But it appears that sibling hatred, that snare of his father's generation, is also replicated in the children – for this brother is so wicked that he won't even consummate the marriage and raise up children to keep his brother's name alive. By practising 'Coitus Interruptus' (last minute withdrawal) he aroused God's anger and he is killed also. After two out of his three sons die, Judah's wife also dies. Now here's the crisis, he is a middle aged man with no wife and only one son to carry on his line. It could be his last shot at achieving his life's purpose; for no heir, no name. No name, no significance; and what is a man without that? Like Abraham and Sarah, Judah is at his dead–end alley, but can you seriously see God using a washed–up has–been like this?

Judah's Diary

Dear Diary,
Things are going from bad to worse, hardly slept a wink last night again, thought living out here away from the family would ease my conscience but I still cannot get the sound of Dad's crying in the night out of my mind. Dreamed again on Wednesday that Joseph was pleading for his life and every time we butcher a goat for dinner my mind is racked with the images of that afternoon, running back and forth, taking the booty out of Shechem. All that blood and the sound of screaming children, I wish I could undo time, I wish I could forget.
But here I am, middle aged, a life come to nothing after such hopes. Always thought that Dad would make me his firstborn after what the others did. I used to try so hard to please him and share his dreams, the

family promise, all that stuff ... until Joseph came along, then the bar lifted higher than I could jump. Don't know if I lost my faith then or before, I think I just gave up thinking that God had a plan for me, I don't think anyone took it seriously after Joseph went. I didn't, anyway, lost any sense of purpose in a larger cause, a wider purpose ... 'the promise and the seed' seems like ancient history, just a nice idea or bedtime story for the grandkids.

Can't believe the others stuck around, they're a thick skinned bunch, I knew that. But I wasn't sticking around, fed up with all Dad's ramblings, was glad to get away from it all; thought making friends with Hirah was the relief I needed but oh ... look at me now, all that independence, what have I to show for it? Three graves and all this social pressure to give my son, my last remaining son ... my last hope, to that poor, wretched Canaanite girl. I don't know whether she's cursed, or we are – probably both – I'm half frightened to death myself, don't know what to do ... Oh God I hate it, the failure, the waste, the unfulfilled dreams, the pain of this guilt, the memories ... if only ... no, forget it, I blew it long ago, no use moaning now. Hirah's turned up, says we should go clubbing, pick up some girls ...

Tamar

Strong Women

When we come to look at the lives of women like Sarah, Rebecca, Leah, Tamar, Rahab and Ruth it throws open huge questions for women about *who* they want to be and *what* they want to achieve with their lives. As a rule of thumb, we must take for granted that whatever model the culture offers as female liberation and fulfilment is going to be a dead end. I'm quite serious. The apostle John had it right when he said 'we know we are of God and the whole world lies under the power of the Evil One'. Actually the literal rendering is that the world systems 'lie in Satan' and if there is anything praiseworthy in our western democratic nations you can bet your bottom dollar it is there because of something God and not Satan did, and certainly not something that we cooked up without God. It sometimes takes strange prophets to remind the church of just how brainwashed she's become by the liberal media machine.

 The Orthodox Jew and political scientist Michael Horowitz lays down the challenge to Christians to discover their history and sense of pride, to stop being frightened by the bigots who say that all we gave the world was the crusades and endless wars. Horowitz cites the origins of human rights, the ideals of democracy and the abolition of the slave trade as examples for starters. Professor Steve Fuller of Warwick University – himself a secular humanist as far as I can tell – lays down a similar challenge saying that Christians need to claim back the history of Science from the secularists who have run off with their own fanciful version of it. But as Horowitz warns, 'it won't happen until Christians reconnect with their own history and stop going round the world apologising to everyone.'

And liberation for women, are you trying to tell me the secret is in the Bible? But everyone says the Bible is anti-women? Yeah, right, you ought to meet them! The 'ancient paths' may look narrow friend, but that's just because they are roads less travelled. Let's start by meeting Tamar in just a minute.

Wife Hunting

These women also shout a challenge across history to the unmarried men, 'What kind of wife do you really want?' Seriously, it is worth thinking and praying this through. Will you be content just to have a pretty Christian woman who goes to church? There are plenty of those but is that the limit of your faith? Might there not be another sort of woman out there, a woman who will live and die for the gospel? A soul-mate who would perfectly balance your ministry and gifting with hers to make an explosive combination in the hand of an almighty God? A lover and friend to grow with, face trials with, to make a part of you whole that you didn't know was warped? The word used of the first wife was, in the old English translation 'helpmeet'. Sounds menial or servile to you? No bit of it, in fact it is only ever normally used of God. Some translate it literally as 'lifesaver'. My friend was contacted by the KGB who wanted a rendezvous. The British security services let him go but suggested he took his wife too. Sure enough when he arrived there was an adultery trap waiting but with his wife right there at his side he was safe. A dramatic illustration for sure but when I consider my own wife I cannot help but think lifesaver is about an apt description as any going. I sometimes catch myself watching my Ruth as we brush our teeth together, for she has been all this to me and more. Basically, lads, I want you all to offer up all your preconceptions of the 'ideal woman' as you read the next few chapters. In effect say, 'Lord, I have my ideas but I know what you have must be better so I'm open to that if you show me.' That was my heart exactly when the Lord told me, almost audibly during a meeting, that I was looking at my future wife. I was not long converted and not really looking for one either, being not long out of an difficult 'pre-Christian' relationship at university. Furthermore the radiant young woman God showed me looked nothing like any girl I had ever dated before either; she spoke differently, dressed differently but I figured God must know what I needed so it wasn't a problem. I gave the matter to prayer and to the test of time, saying nothing to anyone; if this was God's will he would make it happen. So I went back to university to do my post graduate year and then, over a year later I ended up church planting in the same area. The rest, as they say, is history.

A Dark Past

There is no doubt that Tamar was ill-used by godless men in a male dominated culture but it is also noteworthy that she refused to be a victim. She is not alone; recent research by the NSPCC found one in four girls, some as young as thirteen, had been slapped or hit by their boyfriends, one in nine had been beaten up, hit with objects or strangled. The British government wants to use state schools to teach girls how 'not to be victims' – good luck to them. For obvious reasons it is a bit complicated to use Tamar as a role model for assertive womanhood but let's not also miss her incredible courage and ability to act. This brand of tenacity which overcomes a situation by reckless action has often been a pivotal point in history.

It is very possible that Tamar was a Hebrew relation but it is more probable, when we think of where Judah was at the time, that she was another Canaanite girl like his own wife. And let's have none of this live and let live 'noble savage' stuff, these Canaanite people sacrificed their own children to demons; some say every home was founded on a human sacrifice. Even if you did survive, it was not a nice place to grow up or be a goat; bone samples show venereal disease was widespread in cattle and children. It's one thing for Judah to be allured by 'freedoms' of going native, quite another to grow up where paedophilia and bestiality are the norm. It angers me to see all the 'right on' hippy sorts raving about New Age spirituality and never thinking to ask the Hindu Dhalit or women what it's like to grow up in rural India. If you start your worldview with a pantheist deity – one attached to this created order – you will quickly see that nature far from being benign or innocent is vicious and arbitrary in equal measure, an attribute that will then reflect into your ethics and religion. The impressionist painter Gauguin swallowed these doctrines of Rousseau, even abandoning his family, moving to 'innocent' Tahiti and marrying a very young girl. But in the end he saw it for what it was, recorded his despair in the painting 'Where do we come from? What are we? Where are we going?' and then tried to take his own life.

Tamar's despair is Gauguin's despair, for her society's worldview had similar precepts and conclusions. But then she is vastly different for out of her culture's despair and chaos she sees Judah's family – even in the state they are in – and in all that darkness – they, their family promise, their creator God is a massive ray of hope. I think she wants more than anything to be part of that family; perhaps she even dreams that she might be the woman through whom their 'fabled' promise will come. But Judah's problem is her problem too, she had buried two bad husbands, the next one is of age now and by rights he should be given to her but that is not happening. Judah's gone quiet. I think he's in a sort of decision making paralysis, he simply does not know what to do. He wouldn't be the first man in a jam; King Frederick of Prussia didn't know how to appease Napoleon, but while the king was vacillating his beautiful Queen Louise appeared, mounted in armour and wielding a sword to inspire the troops against tyranny. She lost the battle, but you can't blame a girl for trying; at least she made a decision and that is what is desperately needed in our story too.

The Palm Tree

It turns out that the only one who you might think has no choice in the story, or at least has not had one until now, rises up and takes the initiative. It is risky and will almost certainly end up with her being burnt alive, apart from one thing. It is a very small thing and something that everyone, including Judah has overlooked; everyone except the Lord and Tamar. What is that? You'll find out later.

Her name literally means 'palm tree', though figuratively it would denote 'uprightness', i.e. they usually grow sticking straight up! But here's the thing, the real strength of a palm is in its flexibility, an ability to bend low when the storm comes. Have you ever seen those hurricane pictures with palms bent right to the ground? In this case she dresses as a prostitute and seduces her father-in-law without revealing her identity. Now again, as with Rebecca and Jacob's deception, we are faced with an immoral action but if we can look behind the method to the motive, we might be flabbergasted by Tamar's bravery and sheer audacity. Notice she doesn't just go and find any man, she finds the man with the promise; this girl is like Leah, she's in it to be *the one*, to have the line go through her womb. This girl is not getting any younger, there is a time limit on her dreams, are you going to condemn her?

How low will you go? Now, I am not trying to condone sin, but if I am allowed just one sentence to spiritualize this I would ask you, how low will you humble yourself to take hold of your destiny? Would you put out chairs, clean toilets, teach Sunday school even!? Remember David's words to his barren, critical and idolatrous wife Michal, '*I will yet be more vile than thus, and will be base in mine own sight.'* (2 Sam 6v22) David knew the way up is actually down in the kingdom of God, something kingdom life has in common with grave digging! We are literally taller when we bow. There may be someone reading this who knows their life has had little impact and yet there is a strong desire to see it so. Let me ask you, friend, are you willing to be a 'fool for Christ's sake', to give up the vanity that others call middle class respectability, to turn your back on the pitiable peer culture that keeps grown men as fruitless eunuchs to mere career, mere suburbia? Would you be prepared to have all of them, colleagues, school friends, family, spouse and children all think you were a religious nut if you could just have that one chance to do something great with God? If the answer is 'no' then you can still pray, 'God is greater than our hearts' (1 John 3v20), if the answer is 'yes', then watch out world.

Tamar's Diary

> *Dear Diary,*
> *This is probably the last entry I will ever make, but I am past caring now, totally and utterly, my course is set; either I'll get in this 'line-thing' or I will die trying.*
> *One thing's for sure and I'm not going to sit around here any longer wasting my life in widow's weeds waiting for Judah another day, time is running out for me. Even if I did think that the men in my life would do what they should (which I don't!) the kid looks about as nasty as his brothers anyway.*
> *Just read the above ... yikes! Can't believe I'm talking like this, who would have thought it of quiet little me, but I guess even I have dreams ... never used to but being involved with this family has changed me, made me see everything differently. When old Jacob would tell us about the promise God made him, I would tingle all over, like I knew it was true and I could be involved. I made up my mind to live for that, that promise, even when I was abused by Er and then Onan. I just thought 'I can put up with this if I could just have a chance to have my child in that family line.'*
> *So I held on and on ... and on, now the grass has grown over Er and Onan's graves; Shelah is grown; Judah's given up long ago on his faith, anyone can see that, and yet I can see so much depth in him, so much sadness, as if, he shared this same dream that I had once ... I wonder if what I'm about to do will bring him back to God or drive him further away ... if it's the latter, my life will be finished; mind you, it's finished already so what have I to lose ... now where did I put that scarf ... ?*

Revival

In the end there is one thing that she banks on: Judah's integrity. In her desperation she is not unlike the Gibeonites who approach Joshua, banking on his integrity too (Joshua Ch 9). Tamar can see that Judah is ripe for repentance, pure and simple. At the point where she is about to be burnt alive she produces the proof that the children she is carrying are his. Now we see what kind of man Judah is, will he cast the proof aside and have her burnt to remove his embarrassment? Surely everyone has turned up for the event. This thing is going to be talked about in both communities for a long time. The kindling is gathered and anticipation grows. What's he going to do?

> 'But Judah acknowledged them, and said, She has been more upright than me; because that I didn't give her Shelah my son. But he never had sex with her again.' Gen 38:26

It is here that we start to see the man Judah come back to God. Tamar literally causes repentance, confession and revival in Judah and forces him back to confront God again. This is what she gambles everything on and this is what Tamar achieves. She brings repentance and revival to a dying man. It is masterful, and without it, without her, the ground work in Judah's heart would not have been done for the most important decision he will have to make shortly after.

Redemption

Substitutional Love

A young colonel was given charge to defend the north American frontier against the French and their hired Indian mercenaries. It was a vast area and he was woefully under resourced. One day he arrived only too late at a farm to save a young family. When he saw the father and son lying dead and butchered in the field, and the two torn babes lying at the breast of their slain mother, he writes, 'If I know myself, I pledge to God that I would have given my life gladly to save these countrymen of mine'. It is not surprising that a young man like that would go on to be a legend, for that same vicarious love marked the entire career of George Washington, until all the world knew his name.

Those first buds of Judah's repentance would eventually flower into this type of love during the great famine that threatened the whole world. Reuben, limp as ever, offers his first born as a substitute for Benjamin. Judah offers his life, first in word (easy enough) but then in deed when Benjamin is arrested.

Love in Word

> *'I will be surety for him; of my hand shalt thou require him: if I bring him not unto thee, and set him before thee, then let me bear the blame for ever.'* Genesis 43:9

Love in Action

> *v18. Then Judah came near unto him, and said, Oh my lord, let thy servant, I pray thee, speak a word in my lord's ears ...*
> *v32. For thy servant became surety for the lad unto my father, saying, If I bring him not unto thee, then I shall bear the blame to my father for ever. Now therefore, I pray thee, let thy servant abide instead of the lad a bondman to my lord; and let the lad go up with his brethren. For how shall I go up to my father, and the lad be not with me? lest peradventure I see the evil that shall come on my father. Then Joseph could not refrain himself before all them that stood by him; and he cried.* From Genesis 44:18-45:1

It is revealing to see Judah's primary motivation in this is actually love for his father, the man he had wounded so much for all those years as they falsified the death of Joseph. It always interested me that the car magnate Henry Ford never employed men at odds with their fathers. The restoration of family relationships – when it is possible – is as sure a sign as any that God has moved our hearts. If none of the other brothers got it, Judah did; the work of repentance started through Tamar is now manifest in full recovery and revival. Judah does as one of his descendants would do one day, that is, step in on behalf of Israel to be the substitutionary sacrifice. What an incredible picture and who would have thought it of back-slidden Judah?

Well, Tamar for one.

She gave birth to twin boys called Buster and Rising (Perez and Zerah), Buster will 'burst ahead' (as his name means) to be the one continuing the line, though Joseph will inherit the birthright. Chronicles makes this clear; the blessing and birthright are separate now, and the blessing is going through Judah's descendants.

> *'Now the sons of Reuben the firstborn of Israel, (for he was the firstborn; but, forasmuch as he defiled his father's bed, his birthright was given unto the sons of Joseph the son of Israel: and the genealogy is not*

to be reckoned after the birthright. For Judah prevailed above his brethren, and of him came the chief ruler; but the birthright was Joseph's.)' 1 Chronicles 5:1-2

We could re-translate that last verse as '_Judah was more valiant than his brothers because he stood out before them, though the birthright still passed to Joseph._' It is what the Hebrew words mean and it is a very good description of what Judah actually did. The Holy Spirit also mentions God's choice for the line in Psalm 78.

'_Moreover he refused the tabernacle of Joseph, and chose not the tribe of Ephraim: But chose the tribe of Judah, mount Zion which he loved.'_
Psalms 78:67-68

But the most moving and revealing affirmation of Judah's conversion and ministry comes from his own father, the one he had hurt so deeply and yet now the one who prophecies the will of God from his deathbed.

'_Judah , you're the one the brothers will praise: your power will throttle anyone who stands against you; your father's children will bow down to you_ (i.e. not Joseph, nice touch). _Judah is a lion's cub with meat. My son ascended because he prostrated himself, he fell down as a young lion but as an older lion he achieved success. Therefore the ruling sceptre will never be revoked from Judah , nor a lawgiver from your line until Shiloh_ (i.e. Messiah) _come whom all people shall obey. Binding his foal unto the vine, and his ass's colt unto the choice vine; he washed his garments in wine, and his clothes in the blood of grapes_' Genesis 49:8-11

The whole story is a real encouragement for prodigals of every generation, particularly that last line about how Judah washed his garments in the blood of grapes. We may have soiled our clothes, our reputations and families in this world's ways but there is always a place of washing for those who, like Judah find repentance.

'_And one of the elders answered, saying unto me, What are these which are arrayed in white robes? and whence came they? And I said unto him, Sir, thou knowest. And he said to me, These are they which came out of great tribulation, and have washed their robes, and made them white in the blood of the Lamb._' Rev 7:13-14

Conclusion

God can make the *best of us* but we must first be willing to give him the *worst of us* first. He can even weave the dark threads of your worst mistakes, our most inexcusable sin and our deepest pain into his story. So do not fear your past friend, give it to Him and see what he will do. *And we know that all things work together for good to them that love God, to them who are the called according to his purpose.* (Rom 8:28) 'But what have I got to give?' you say.

Prodigal Judah had nothing but a wasted life and an impossible problem to bring to God, that was enough for God. Tamar brought nothing but her broken heart, her broken dreams and the broken promises of faithless men, it was enough for God. He used both this pitiful material and these fallen people to change history. Why should you be any different?

> *For whatsoever things were written aforetime were written for our learning, that we through patience and comfort of the scriptures might have hope.* Rom 15:4

At the weekend our local town made the national headlines for five days when a one in a thousand year flood event swept through our lives. A month's rain fell in thirty-six hours and a deluge swept through the town taking out bridges that had stood for centuries. Friends of mine lost everything they owned, but not as much as PC Bill Barker who was swept to his death when a bridge collapsed. He died giving his life for others but it is not something we are all called on to do everyday for we're usually called to living first. And we can take a leaf out of Judah's book and start to seek that kind of love that gives itself to others. It may not be giving up your life to the lions on the first occasion, perhaps just giving up your time to your spouse, child or parent. From little acorns mighty oaks will grow if you are faithful.

For example there is a type of prayer where we can share in the sufferings of others, where our hearts and lives are so bound up with our loved ones that we feel and so help carry their anxieties. This is the high calling we have in Christ, in fact it was and is the entire focus of his heart towards you, 'Bear one another's burdens and so fulfil *the law of Christ*' Gal 6:2

The word for *law* here can describe a 'parcel of land' suitable for a grazing animal. We keep goats in an acre patch at our ranch, that patch is their total life within which they live, move and have their pasture. Lifting burdens from sinners is Jesus' *patch*, the focus of his whole being, his meat and drink, what his father called him to.

If we share this patch – this heart – with Jesus; the church and the world will never be the same again. Oh Lord change our hearts.

The Palm Tree

Judah and Tamar's song from the stake – Tamar's words in italics

(From 'THE LINE' album, words and music by Henry Brooks)

Oh Tamar, I have done you wrong, but you tell me what else could a man do?
Standing at the grave of a wife and two sons and he sees all his life is and it all shot through
Now I'm not saying that I'm a saint, gave up my faith long ago
Done things that make heaven weep, Things I can't undo and only God knows

There was a time when I shared Dad's dreams, about our promise and all he said that it would mean
But I couldn't make it as a favoured son, since Joe was born and became God's chosen one
So I gave up God and ran to the world, made cool friends and found a pretty girl
Knew I was running but I didn't care, needed love and I found it so easy there

Now all that's left's a disillusioned man, coming with nothing but his sins in his hand
Cos you've prevailed, Tamar and made me see, that God's not run out on me

Now this might sound weird to you, you took for granted all that your family were
But I knew that the promise was true, grow up where I did, you can tell light from dark
And I yearned to have a part, that my life could mean something more than this
When the boys died it crushed my hopes too, but the dream lived on and so did I

And I waited for all you promised me, but I grew older and time was running out for me
If I was going to be used by God, I had to seize my chances while I could
So I'm not ashamed I had to stoop so low, a palm tree bends when the strong wind blows
Being in the line was worth all I've been through, I trust my judgement to you

Oh my dear, you're more righteous than I, you risked your life and made me see
Some things are really worth dying for and you've birthed revival in me
And God has given all you asked of him, to me what I'd only dreamed

Now it's time to fix these sin-filled lives; that he's turned around and redeemed

Not know what will become of us or to the babes that will be born
But our faith is in the living God, whose grace has covered all
And we will not doubt again God's heart for us whose lives are spent and worn
He has no scrap yard for open hearts, and now mine is open for sure.

Life Application Devotional Guide

Chapter 5 – Counting the cost

- The sort of faith shown by Tamar and then Judah in this chapter might be spelled 'RISK'. Can you remember a time when you staked something (or everything) on God 'coming through' for you?
- Do you *feel* that God has ever let you down? If the answer is yes, then please record this event or situation in your journal and talk through your feelings about this with the Lord.
- Between where you are now and where you believe God is calling you (i.e. that place of relationship or fruitful ministry that you may have already recorded in your personal journal entries from previous chapters) what three things might you have to risk?

Prayer: (Start with thanksgiving & praise, particularly for God's faithfulness to you.) 'Sovereign and faithful God, I see where you are calling me and having counted the cost I still want to obey your call. Please give your servant courage and strength as I step out in obedience. I confess that the safest possible place for me is in the centre of your will for my life. Lord teach me your ways.

Abraham
Isaac
Jacob
Judah
Perez
Hezron
Ram
Amminadab
Nahshon
Rahab —— Salmon
Boaz
Obed
King David
Solomon
Rehoboam
Abijah
Asa
Jehoshaphat
Jehoram
Ahaziah
Joash
Amaziah
Uzziah
Jotham
Ahaz
Hezekiah
Manasseh
Amon
Josiah
Jehoahaz
Jeconiah
Jehoiachin
Shealtiel
Zerubbabel
Abihud
Eliakim
Azor
Zadok
Akim
Elihud
Eleazar
Matthan
Jacob
Joseph; *the husband of Mary; the mother of Jesus; who is called the Messiah.* (Matt 1:16)

Chapter Six

The Prince and the Prostitute (Read Joshua 1-6)

We pick up 'THE LINE' again on the verge of Jordan four hundred years after Judah and Tamar's story. We have the names of those in it (Perez, Aminadab, Aram, Esrom, Nashon) but nothing much else to go on. The delay in receiving the land was necessary for, as God warns Abraham:

> '... Know of a surety that thy seed (your descendants) shall be a stranger in a land that is not theirs, and shall serve them; and they shall afflict them four hundred years; And also that nation, whom they shall serve, will I judge: and afterward shall they come out with great substance. And thou shalt go to thy fathers in peace; thou shalt be buried in a good old age. But in the fourth generation they shall come hither again: for the iniquity of the Amorites is not yet full'. Genesis 15:13-16

In other words, you must suffer in Egypt until the ethnic groups in this land have forfeited any further right to live in it. Archaeologists have uncovered the graves of some of the Hebrew babies in Goshen, some buried in the Hebrew's houses. It has been argued that theirs is a classic case of the righteous suffering for the guilty. But that suffering did not give them any right to annihilate the Canaanite nations, God was very clear that they were merely tools of *his* judgement. I know many ethnic cleansers have hidden behind religious rhetoric to achieve their political or anthropological ends, but for the Jews this really was not the case – though God anticipated they might think so:

> ' ... do not say to yourself, "The LORD has brought me here to take possession of this land because of my righteousness." No, it is on account of the <u>wickedness of these nations</u> that the LORD is going to drive them out before you.' Deuteronomy 9:3-5

I touched on the 'wickedness of these nations' in the last chapter but lest we sit back in our armchairs and feel a glow of self righteousness at their abominable society, let us not forget our own. One area of western civilisation that would surely stand out is 'unwanting parents' (though I notice they mostly project the problem by saying 'unwanted children'). Who's worse in God's eyes, a savage Iron Age culture built around very genuine fears of starvation if they didn't sacrifice to the fertility gods and goddesses – or ours? By abortion we sacrifice 26% of conceived babies to our cult of socio-economic freedom. That is forty six million a year, 200,000 of which are in the UK. That works out at over 800 babies on the average working day in the UK, one every forty seconds, not because anyone's afraid of starving but out of sheer convenience in over 99% of cases.

Even worse, over two thirds of U.S. abortions are done for women with a Christian affiliation; in fact 18% of their national total is done for women who claim to be evangelical, born again, Bible believing Christians. That's a mountain of 250,000 infant corpses annually, from women who claim to believe the same God who judged the Canaanites and Jews for sacrificing their children to idols. (And none of these statistics mentions the billions of fertilised eggs that have been destroyed by abortificiants in some contraceptive pills and devices, humans every bit as alive to God as you or I). Ezekiel told the Hebrews that as far as God was concerned children born to his people were his, literally 'borne to him'. *'Then you took your own sons and daughters – the children you had borne to me and sacrificed them to your gods'* (Ezekiel 16.20) If God judged the pagan nations around Israel for such things, he would be doubly hard on his own people. And just because Molech and Baal have changed their names to 'Career', 'Sexual Freedom' and 'Materialism', let's not delude ourselves about the innocent blood that screams to heaven for justice from the bins of our western hospitals. (For a broader view of this subject please read my international thriller, *The Cradle Snatchers* from the Will Houston Mysteries, 2012.)

I mention all this because it does us no good to imbue our culture with some innate Christian saintliness which no longer exists. A culture's nature is seen in how it treats its weakest citizens, and in that we are streets ahead of the Canaanites for sheer barbarity! So when we read of Jericho in this chapter, make a mental note to think, 'Ah yes, Jericho, just like the west, only we've got even less excuse.' Western civilization has no cause to be optimistic if history is anything to go by.

Salmon

No Country for Old Men

Salmon's dad saw it all, a bit like my grandparents' wartime generation, they'd been there, seen it all happen. You might think that seeing the reality of war and the deliverance of God would make a more 'whole', i.e. more holy people but that wasn't the case for them. Nashon – Salmon's dad – walked with Moses and saw Egypt fall and the waters part. It was something talked about by nations for generations to come and yet the impact on him and the other dads appeared minimal.

They'd effectively agreed a kind of nation/God marriage at Sinai. They'd seen the golden calf and the three thousand slain, they had eaten quail and manna, rebelled at Meribah and Kadesh. Moses had brought Nashon and his friends out of Egypt but could God get Egypt out of them, that slavish, moaning mentality?

Unfortunately not, it is very often the case with us also.

Salmon's dad was part of a generation that had persistently hardened their hearts in disobedience. They could have had so much but fear, unbelief and worldly hankerings left them sitting out their days in the desert, destined for no more than wandering in circles, making excuses for their failure and blaming everyone but themselves.

The very name 'Nashon' comes from the Hebrew root 'whisper' or 'procrastinate' and it is interesting that he had not even taken a wife for his son, Salmon. Why not? Well, you might conjecture that it suggests he'd given up his faith, his purpose, the responsibility and vision for his family. I've met men like that in churches, too worldly, lazy and fearful of men to go on with God and after a life spent in smallness, they pass on their own stern view of an angry God to the next generation. But though this could be true, another reason might also be that his dad was in fact executed by the people at Peor. You see Salmon's dad is not just any man, Numbers 1:7 tells us he is the head honcho of the tribe of Judah, a social contemporary of Aaron, Joshua, and Moses. Later we can see in Numbers 7 that it was Judah's clan chiefs (i.e. Salmon's dad and his mates) who were the first of the tribes to make offerings at the dedication of the new altar. It must have been a proud day for little Salmon to see his dad leading that cart load of silver and gold to the tabernacle. Later again Nashon watched Joshua and Caleb go to spy out the land. Forty plus days after that, he must have watched or perhaps even been apart of the rebellion. Perhaps Nashon died then or perhaps, as I said above he indulged in a fertility sex orgy with those pretty Moabite girls, for certainly in this instance the clan leaders were executed.

> 'And the LORD said unto Moses, Take all the heads of the people, and hang them up before the LORD against the sun, that the fierce anger of the LORD may be turned away from Israel.' Num 25:4

So my best guess is that Salmon saw his father executed by stoning at Peor or perhaps in one of the earlier rebellions when . Yeah, that's right, not pretty. I wonder what it would have been like to grow up with a dad like that?

A New Generation

> 'When I was a boy of fourteen, my father was so ignorant I
> could hardly stand to have the old man around.
> But when I got to be twenty–one, I was astonished at how
> much the old man had learned in seven years.'

The quote from Mark Twain is deservedly well known for it is an all too familiar lesson we have learned or – if we are younger – will learn. But there have been one or two generations in history who may have known better than their parents and I think Salmon's might be among them. He was the descendant of Pharez (or Buster) mentioned in the last chapter. He had grown up living like a gypsy on the backside of the desert, paying for the sins of his father's generation. Salmon probably saw the cost of rebellion in his father's eyes every day, the look of a man who might be able to look back and see his error, but like Esau before him, find 'no place for repentance though (perhaps in Nashon's case too) he sought it carefully with tears'. Remember repentance is not just a 'sorry'; notice even Judas Iscariot said 'I have sinned in betraying innocent blood.' Now that would get him restored in most churches but we should notice that it is God who 'grants repentance unto life'; it is nowhere merely an expression of our remorse or regret. Salmon's dad and his friends must have been crushing role models to grow up with. But it was not just his father, think of the uncles, the elders. Salmon had grown up surrounded by a cold, hard faith that refused to trust God or take what he had given. He may have seen the armies of Bashan defeated, the sexy Moabites girls infiltrate the camp, the heroism of Phinehas. He definitely saw Balaak and the Moabites defeated, Balaam slain, and would no doubt have been with the 1200 men who destroyed the Midianites with no casualties to their own army. He saw Moses die, Joshua rise up, and the Jordan dry up.

When looking back at that wartime generation in his inaugural speech John F. Kennedy said, 'The torch has passed to a new generation.' And that is how it

was for Salmon and his friends. He was part of a new generation in every
sense; where the dads had failed they would succeed. Where the dads had
eaten manna, they would eat fruit and meat. Where the dads had trod the
aimless deserts, they would 'tread the verge of Jordan', they would bid their
parents' anxious fears subside, they would come clean over to Canaan's side.
And they did; youthful optimism is a great stimulant. And it wasn't all hype
either, there was the revival at Gilgal where they dedicated themselves by
circumcision and celebrating Passover, a new year, a new beginning.
But as we have said, despite all this he was not married, why not? His family
were certainly not poor nor lacking social position. My only conclusion is
Nashon had been derelict in his duty as a father and head of the house,
though this is pure conjecture. One thing we do know is that Salmon is about
to meet a woman of faith, and there are few more attractive qualities to a
searching man. And I wonder as he walked around the walls of that city
whether the scarlet cord made him rethink everything? Again that scarlet cord
sends out the big question to unmarried men and women reading this: what
kind of spouse are you looking for?

Salmon's Diary

Dear Diary,
God only knows I can't wait to get in this land, get all God's giving us,
hang up these wandering shoes. But I can't see a whole lot of point in
any of it without someone to share it with. I wanted to express this
wonderful redemptive love that I'm experiencing, this love that is
blowing my mind. God is going to give all this to us – for free. But what
good is a fancy new house, without someone to share it with. What good
is anything if I cannot pass on my name through a son, if I could not
hold him in my arms and dream that my own flesh and blood might be
the 'seed' promised to Abraham.
Then Rahab, I noticed your scarlet thread as I marched around the
walls and I began to think about the kind of woman I'd prayed for since
being a teen. Later I watched where they quarantined your family
outside the camp, and that's when I first saw you. Saw your nervous
happiness at the new freedom found under the wings of the God of
Jacob. You were like a calf let out of the winter stalls into the spring
sunlit meadows. I watched at a distance when you received instruction
and blessing from Phinehas, who told me how the Lord had healed your
diseases the moment he spoke our nation's blessings over you and that's
when I knew, just knew you were the one.
Courting you was a major controversy and many disagreed but
Phinehas, who's stricter then most said that God was really with you,
that he had shown you great favour in joining you to our people. 'What

*God has cleansed,' he said, 'we should not call common' and then I just
knew with all my heart he was right, you were right, the world was all
right ... I had found my soul–mate at last.'*

Rahab

*'Likewise also wasn't the hooker Rahab made innocent by her actions,
when she had received the messengers, and had sent them out another
way?'* James 2:25

Once again we are dealing with a certain type of woman, one who takes
decisive action and refuses to go with the crowd, refuses to be a victim when
there is the faintest chance of something better. It seems to be a recurrent
theme in our story; one we cannot escape. It will be the same with Ruth in the
next chapter and others. So what is it that God likes about them? You could
say that he is not picky over some things but he is definitely is drawn to 'can-
do' girls. I'm not into feminism (we'll look at that later when we deal with
Athaliah) but I do like to see strong women, the kind of women who have
been 'liberated' to *be* women, not just imitations of men. The very suggestion
that a woman would have to alter or reject her biology to find fulfilment and
equality should be dismissed out of hand for obvious reasons. We may be
appalled at the Amazon women who cut off their right breast so they could
use a bow like a man, but modern women are being told to cut off far more
than that. A substantial blame here is laid at the feet of weak and unloving
men, particularly in the west where we have done so little with the Bible's
command to 'Love our wives as Christ loved the church', but notwithstanding
it will be right thinking women who will affect this debate more than us.
You can keep your Cleopatras, Zenobias, Boadiceas or Margaret Tudors; give
me a Susanna Wesley, a Mary Washington or an Abigail Adams any day. They
are the women who benefit nations most and affect the world for good. Who
wants a Jezebel when you can have a Gladys Aylwood? She didn't wait around
for the men at the missionary society to catch up with reality, she bought her
own ticket and went to be a mother to a lost world. It was the same for Jackie
Pullinger; no waiting around for officials to rubber stamp her mission, she'd
been called by God and that was all there was to say. These are - what I call -
'Proverbs 31' women; women like Rebecca (Gen 27:8), Jael (Judges 4:21),
Abigail (1 Sam 25:18); women who see what is to be done and do it. Rahab is
such a women too and it is something this world desperately needs.
'Forgiveness is better than permission' is not a bad maxim on occasions, after
all no one ever followed Jesus too much. My friend Annie had a good career

ahead of her as an educational psychologist but she knew God wanted her for something else, though she had to leave her job before He revealed the vacancy at Tearfund. Later her dad got the phone call, 'hey dad, you know that place Darfur, the one in the news? Well I'm off there in two weeks.' And it was there among a man-made hell that she led her tiny team to serve 78,000 children. When they arrived in the camps or towns the children would flock to the vehicles in their thousands shouting, 'Annie, Annie, Annie.' Apparently it has even become a common name for baby girls in that part of the Sudan! My wife is currently reading the historian Antonia Fraser's *Warrior Queens*. The book examines the miserable lives of the supposed *great* women who ruled empires and led armies. Not one of them experienced a tenth of the fulfilment that Gladys or Annie had, though they pursued meaning and significance more than most women today.

Rahab turns out to be that kind of strong woman though when we find her she is at the very bottom of society's pile. She may have been born into it, or sold into it by a parent at an early age. She may have known nothing but brutality in her past and sexually transmitted disease in the present, but her future is going to be a whole lot different, if she has any say in the matter. And she does, we all do and if there is any aspect of your life that you think binds you from the freedom to pursue God fully, I would really urge you to take a good hard look at it. It needs a good kicking. Something like repentance will be needed to break that thought pattern.

I recently heard the testimony of a man who survived a plane hijacking. He said the passengers divided into three distinct groups; the majority descended into fear and inaction, others went into denial and tried to carry on reading their newspapers, and the remainder started to make their contingency plans. It is interesting to me that almost the entire world at present would fall into the 'denial' category. Be that as it may, Jericho under siege must have been like that, some in fear, some in denial – but there was only one family that got out alive, and that was because of just one woman. Why is that? I think 2 Corinthians 2:16 shows a similar mechanism at work, to everyone else in Jericho, the coming of these Hebrew Slaves smelled like '*death unto death*' – a fact that might explain anti-Semitism generally – but to Rahab, they smelled of '*life unto life*'. But what exactly could she find to be optimistic about, or more precisely, on what ground could she possibly hope that a pure and just God would have somebody like her? It's a big question and though we can never be 100% sure about these things, I have offered my best guess below.

Rahab's Diary

Dear Diary,

The tension has been unbearable.

The king sent his thugs round again today to hassle us. I know that underneath their big–man talk, feverish activity, their military reconnaissance, their interrogations and posturings, that they're all running scared. They now know it's all true, there is now incontrovertible proof that a righteous God is alive and is at our very doors to judge us.

But what caused them fear has caused my faith and hope to rise for tonight as I dare to believe that this God might take me and my family too. When I heard how this Jewish God rescued them from the powers that they had no strength to fight, I thought, wow, why could he not do the same for my family?

I know there is nothing worthy to salvage in my life and that I will not last long anyway the way my health is but I have long dreamed of a better life for my children, even if I die getting them out it would be worth it. Oh, God of these Hebrews, be my God tonight, for my children's sake. Please join us to these other rescued slaves you've had pity on. If you would do this one thing, I would not ask anything else again.

Fallen, Fallen is Babylon the Great

'Behold therefore the goodness and severity of God: on them which fell, severity; but toward thee, goodness, if thou continue in his goodness: otherwise thou also shalt be cut off.' Rom 11:22

The destruction of Jericho – and the rest of Canaan – is not an ethnic issue per se; God's intention for Israel was always to be a missionary nation and that others should join them (see Ezekiel 5v5-7). And many did, mostly the repentant individuals we see in THE LINE, but others were to come en masse, for example, Zechariah says God would one day join the remainder of the Philistines to Israel like he had done with the Jebusites. God is expert at *'rescuing the godly out of temptation'* but we must not overlook the rest – *'the unjust who are guarded and brought down on the day of damnation.'* (2 Peter 2:9) Lot's righteousness saved his family, Rahab's faith saves hers, but in our day each must come out alone out of their unrighteousness. Sodom, Gomorrah, Tyre, Nineveh and Jericho are all massive warnings to modern – or should I say post-modern man. The issue of divine judgement is perhaps the most offensive teaching Christians hold to in our present age. In other cultures and times it has been other things; for example 'divine judgement' for the Anglo Saxons was a given, but they would have been scandalised to hear of Peter being forgiven after having broken the honour code (i.e. betraying Jesus). But for us, at this point of history it seems *judgement* is the unmentionable topic and yet when you dig a little deeper you will still find that your friends are every bit as full of moral indignation over injustice as any that have ever lived. Indeed when you pin them down to it, they would certainly never worship a God who let evil go unpunished – just so long as it does not include them! This apparent inconsistency is picked up by the Polish poet Czeslav Milosz, *'The true opium of the people is belief in nothingness after death – a huge solace of thinking that for all our betrayals, greed, cowardice, murders, we are not to be judged.'* Milosz speaks here very much in the tradition of the Hebrew prophets, listen to Zephaniah;

'The Lord says, "I wiped out entire civilisations, destroying their cities leaving only walls and ruined towers. Their cities are deserted now – check out the streets – there is no one there. I thought my people would never forget this lesson, that they at least would reverence me and accept my discipline, but soon they were behaving worse than ever." ' Zeph 3:6-7

Take a boat over the southern end of the Dead Sea and you can still observe the tree stumps that were the woods where Lot would have grazed his sheep. These things really happened, God really does bring judgement on wicked civilizations. A quarter of Bible verses contain a prediction about the future and 81% have come true to the letter. The remaining 19% concern the future coming of our Lord Jesus and the final judgement. Although I don't participate myself, I come from a long line of betting men, it's in my blood to sniff out good odds ... these are very, very good odds! God's unwillingness and slowness to do this should not be interpreted as weakness, it is mercy and love. But when it comes, it comes swiftly and with overwhelming force. I imagine that when the apostle Paul spoke to Felix and Drusilla about 'righteousness, self control and the judgement to come' in Acts 24 they assumed they had all the time in the world to decide. They thought there would come a 'convenient season', rather like my college friend who felt conviction after seeing a Ken Ham video, but thought he'd 'wait until he was forty and live a little first before becoming a Christian'.

How crazy is that!

History records that Drusilla was killed in the destruction of Pompeii. It would be lovely to think that she remembered Paul's words and repented at the sight of the pyroclastic flow, but I have my doubts. God gave seven extra days after the animals were in the ark, presumably days of grace to allow men to change their minds. But just as God is kind, so men are stubborn.

> '....when the people heard the sound of the trumpet, they shouted at the tops of their voices. It was then that the city wall fell down flat, leaving room for the whole army to rush in and take it. They totally destroyed all that was in the city, both male, female, young and old, even the cattle, sheep, and asses. Joshua said to the two spies, 'Go into the prostitute's house, and rescue her and all that she has, just as you promised'. After that, the army torched the entire city and all its contents except for objects made of silver, gold, brass and iron, which they put into the treasury of the house of the LORD.' Josh 6:20-22, 24

Rahab must have lived on the northern section of the wall for in 1907 Italian excavators found it still intact. What incredible courage to trust the words of God's messengers and stay put as the proud walls of her civilization collapsed around her. I think there may be a lesson here for us too when we think of all that must come upon 'so-called' western civilization in the end times. Other, British archaeologists, Garstang and Kenyon, confirmed the massive devastation as follows:

'Wherever the archaeologists reached this level they found a layer of burned ash and debris about one metre (three feet) thick. The destruction was complete. Walls and floors were blackened or reddened by fire, and every room was filled with fallen bricks, timbers, and household utensils; in most rooms the fallen debris was heavily burnt, but the collapse of the walls of the eastern rooms seems to have taken place before they were affected by the fire. Both Garstang and Kenyon found many storage jars full of grain that had been caught in the fiery destruction. This is a unique find in the annals of archaeology. Grain was valuable, not only as a source of food, but also as a commodity which could be bartered. Also grain jars full, not a long siege.'

Only that which could pass through cleansing fire could leave that city and the same could be said on a spiritual level about this tenacious woman as she clung with total abandon to her faith in a redeeming God. Having passed through a fiery trial herself, Rahab was found to be more precious than any other gold the Jews rescued. The same walls that were the defence of the enemy were the prison of this woman. It was these enemy walls that God broke down, liberating Rahab into her own promised land. For us too, there are certain walls we assume give protection to our lifestyle and mindsets, but many are the very enemies of God, and keep us prisoner in lukewarm faith and mediocre Christian experience. Our Jericho strongholds will not be made of bricks, but of insecurity, inadequacy, loneliness, self pity, self criticism and myriad other sins. These walls are dismantled by repentance and faith in Jesus Christ. They are 'thought–ifications' – mental or spiritual strongholds – that keep us from the fruitful land of God's promises and he wants to break them down and rescue you. Listen, when Jesus cried 'My God, my God why have you forsaken me' he was experiencing total rejection so you could have total acceptance. Jesus can liberate you from all the hurt that holds you back from your life. He gave everything for that and all power in heaven is poised to make it happen for you; but it will never happen unless you permit it, unless you renounce the evil of Jericho and every part you have played in its ways, its kingdom. Oh Lord Jesus deliver us from these walls. Friend, remember that what was said of Joshua is doubly true of Jesus: that no one would be able to stand before him all his days. All power in heaven and earth will move for you when you pray and fast to your 'Joshua' (i.e. Jesus) for this type of liberation.

Coping in Canaan

'And Joshua saved Rahab the harlot alive, and her father's household, and all that she had; and she dwelleth in Israel even unto this day.'

Josh 6:25

I wonder how she got on, how they both got on?
Can't have been easy in a small village like Bethlehem but I get the feeling Salmon turned out to be one of the good guys. In Revelation 3:18, Jesus is the one who provides, *'white raiment, that you can be <u>covered</u>, and that the shame of your nakedness be hidden.'* Salmon's name literally means 'to cover,' and that of course is exactly what he became, what he did. He covered the naked shame of this woman's past life and loved her tenderly. This much I assume from the fruit of their marriage: Boaz – another considerate, loving man.
But to cling to God when he is all you have, is easier to do than when you have other options. The comparative luxury of walking into a farm you never built, with crops, vines and figs you never planted may well have presented its own challenges to their flesh. As with us, the test is to stay with God when you come out of the desert situation. I remember a lovely couple who had business difficulties; for years we prayed for their business to sell, and when it finally did sell they never came back to church. Another widow who became a believer wanted a new husband; again the church prayed and she married a man on the periphery of the congregation, they never came back either. But that wasn't the case for Salmon and Rahab. How do I know? Well, when the

great famine came (the one in which Naomi and Elimelech took their boys east to Moab, see Ruth 1:1–2), Salmon and Rahab must have stuck it out with the Lord in the land that God had promised to them.

I love the way Abigail Adams used to sign her love letters to her husband, John, during the American War for Independence: 'your beloved Portia'. Portia was the wife of 'that noble Brutus' who killed Caesar, 'not out of private malice, but to recover the glory of the republic' – so the historian Plutarch says. She has become famous as a woman who insisted on sharing her husband's sufferings and anxiety as well as his pleasures. Rahab was that kind of wife, in it for the long haul; though staying probably took more faith than turning traitor to the king of Jericho ever did. With grit like that came the royal line of David, and from there the Saviour of the world.

You unmarried guys; you should pray for wives like this, faithful women that burn to be part of what God is doing. And not just the guys, my friend Jan was shocked when, as part of a prison visiting ministry, she found herself drawn to an ex-mafia henchmen, who after a dramatic conversion would become her husband. To this day they have a beautiful and dynamic ministry. So don't settle for safe, certainly not when you've pledged your life to a God like ours, it will leave you on the wrong side of the Jordan.

You were made for adventure, don't be a victim any more – Canaan is calling.

Walking in Canaan

Salmon and Rehab's song – Rehab's words in italics
(From 'THE LINE' album, words and music by Henry Brooks)

I grew up like a gypsy in a desert place and my old man would say
'Don't your waste your life, son, as I did mine those times I disobeyed.'
Well Dad, I trod the verge of Jordan's banks and bid those fears subside
And when I came over to Gilgal's shore, man, I broke down and cried

Cos I was walking in Canaan, walking with my feet 10ft off the field
Walking in Canaan, can't believe I'm actually here
Walking in Canaan, the manna is gone and the fruit tastes fine
Walking in Canaan, the baton's been passed and the future's mine

Well, I never thought it'd end up here on the darker side of town
My life's so screwed up, my heart's so broke and my health's nearly gone
Then I heard of your God who rescued you from the powers you could not fight
And if you'd asked if I was a woman of faith, I'd'a said, 'I was that night …'

When we came walking through Canaan, you began to dream of a world that
was new.
Walking through Canaan, you wondered if our God would take somebody
like you,
Walking through Canaan, you hated all you'd been and everything that you'd
seen.
Walking through Canaan, you hungered and thirsted for a life that was clean.

See, I pledged to wait for a pure wife that God would bring to me and
When I saw that scarlet cord hang down, I began to see … that what
God has cleansed is pure indeed though many disagreed
I gave you white to wear on our wedding day cos God had set you free

And now we're walking in Canaan, spent a lifetime dreaming of days like
these
Walking in Canaan, can't believe I found someone to share it all with
Walking in Canaan, it's becoming like Eden everywhere I go
Walking in Canaan, wouldn't trade the world for this peace I know

My cousin brought some figs round the other day, he got a nice new place just like ours
Can't believe God gave us farms like these and the size of baby Boaz
I'm praying for him now every day, that he'll grow just like his dad
To display this covering grace of God, in a world that's torn and mad
(Previous Chorus)

But now this drought has struck, the stock are dying and my faith's going that way too
Used to be so sure of God's plan for us, now I don't know which way to go
Naomi called to say goodbye today, gonna take the kids back east
But I trust God's still got plans are still good for us and Bethlehem at least ...

We're still walking in Canaan, spent a lifetime hoping for a life so real
Walking in Canaan, I can see you feel the way I feel
Walking in Canaan, his promise is as good as it was back then
Walking in Canaan, I know we can trust him for the years ahead

Life Application Devotion
Chapter 6 – A Love that Covers

- <u>Taking your time</u>, make a list of the people in your acquaintance that you think are least likely to become Christians.
- Examine this list and search for any correlations. (i.e. Is there any particular category of person here, whose lifestyle or religion has placed them beyond your faith for their conversion?)
- How has this understanding affected your behaviour and prayer life toward them?
- Considering Jesus and Salmon's example of a love that 'covers' the sinner, will you prayerfully now ask the Lord to point you toward someone each day of the next week for whom he wishes you to pray for or show *his* love to.

Prayer: (Start with thanksgiving & praise, particularly for God's tender heart toward the prodigals.) 'Oh Lord Our Righteousness, thank you for clothing all my nakedness by the blood of Jesus my Saviour. Lord, give me a heart like yours toward everyone I meet this week. I confess my hardness toward certain people, please show me how to love people the way you love them, how to think and feel the way you think and feel about them. Lord, I beg you to give me your love and your heart for the lost in increasing measure.

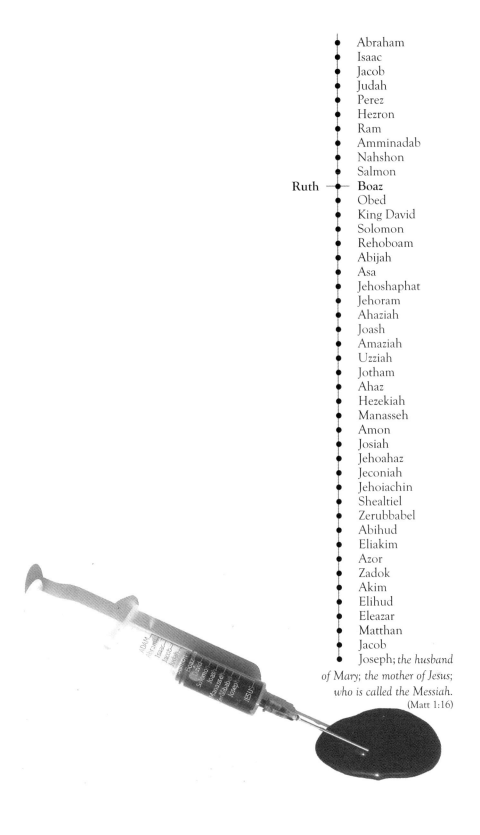

Abraham
Isaac
Jacob
Judah
Perez
Hezron
Ram
Amminadab
Nahshon
Salmon
Ruth — Boaz
Obed
King David
Solomon
Rehoboam
Abijah
Asa
Jehoshaphat
Jehoram
Ahaziah
Joash
Amaziah
Uzziah
Jotham
Ahaz
Hezekiah
Manasseh
Amon
Josiah
Jehoahaz
Jeconiah
Jehoiachin
Shealtiel
Zerubbabel
Abihud
Eliakim
Azor
Zadok
Akim
Elihud
Eleazar
Matthan
Jacob
Joseph; *the husband of Mary; the mother of Jesus; who is called the Messiah.* (Matt 1:16)

Chapter 7

The Immigrant (Read Ruth 1–4)

*'It's not vast scenery that makes a great landscape ...
no, humanity is the thing.'*

William McTaggart was a rare dude – never mind Captain Ahab lashing himself to the mast – this guy lashed massive canvasses and easels to the beach and painted the finest, stormiest Scottish seascapes of the nineteenth century. The quotation above is his, for he would always paint people in his landscapes, whether it was lifeboat men struggling against the storm to do a daring rescue, or a ship of immigrants leaving for the New World. The human story was 'where it was at', just like the Bible.

When Ben Franklin was in Paris he would often converse with members of the 'Infidels' Club', a group of philosophers who spurned the Bible. These intellectuals spent much of their time searching for and discussing masterpieces of literature and art. For his amusement, Ben Franklin announced that he found an ancient manuscript worthy of their consideration. 'We must hear it!' they exclaimed. Franklin then read to them a story of one family's tragedy and triumph, of an immigrant worker who found love in a country and culture where she was despised. When he finished, Franklin's hearers were unanimous in their praise. 'We have never heard anything like it', they said. 'It is one of the most touching stories we have ever heard.' 'You must tell us where you found it!' You can imagine Franklin's delight when he announced that it was a story of Ruth from the Bible.

Naomi

The Ski Pommer

On our tenth wedding anniversary we went with friends to the Hardanger mountain plateau in Norway for a ski trip. It was magnificent country, the same country where the Heroes of Telemark scuppered the German nuclear programme. I have fond memories of the people, the hot chocolate, the reindeer, the moonlit ski treks across that sub arctic wilderness. The whole thing was just magical. Trouble is, it's so pristine and grand, that you can't help looking around at the landscape when you're on a pommer ski tow. In my case it is a big mistake. Usually your skis cross or one foot just wanders off, next you slip off the pommer – and that is the beginning of the end.

If you're generally optimistic, or a real fighter, or just very naïve, you'll try to recover your position, but after ten metres of being unceremoniously dragged through the snow with your legs flailing like a duck and everyone looking, you let go and do your best to stop being run over by the person behind you! Sometimes there'll be no one around and that gives you the morbid opportunity to watch the pommer going higher and higher up the mountain without you. This was particularly painful when I was learning to snowboard, I mean it took every ounce of skill just to get on the pommer and survive the first few metres, but to have gone through all of that for nothing is so disheartening. When the pommer disappears into the mist there is nothing at all that you can do, you just missed your chance, it's back to the queue for you!

Dark night of the soul

My ski story is nothing, but I know some people who have watched every object of their hopes, their motivation, their security disappear into the distance while there was nothing they could do about it. Maybe they took their eye off their pommer, maybe not, maybe they did nothing wrong whatsoever at that moment when life dealt them a cruel blow, a car crash, a cancer, a family crisis, an economic catastrophe. Elimelech and Naomi were two such people. They were part of that 'new generation' we talked about in the last chapter who walked into God's big blessing. But they'd outlived Joshua and seen the nation go to the dogs. (Though as far as most of their day were concerned, it was not that anyone did anything *wrong*, but more like *every man did what was right in his own eyes* (Judges 17:6) – all strangely post–modern. You can read all about this in the book of Judges, it's not pretty and soon God's anger 'boiled over' and famine came knocking.

Fight or Flight?

I can imagine that Mr King and Mrs Splendour (as their names mean), were just getting on with their lives in Bethlehem, planting their crops and raising their two lively boys. But then those rains didn't come in the spring or autumn and everything changed in a moment. It is how trouble often comes to us too, without warning, but it is a very big deal if you have nothing laid by. For Naomi's family it could mean starvation. They didn't stick around: 'there's no bread in the-house-of-bread (Beth-le-hem) but they've got some in Moab, what are we waiting for?' So at a time when Salmon and Rahab waited it out, Elimelech and Naomi gave up on the promised land and all that it meant; they swapped cultures and married their boys into the new one. Trials can do that, either drive you closer to God or further down the road to Moab. A friend of ours got a broken heart and quit coming to church; another guy I spoke to at the weekend lost everything in the floods and now wants to get serious with God. (When he asked about baptism I said water wouldn't be a problem!)

Do you think Elimelech and Naomi sinned in going? It's a very hard call; my feeling is that they would have been alright if they had stayed in Bethlehem. Sometimes sticking it out, though counter intuitive, is the best solution. In a desert survival scenario, staying with your vehicle is 99.9% the right thing to do. Habakuk's prophecy to the generation that would face Nebuchadnezzar's sword was that even during that fiery punishment of the guilty, *the just would have their lives preserved by faith*. After the city was sacked, the remaining Jews forced Jeremiah to run away with them to Egypt, but he told them in no uncertain terms, *'Stay and submit to Nebuchadnezzar or the sword you fear will follow you to Egypt.'*

I believe we need to make a distinction between the times when we are to run from persecution (as our Lord tells us) and when *'having done all'* we are to stand. Elimelech and Naomi run from the famine but later she says, *'Don't call me splendid any more, call me bitter because God has made me utterly bitter.'* There are plenty of people – even those who claim to be irreligious – who blame God for events in their life, many of which are self caused, many which come to us all in a fallen world. But we must be careful not to say, 'God never allows nasty things' for the truth is, he does all the time. Who drew Satan's attention to Job in the first place? On a national level the Lord wanted to make Israel a beautiful 'vase of his mercy' (Jeremiah 18:1-12) but, because of their unbelief, had to make them 'crude pots of his judgement'. The parable of the potter's house in Jeremiah is all too clear; it's not *just* the potter who decides, for the clay must run in his hands too. If that clay is lumpy and won't run it will never be what he wanted, pure and simple: we *both* decide. It was the same for Naomi and it is the same for us. Lives of loss and suffering have made some people sweet and others 'utterly bitter'. She also said, *'I went out full but the Lord brought me back empty'*, but I believe here she makes a category mistake like many in our own day, in attributing her circumstances in a fallen world to a direct action of God.

Who sinned, this man or his parents?

Naomi says God has '*testified against her*' and '*broken out against her*'. Now this either shows a high degree of self awareness, for perhaps he did; or more likely, somewhere down there in Moab she has picked up a warped sense of God's character. That is not say the God never punishes evil in this life; for some men's sins really *do* go ahead of the to judgement; some *do* get illness and an untimely death as payment for sin (1 Cor 11v30) but it would wrong to apply this as the norm. Everyone assumed it was the '*fire of God*' that fell on Job's house, when actually it was Satan's fire. Even after all Jesus said on the subject, most people – even Christians – still use the 'wisdom' of Job's comforters, the 'what goes around comes around' view of suffering. I was once on the receiving end of this 'wisdom' when my wife was very ill. It's not nice when your back is already against the wall and someone in a position of spiritual authority puts the word out that it might be a 'sin' issue. I mean, who's going to stand up and say, 'No, that's not right, my life is so pure that I don't deserve to suffer?' As it was, God overturned that particular accusation with a most extraordinary healing miracle, but I realize that doesn't always happen.

Friends of mine lost their son in a car accident.

Two Christian boys with their lives in front of them, one survived; one didn't. The other parents praised God for his mercy in saving their son, but where did that leave my friends? The reality of life in this fallen world is usually bigger than our sound–bite theology. I survived cancer; another friend at church didn't. On another occasion my wife received healing – without prayer even – for the same illness that another woman at church prayed for and saw no result. Though life is full of imponderables, we are not questioning that God is good and we are certainly not questioning that he doesn't empathize. As we have already seen Psalm 69:2-3; in those lonely Nazareth trials Jesus was so weary of intense crying out to God, that his throat was burnt dry and his eyes had almost ceased to function. In his case it was all the people who were coming against him; as Anna prophesied he was a 'sign from God that many people would speak against' because he exposed the darkness in their hearts. Friend, Jesus knows the pain of delayed answers to prayer, you are not alone in your suffering. You may think that your situation is as hopeless as Naomi's, perhaps worse, but remember she hadn't reckoned on God's heart towards her, and she hadn't reckoned on the calibre of her daughter-in-law either.

Ruth

Friends

Her name means 'friend' and that is what Naomi needed when everything else was taken away.

It was the same for Jeremiah. When he was about to die in a dark hole (an empty well in his case) it wasn't another prophet or a cousin or a social worker that got him out, it was a friend. I thank God for the close friends in my life; 'iron sharpens iron', although in the missionary environment of church life some have had to be temporary on occasions. For different seasons in your life God may yoke you with different people. If you find this is a deficit area in your life, don't whine on about how 'nobody is ministering to me', ask the Lord to show you someone else who needs a friend and go and be a blessing to them instead. Who knows, perhaps your friendship will change their life like Ruth's did to Naomi's. The people of Bethlehem witness that Ruth's friendship filled Naomi's heart more than seven sons would have done. Now that is an extraordinary achievement; to be on someone's Christmas card list is one thing, but to be have been the means for another Christian to achieve God's plans for them is something worth living for.

God make me such a person. (I will say more about Friendship in the next chapter.)

Choice

Ruth is already in her early twenties by the time she chooses to forsake her people, her culture and her god. I see her as a bit like Rebecca, Tamar and Rahab - the outsider getting in on what God is doing. She had already been married for maybe ten years when her husband dies. It struck me that it was strange that neither Ruth nor Orpah had borne children and yet you can tell it was the main thing on their minds, the main thing that balanced their decision making.

How do we know?

Well, Naomi sums it all up by saying, 'Don't bother following me, there's no way I can give you another husband, get back to your own parents, your own gods, you've a better chance there.' On the face of it sensible advice but 'sensible' rarely signals the onset of a great story, and this is one of the greatest!

Ruth, like so many before her, does the one thing which is against the conventional wisdom, the one path which the culture would have told her was a dead end. She chose the narrow way, to join a narrow minded people and exclusive religion, and you have to ask 'why?' It must have been that she saw through her own culture and that maybe, just maybe, this God of the liberated slave nation was who they claimed he was. Ruth's mother might have been one of the girls sent into the Israelite camp to tempt the young men. All that stuff and the battle that followed would be in living memory; Balaam, Balaak, the blessings, Phineas' spear, the Jordan drying up, Jericho tumbling. The Moabite refusal of water and hiring of Balaam was so serious that Moses says in Deuteronomy that the Jews were not to let a Moabite into the people of God until the tenth generation.

Ruth would be the second or third generation, so how did she 'overcome' the word of God?

In the same way the Syrophonecian woman 'overcame' Jesus' words, by a determined faith. If all you've got is mumbo jumbo fertility religion built on rancid fear, then *'a living God who sees me'* can seem like an attractive alternative. Maybe her deceased husband told her about their childhood friend Boaz, the man whose mum had been a Canaanite prostitute before she joined the people of God. Now that is the stuff of dreams. Whatever it was, Ruth gives up her comfort zone and possibly her chance to ever have a baby in order to journey west across the river with Naomi and her invisible God. 'Journey west across the river' haven't we heard that somewhere before? Ruth walks in the footsteps of Abraham, Sarah, Rebecca, Rachel and Leah. Ruth is like Elisha with Elijah too – and the Syrophonecian woman with Jesus, for that matter, as she treats the command to stay as a veiled encouragement to go further. God give us wisdom and tenacity to know when he's really wanting us to push the door. And not just wisdom; for to act on such occasions takes a 'blood'n'guts–heart–in–your–stomach' sort of tenacity that is almost impossible to describe on paper. Make no mistake, those women like Ruth, Rahab and Tamar had it, God give us such a heart too.

Boaz

Casablanca

If Boaz were Bogart he would have said something like 'of all the fields in all the towns in all the world, she walks into mine.' It's one of those 'God moments', Ruth was doing what she could, and God was turning the circumstances in her favour. Mind you, it is easier to steer a car when the wheels are already moving.

Stigma and Ostracism

Boaz is a middle aged farmer and it seems his parents have done well for he is a *'mighty man of wealth'*, though it could also mean valour or virtue too. Now considering that his parents have succeeded in other areas we have to ask – as we did in the last chapter – why this man wasn't married. My only answer is his lineage: he was the son of Rahab. Don't forget Rahab's mother, father, brothers and sisters were all rescued from Jericho too. How do you think they would be treated in Bethlehem? Different language, different manners, and human nature being what it is I would say Rahab had a pretty rough time. And as for Boaz, their son, which pure descendant of Judah would let their daughter marry the 'half-caste spawn of a Canaanite prostitute'? He may have been loved at home but I think Boaz was ostracized by the community. He was an unclean man, neither Jew nor Canaanite. Yes, he may have been useful as an employer and respected for his wealth but never accepted as an equal. David would experience a little of this a few years later in the same village, but our main comparison here is Jesus. For if I am right, both he and Boaz were *'despised and rejected'* because of their lineage; for Jesus it would haunt him into adult life – I imagine it did for Boaz too. But did it make him small or bitter? No, like an aircraft, the pressure forced against the wings make it take off and fly.

His Name

It's hard to pin down the exact meaning of Boaz's name; some say it means *'in him is strength'* which I like and think sums up something lovely that he inherited from his father, Salmon; the one who 'covered' and protected Boaz' mother Rahab. I have four sons and we have good playfights. When my oldest wrestles me onto the sofa and asks, 'Dad, am I strong?' I always affirm it with this caveat, 'Yes, Tom, and why did God make men strong?' The reply I've drilled him with is, 'to protect people who are weak.' It's a big part of being a man, a lover, a father, a fighter, that we are trained to use our strength on behalf of others. This is a high calling and certainly not for the selfish and lazy. As C. S. Lewis points out in *The Four Loves*, feminists need not begrudge the crown of 'headship' that is laid upon the male sex; for under the pagan system it was but a paper crown and under the Christian system it is a crown of thorns. A Christian is charged to love his wife as Christ loved the church; and how was that? He gave himself up to a crucified life for her and now lives to extend his inexhaustible forgiveness. That, very approximately, is the *only* 'crown' offered to Christian men as heads of their wives; it is a crown of thorns, gentlemen! God help us remember it, and live it.

Boaz Models 'Sacrificial Strength' in Five Ways.

Boaz offers protection

Boaz orders his workers not to persecute Ruth but he also commands her not to go to another's field, *'abide fast by my maidens and keep an eye on where they reap'*. Someone once asked Reinhard Bonnke why he was so fruitful. His answer was, 'Well I just see what the Lord is doing and join in.' God has a field of service for each of us that will be uniquely fitted to our personality and gifting. It takes real tact and insight at times to just stay there. A very gifted friend of mine has an apostolic calling on his life. We went sailing and camping in the summer and he said he'd had two job offers, one in the United States. The week following I felt obliged to write a text reminding him of his calling when considering what course to take. You can bet if you're supposed to be in one field, there'll be three guys in the other fields calling to you to join them instead. I'm all for duty but I know in the past I have signed up for everything at church and burnt myself out. Take an inventory and take it to the Lord; you have one life and it's as clear as day: 'If you're doing one thing you ain't doing another.'

Boaz offers water

Boaz is not content to leave Ruth on the outside with the minimum. He starts to draw her into the centre of his sphere of influence, his mini-kingdom where the hungry are not just protected but also given water. Of course this giving of water is something we see of the Messiah in Isaiah 55 but I also want to point out that what he does, we can do too. It's a very dry and thirsty place outside our church doors and sometimes inside too. People have different ways of hiding their thirst, but to be a man like Boaz is to see the opportunity and bring that soothing water of God's word. The greatest famine in the western world in our day is a famine for the word of God; armed with a 'bucket and ladle' you will never be short of opportunities to share it.

Boaz offers bread

I love this guy's sensitivity, he doesn't do outright handouts but lets the sheaves fall. If we are to be like this man we need that same sensitivity in ministry, the world needs the salt of the earth, but not rubbed into the wounds of their need. Boaz goes as far as he can to give Ruth help without overriding her dignity to help herself, a very hard balance to strike sometimes. We had a friend who was an alcoholic living with us and this was a major difficulty. As with parenting, there are times when letting someone lean on your strength too much does them no favours. We all need wings as well as roots.

Boaz offers encouragement

Boaz sees things in Ruth that no one else sees. The other men see sexual prey; the women see an object of gossip, a despised immigrant. But Boaz sees more because he has been on the other side of all that himself. The same word 'virtue' used of him is what he used of her. 'It takes one to know one'. Someone said that 'a flea doesn't know if it rides on giant shoulders or ones of ordinary size', how true! Don't be overly bothered if no one affirms your gifting and ability, go to Jesus for he – just like Boaz – was done down all his life and he will always have something encouraging for you. And when you've done that, look around you, there is a whole world of people who are weak through lack of encouragement; why not ask the Lord to show you how he sees them, then go and speak Jesus' affirmation into their lives? It is a powerful ministry, something we can all have. I can still remember when my big brother praised me for doing a good gear change when I was learning to drive. It seemed to just lodge there. Bear Grylls once wrote that 'I was a gentle man of God who had faced life's great mountains.' Sometimes these 'Boaz' words can have a prophetic and creative power; I remember David Powell's encouragement to me like it was yesterday. He was something of a patriarch in the Pentecostal movement. He had lived with Smith Wigglesworth and also wandered the streets of London during the Blitz preaching in the air raid shelters, and believe me, when this guy preached his face shone, no kidding. I went to stay with David at the beginning of my first 'missionary post'. Being very young in the faith I had real anxiety about my fitness to lead this new church plant, so I took a huge list of questions with me. He said many things I have since forgotten but never the assessment he sent to the church, for it became metal to my insecurity: 'Henry is a man of exceptional character who will go far in the kingdom of God'. God give us all hearts to bind up weak knees, Lord use the words of our mouths to lift up drooping hands.

Boaz offers commitment

Boaz seems genuinely flattered after Ruth proposes to him on the threshing floor, 'God bless you for not choosing a younger man.' It must have been the answer to his prayers too. Boaz did not rest until he had secured her for himself; he is the one making the moves on her behalf but he would not let it settle until he has her. Like Jesus coming to wed his bride, Boaz must wait until the harvest is brought in. The delay for Ruth was a time of excitement, provision (he fills her shawl with wheat) and preparation; and it should be for us too.

There has always seemed to me a 'commitment deficit' among the majority of men in the church, a lot of pious talk, but not so much *stickability*. I include myself here and I don't just mean the church either, it is rife in western life. I think we're raised too much on the Hollywood paradigm where the unglamorous nature of true courage, seen in dogged 'faithfulness' and fidelity, has been replaced by the courage of the big shoot out or punch up. I wish we could hear again Charles Bronson's words in *The Magnificent Seven* to the village boy who thinks his farmer dad is a coward,

> *'Don't you ever say that again about your fathers, because they are not cowards. You think I am brave because I carry a gun; well, your fathers are much braver because they carry responsibility, for you, your brothers, your sisters, and your mothers. And this responsibility is like a big rock that weighs a ton. It bends and it twists them until finally it buries them under the ground. And there's nobody says they have to do this. They do it because they love you, and because they want to. I have never had this kind of courage. Running a farm, working like a mule every day with no guarantee anything will ever come of it. This is bravery. That's why I never even started anything like that ... that's why I never will.'*

I believe it is this type of commitment that causes the angels to sing, 'holy, holy, holy', as millennia by millennia they stand astounded at the 24/7 paternal care of God for his creation. C.S.Lewis said that courage is the testing point of every virtue and this is supremely seen in our heavenly father's dedication to us, completely selfless – if only he might share with us the riches of his mind in the ages to come. This is the commitment of true love, not blind but bound; the spirit of the true lover that we see in Boaz too, for like Jesus, he is a 'lover' and not just a consumer.

Narrative Symmetry

God knows how to weave a great story and his endings beat anything at the cinema. I think I prefer Ruth's marriage to Haman's gallows in Esther 7:10 but I'm still open to persuasion.

Naomi turned back and in her repentance and emptiness was filled by God. In fact he was able to give her more joy and fulfilment from one daughter-in-law than seven sons. Ruth's friendship became a 'restorer of Naomi's life' and when little Obed is born, the village says, *'A child is born to Naomi.'* The bitter woman was made sweet again. God can fill the gaps in our emotional, spiritual and physical vacuums if we turn back to him.

Ruth got a place with God's people which was all she asked for in the beginning but, as with so many, when you journey into Jehovah's world and see what he can do, you end up asking for a whole lot more. She not only got a husband and then a baby but also a place in history. Of course she and Boaz never knew that they were part of the most important line in history; they were arrows hidden in God's quiver - like you perhaps. All anyone knew, including Satan, was that the promise would come through Judah's line. It would not be for another two generations that the Lord would finally reveal his hand. Obscurity is an essential part in God's toolbox, I would encourage you, whatever you feel your gifting is, to remember Ruth and Boaz. When most others in the nation were back-slidden, their home was the nursery of the coming kingdom.

Boaz overcame the opposition of small minded ethnic and religious persecution to become a pillar in the house of God, both figuratively and literally, for they named one of the two pillars outside Solomon's temple after him. And that from the kid no one would play with! Jesus gives encouragement to Christians in Philadelphia and to us when he said, *'Him that overcometh will I make a pillar in the temple of my God ...'* (Rev 3:12)

God knows how to write a good story, but if we think it just ends at the leather bindings then we are missing the point. Our lives are the stuff of his narrative; our hurts and broken dreams, the fabric where he wants to weave his salvation threads. Imagine if Ruth had turned back with Orpah or if she'd chickened out at the threshing floor. Imagine if Boaz had been too busy building his business or cared too much about popular opinion. Think about your life friend, you only have one and this is not a dummy run. If God has called you to do something, for his sake, for your own sake and for the sake of generations unborn don't let the opportunity slip by.

At His Feet

Boaz and Ruth's duet – Ruth's lines in italics
(From 'THE LINE' album, words and music by Henry Brooks)

Who's this at my feet in the darkness of the night and why are you crying?
It is me my Lord and I want you to spread your robes around me this night
and all nights and for evermore

the Lord bless you my dear,
I'm not the youngest or most handsome dude, or the richest guy round here
And, precious one have no fear,
I will do all that you ask of me, I'll take it all from here ...

But stay at my feet tonight, and you'll soon be by my side
If you can bear it 'till the harvest ends,
one day I'll come and take you home to be my bride
... just stay at my feet

I bless the day you turned in at my place for some bread,
the first time we spoke you fell down at my feet and said,
'Why have I found favour in your eyes, seeing I'm despised
in this small town, where only you have empathized'

We're both strangers here my dear,
I've been despised, rejected all my life for the lineage that I bear
But, God's our refuge, do not fear,
under his wings we've both learned to trust and he has brought us here

So let's stay at his feet tonight, and we'll soon be by his side
If we can last out 'till his harvest comes, he'll soon come and take us home to
be his bride, ... if we stay at his feet

Now it might seem like long hard times 'till I can make this right,
but just hold on for me, keep pure as morning light
Cos I'll not rest one minute until I have made you mine and taken you home
with me, and that is why I say

Stay by my feet tonight, and you'll soon be my bride
If you can bear their looks and cutting words, I'll dry your tears and stand by
your side, stay by my feet tonight, I will not let you down
In the pain, fear and loneliness, I will carry you, protect you as my own, just
stay at my feet.

Life Application Devotion
Chapter 7 – Dealing with Loneliness

- List the ways in which you have experienced loneliness, ostracism or bullying in your life.
- Think of what you have learn in this respect about Jesus, Rebecca, Jacob, Leah, Rahab, Boaz and Ruth. Who do you identify with the most and what have you learnt from them?
- List your usual responses to loneliness, ostracism or bullying; start with the least helpful, to the most helpful things you usually do and then finish by asking the Lord for further insight. (Journal what He shows you.)
- Prayer: (Start with thanksgiving & praise, particularly for God's tender heart toward 'bruised reeds' and outsiders.) 'Oh Lord Our Comfort, thank you for accepting me into your family, for giving me purpose in the present and the hope of a glorious future. Forgive me Father where I have exchanged the acceptance of heaven for the approval of men, I confess this idolatry and ask with all my heart that you will empower me to derive my primary sense of belonging and security in you. Lord, is there anything that you want me to do in response to this prayer

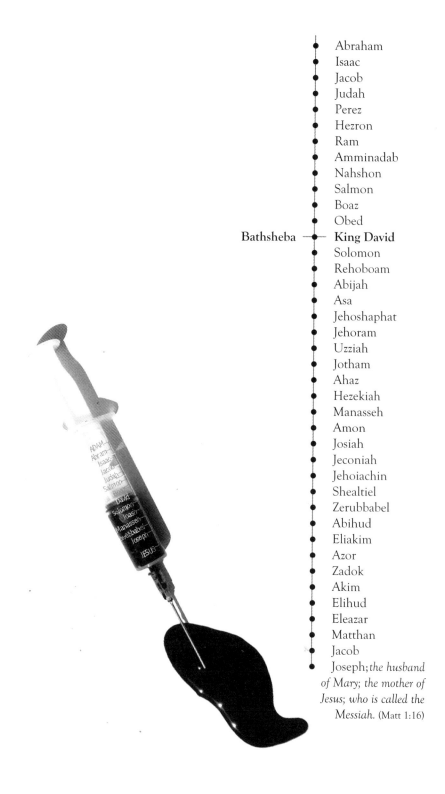

Abraham
Isaac
Jacob
Judah
Perez
Hezron
Ram
Amminadab
Nahshon
Salmon
Boaz
Obed
Bathsheba —•— **King David**
Solomon
Rehoboam
Abijah
Asa
Jehoshaphat
Jehoram
Uzziah
Jotham
Ahaz
Hezekiah
Manasseh
Amon
Josiah
Jeconiah
Jehoiachin
Shealtiel
Zerubbabel
Abihud
Eliakim
Azor
Zadok
Akim
Elihud
Eleazar
Matthan
Jacob
Joseph; *the husband
of Mary; the mother of
Jesus; who is called the
Messiah.* (Matt 1:16)

Chapter 8

The Promise (Read 1 Sam 17–18)

'Your house and your kingdom will endure forever before me; your throne will be established forever.' 2 Samuel 7:16

Who are you going to vote for? Sometimes that is a hard question to answer when more of your nation votes for a contestant on 'Strictly Come Dancing' or 'X factor' than in a general election.

Even so, in more serious times the history of Britain had been one long search to establish a right model of government. Men lived for it, fought for it, died for it even. And we really have tried everything, even a most earnest attempt to establish a millennial style reign of Christ following our bloody civil war, which – without Jesus actually being there – turned out a bit messy. The kings and queens we've had – and we've had a few – all shared the belief that they were given the sceptre by God who commanded them to *rule the waves*, which they did with varying degrees of success. This doctrine became known as the 'divine right of kings' and was vehemently clung to by all of them – as you would expect – even men like Charles II who believed in little else.

Of course, what we Brits wanted desperately was God to show us the same favour he once showed the Hebrews – that is to select a dynasty through whom he himself could be literally seen to manage the affairs of a nation. (And even then, in Israel's case it met with varying success.) Now we can argue all day whether certain English monarchs – or American presidents – were raised up by God, but we can all say for sure that there was one king, in a land far away, who definitely was. But he was not of the house of Alfred, William, Godwin, Anjou, Lancaster, York, Tudor, Stuart or Washington but of a Hebrew peasant call Jesse. Think of that, a sheep farmer!

So when we come to study the actual man that God selected from obscurity to be the divinely appointed king over – what would become – a great Israeli Empire, we, in Britain are no strangers to this story, for it is what we have sought for two millennia in our own land. It is what every nation has sought. Freedom without chaos, leadership without tyranny. The West has come closer to that than other cultures because their legal systems – systems that bound their rulers too – were based on the absolute moral base given in the Bible. I know this seems all too quaint to modern and post-modern men but we shall soon see, even as we are seeing right now, that our departure from that base eventually leads to arbitrary law making, and then tyrannical government. Of course democracy is not really the answer, as Churchill said, it is 'the worst form of government apart from all the others.' And, as we shall see, our study of David is not mere academic enquiry either, for in the final analysis, it is one of David's Jewish descendants who will one day assume the throne of England, Scotland, Ireland and this whole troubled world, sweeping aside all constitutions and amendments in his exercise of unlimited power. From the school yard bully to the knife-carrying hoods; from the armed tribal militias, to the United Nation's armies, men seek control and mastery, though in the end this will only be given to one man, and that only because he will care for the weakest before his own wants or needs. In the light of this it is well worth calibrating our own priorities and life goals as this poem suggests. It is one I wrote after reading in the National Geographic yet another unsettling article about armed militias in Africa.

An Ode to the Mighty

You despots and dictators, god fathers and God haters,
Who rule your little empires as if the first ones,
As if your muscles, fists and armies made you heaven's favoured sons.
You should have learned your history instead of playin' with guns –
a sure cure for amnesia if you had done your sums

See Rameses, your great tomb's pillaged, your city lies in ruins,
Alexander's empire's chopped up, is swallowed by the Romans.
Cyrus, Sulla, Caesar where are your armies now?
You bent men for moments before you took your final bow

And Britannia no more ruled the waves than Canute would turn the sea
As she plied that bitter, bloody trade to sweeten up her tea
And you, society's great engineers
Consenting Fuhrers of this brave new era
These final solutions are nothing new;
Oh Plato's sons, you chosen few,
Your guardian stock will no more endure

Than one small wave break on time's shore

So away, vain tyrants for whom the world was just too small,
Away, magnified exemplars of Adam's tragic fall.
And away vain thought that tells that you live on in verse and stone,
what mocking payment must this seem for pains that you now know.
For only rock cut from Zion's mount, stone rejected by you all,
Will God establish and exalt to build his empire on.

And do you offer cruelty, histories crammed with sin and crime,
As materials to that builder of God's temple for all time?
No! Away I say, you stubble'n'straw who'll whither before his eyes
'tis only a meek and contrite heart that God will not despise

And oh my God, oh what of me and all that I pursue?
Do I daily trade my birthright for suburbia and stew?
Oh Sovereign Lord please save me from all those men enjoyed
For hearses have no tow bars for trailers filled with toys.

At the time of writing one of my sons is approaching his fourth birthday and will often bring me his Bible and, sure enough, he will always ask the same thing, 'Daddy, please read me David and Goliath.' David's story has that fascination for all of us and who has not seen themselves in the life of David – I know I have many times. When I see him, I see a life lived to the 'max', rich and broad in exploit and attainment. Not one of Teddy Roosevelt's, 'cold and timid souls who knew neither defeat nor victory', but very much 'the man in the arena, his face marred by dust and sweat'. You have got to love this about him. Stuff the critics, this is what you want isn't it? The demand for men and women like him has never been higher, particularly in the West where David's gritty 'Monday-morning' spirituality is so much under attack from that Far Eastern 'navel-gazing' brand that seems so popular. The answer is not 'in here', it's in him, as Chekhov wrote, 'The Lord God has given us vast forests, immense fields, wide horizons; surely we ought to be Giants, living in such a country as this.'

So I hope we might recover something of our truer selves in this chapter, but even more I hope we also see some prophetic shadows casting forward a thousand years, to that 'son of David', our saviour Jesus.

David's Early Influences

David's Purity

There is no doubting here that David had it easy compared to us. In the UK it is hard to pay for your petrol without being confronted with pornographic images. What do you do when your daughter asks you why there is a half naked woman in a suggestive pose on the front of a newspaper or a car magazine? I won't go on for fear of sounding like an old man but I'm sure you get the point. The assaulting of conscience through the mass media has never been greater, the minds of children and adults have never been so assaulted, or corrupted with such ease. We are told what to buy, what to believe, and what to fear, with such reason and affability that not to recycle your cardboard would seem altogether a greater crime than murdering an unborn baby.

Fear is the great enemy of faith, always has been. On the same day that I wrote this chapter I was speaking to a diplomat from Cuba at a funeral. He raved about the charisma oozing from Castro, but also said that behind the rhetoric that entire Communist state is run on fear, secret police and uncertain justice.

But we are too apt to look at repressive regimes and think we are free when we are anything but. Global pandemics, global terrorism, global warming; all current fear inducers that cause western nations to forsake centuries of civil liberty, national sovereignty and part with vast swathes of cash to save the planet. In, what the Duke of Gloucester called, his 'damned, thick, square book', *Decline and Fall of the Roman Empire*, Edward Gibbon wryly observed, 'The fabric of a mighty state, which has been reared by the labours of successive ages, could not be overturned by the misfortune of a single day, if the fatal power of the imagination did not exaggerate the real measure of the calamity.' And of Augustus, the cunning tyrant who turned democracy into dictatorship, Gibbon says he was 'sensible ... that the senate and people would submit to slavery, provided they were respectfully assured that they still enjoyed their ancient freedom'. Not having a television to tell me how afraid I should be of everything, it can be alarming to see how dominated my friends – even Christian friends – are with anxiety about the future. I've tried to teach a Sunday school class when the children cannot focus on Jesus for fear of bird flu. The stress they carry will become part of the 'fear-culture' of their adulthood. This was the atmosphere of the Israelite village and military camp, but was not so for David who spent his time apart from them with the Lord. The day he walked into the valley of Elah – amongst the men polluted with fear, dominated by public opinion and media lies – all the paralysis seemed absurd to David coming from his 'narrow' and 'parochial' mindset. It is narrow in that it disallows phobia and peer pressure but it is heavenly broad and expansive in that it captures the immensity of God's viewpoint. The size of God impresses David, not the size of Goliath. The freedom of having a *narrow mind* is something Christians desperately need in the twenty-first century; the great cry of being 'contemporary' in outlook seems a bit limp when someone comes with a Goliath-size prayer request, for it is then you need big faith in a big God. We are the gatekeepers to our hearts, minds and homes; some things we cannot reasonably avoid but so much we can. It is so tempting to give a 'helpful' list of 'dos and don'ts' at this point, but I must resist becoming legalistic. I suggest you ask the Lord for yourself, perhaps go from room to room in your home and take a list of what he wants you to throw out. I can assure you that you will hear the whisperings of the Holy Spirit, even if you claim not to be the 'spiritually sensitive sort.'.

For seeing we are compassed about by such a cloud of witnesses (which includes David), let us cast aside every weight that can so easily thwart us. Friends, we must be serious about this, great power falls on great purity and for those who, like you, have set their hearts on being *great in the kingdom'*, the excess baggage must be negligible. This separation from our cultural thought-ifications can be like you achieving your own 'exodus' in no less real a way than Abraham, Rebecca, Jacob, Leah, and Ruth did. You may not see it now, you may scoff at what I have just said, perhaps I would have a few years back, but for those who choose to pursue a truly biblical world view, to truly *'come out and be separate'*, yearning to see the world and people as God sees them, the paradigm shift is quite astonishing.

There was one Christian Lawyer who no doubt people thought was very generous; for he gave his sister – a missionary in India – $5000 a year for her support. But he realised after a few years that he had spent over $175,000 on his flash Mercs and 4x4, and the latter he hardly ever used because he worked such long hours for the firm. He felt convicted of this and so he sold the cars, bought a second hand one and gave the money to his sister instead. With that money she was able to start four rescue houses for child prostitutes and within a short time over 400 had been saved. This lawyer was starting to achieve his exodus from the stranglehold of the culture but he found that it is only when you try to get free that you see the strings; a partner in the firm saw his second hand car and assuming he'd made some bad investments offered to loan him money to get a Porsche and so not disgrace the firm. He refused, and that was not all – for he then felt convicted that working 14 hour days was betraying his primary responsibility to his family. But when he started leaving work on time he was taken aside and told in uncertain terms that if he didn't put in the hours he would never be a partner at that firm.

Mild stuff I admit, but you see my point. Ronald Sider said the *'Western middle class life is a structural evil'* in itself, and that we must learn to *'live more simply that others may simply live'*. Could you agree with him, that our culture is just as anti-Christ as say that of North Korea or Saudi Arabia? If we cannot feel or experience that hostility, to Jesus through us, then we should ask why. I grant that there was a period when even the early church was *'praising God and having the respect* (favour) *of all the people with God adding to them daily those who were being saved.'* But let us not forget that this was an 'Acts 2' church; they were young but still not far away from those later chapters of persecution. If you or your church are not persecuted at present, then you may not have done anything wrong – but my advice is still be prepared for it, in the words of Paul to Timothy, *'all who would live godly in Christ Jesus will suffer persecution.'* Of course it might be that we or our church pose no threat to the culture or the powers that be and that is why we are 'kept at peace'. This is a real challenge to us, in China one house church leader said that if all they did was worship and study the Bible together then they wouldn't get in trouble. It was another matter however if they made converts. Pastor Haik in Iran told Brother Andrew in 1993, *'Andrew, when they come to kill me it will be for speaking, not for staying silent.'* When a Muslim converted to Christianity and was sentenced to death, Haik stood up for him, stirring up such an international outcry that the convert was released. Later however Haik was himself abducted and knifed to death.

William Barclay said the three hallmarks of a genuine Christian are that they are absurdly happy, they have an irrational love for everyone and that they are always in trouble. The question here is: how much trouble are you in for Jesus?

David's Obscurity

Remember this is before Micah's prophecy about Bethlehem being the birthplace of the king. No one thinks of the hill village as anything special, certainly not Jesse's family with their dubious mixed marriages. David was always aware of this, and later referred to himself in the royal court *'as a poor man and lightly esteemed'*. That is no mock humility; to have a Canaanite prostitute and a Moabite asylum seeker as relatives was not exactly a plus on your CV in those days. David grows up in a nowhere village despised by his tough brothers. We have touched on Isaiah 49 before but it bears repeating, for as it was true of our Lord, so it was true of David and perhaps of you too.

'And he has made my mouth like a sharp sword, in the shade of his hand he has kept me as a secret; he has made me like a polished (or tested) arrow, keeping me in his secret place.' Is 49:2

Some were never able to acknowledge what God was doing in David though it's good to see some of his brothers in the army later on. We can also be obscure to those closest to us, they can be the last to acknowledge what God is doing. I think it is safe to say that David was despised (thought little of) by his brothers, and perhaps even by his father, and yet was anointed in the midst of them as jealous eyes looked on. The parallels to Joseph are all too clear but this is also a direct foreshadowing of the treatment Jesus would receive from his half brothers and sisters, and townsmen. I love the way God hides his greatest treasures and I was deeply moved when reading Thayer's biography of Abraham Lincoln recently, particularly when it came to his dealings with Rebecca Pomroy.

It was a year into the war and a deciding night in the battle for Port Hudson. It was also President Lincoln's dark night of the soul as his son, Willie, had just died. Another son, Tad, lay critically ill with typhoid, and Mrs Lincoln was sick in bed. Lincoln was broken hearted and beyond despair when this frail woman, Rebecca Pomroy, arrived at the White House. She had come quite unwillingly, having had to leave thirty dying soldiers with someone else at the hospital. Lincoln was amazed that she was reputed to do so much and yet look so feeble but his enquiry led to her giving him her testimony. She had nursed her own husband twenty years ago, and just before his death, she also lost her two sons and one daughter ('the light of her home'), before all her worldly belongings were sold off to pay her creditors. It was after this, when her own health was crumbling under the strain that Rebecca was born again at an evangelistic crusade and found God calling her into nursing. She spoke of being supernaturally sustained by God, the power of prayer, and the joy of having a living faith in a living Saviour. Lincoln was fascinated and asked whether the born again experience was 'exceptional'. She told him it was for everyone, and that he ought to go and pray himself. He did, and she heard him interceding for his family and then his country, and at that moment she knew things were about to change.

By that morning news came of the decisive victory at Port Hudson, and pretty soon Rebecca had nursed Mary and Tad Lincoln back to health. The effect on honest Abe should not be understated; he would often call in at the hospital thereafter to ask her again of some finer point of her conversion. 'Oh, I pray God would give to me also your childlike faith, Mrs Pomroy,' he once said to her. He would also send senators to see her on occasions, 'be sure to introduce yourself to Nurse Pomroy, my conversation with her did me a great deal of good.' Who would have thought that this woman, a polished arrow, tried and tested – and yet quite secret, would have been the evangelist to reach a United States president and many senators? Friend, we must labour to entrust our lives, our reputations and our gifting to the God who sees what is done in secret. In the final analysis we are only what he says we are, and that might be an awful lot more than our friends and family say, but equally it might be less than we try to make ourselves out to be. We must keep our counsel, saying along with Job, that God alone knows the path we take and when he brings us out we shall be as polished gold. Amen to that.

David's Training in Faith

Training in the 'Word'

But for David it was not just the absence of worldliness that formed him, it was something far stronger. It is apparent David has a biblical heritage – from his psalm writing. He is trained in spiritual understanding and also has the ability to process (meditate on) these things. Romans 10:17 says, 'faith comes by hearing' and there is no automatic download to have your mind renewed if you want to serve God, study – not merely listening to worship CDs – is the only way. I know, I know, study sounds untrendy, surely there is something more contemporary for generation X – but that is just the way it is, get used to it! Even Jesus sought God with diligence for theological answers, as we saw in a previous chapter. Horace Mann said, 'There is nothing so costly as ignorance' and quite simply, if we spend more time on TV soaps than we do in being washed in the word of God, our minds will be conformed to the culture, not heaven – and our impact will be small. Abigail Adams said 'wisdom and penetration are the fruit of experience, not the lessons of retirement and leisure. Great necessities call out great virtues.' C.H. Spurgeon said, 'If you wish to know God, you must know his Word. If you wish to perceive his power, you must see how he works by his Word. If you wish to know his purpose before it comes to pass, you can only discover it by his Word.' Forget paperbacks, (even this one); pursue God through his word and by prayer.

Training by 'Doing'

Jesus once said that 'My food is doing the will of the one who sent me and completing his work', so we could say that if faith 'comes' by hearing, it stays by 'doing'. Faith is not theory; to quote Luther, 'Salvation is by faith alone but not by a faith which is alone'. David learned by life and death fights with bears and lions that God is real and reliable. Goliath was not some great pinnacle of achievement to David, but a natural progression of a life he was already living. We must not resist the Holy Spirit's call to 'get out of the boat' for ourselves. Also for our children, there is no growth without proven experience.

In Bristol a hundred years ago you would have been laughed out of the pubs if you had suggested that God was not real. Why? 'Well where have you been? Haven't you heard of George Müller?' A former rich kid who ended up in prison after stealing from his own father, Müller was converted and exercised his apostolic gifting across the world with great effect. He is mostly remembered in history as the man who built up the Bristol orphanages for 2000 children; he never once made an appeal to any man for money, only to God. After being a father to the fatherless, Müller's whole aim was to prove to the world beyond any doubt that there was a 'prayer hearing God' in heaven. There were few deluded enough to deny it. Müller once said, 'I have learned my faith by standing firm amid severe testings', and 'If the Lord fails me at this time, it will be the first time.' How does a man reach such a godly state? We may not want the answer for he says of himself, 'There was a day when I died; died to self, my opinions, preferences, tastes and will; died to the world, its approval or censure; died to the approval or blame even of my brethren or friends; and since then I have studied only to show myself approved unto God.' To learn strong faith is to endure great trials.

George Müller proved God by what he did, so did David, and so will we.

The pressure and adversity that will come on you as a warrior in training should be taken, if possible, as a good sign. Make it your whole aim at these times that 'your mouth reflects what your faith detects'. By this I mean, do not whine and whinge, as I know I have done in the past, about how tight things are financially for example. Just smile like Müller would, when someone asks you how you are, and say, 'They are as great as the Lord pleases'. Like the saintly James Hudson Taylor who wrote to his wife, 'We have twenty–five cents – and all the promises of God!' To be under God's discipline (literally, his 'discipling') is to share Jesus' triumph over all things: 'In the world you will have great troubles but don't worry I am on top of it.'

Training by Role Models

This is a much neglected area and it is so much more than the modern fad for 'mentoring'. You don't have to appoint mentors when there are men and women about that everyone wants to be - they are just copied, it's that simple and that powerful. We're not called sheep for nothing, it's just the way we are wired. I have known some extraordinary men and women of God, but I must admit with sadness that they have been few and far between. By the time teenage David forms a deep friendship with the king's son, Jonathan is already middle aged, possibly in his mid fifties. Jesus was once referred to as the *pioneer of faith* for us, and that is exactly what Jonathan was for David. As my son reads and rereads the Goliath story with awe, so Jonathan's Mishmash victory was something of that order for David. It was the one major headline event that David would have been weaned on; the prince of Israel who took on a Philistine garrison single handed.

We see these extreme sports guys egging each other on to do the next biggest bike jump; well, this is no different, Jonathan sparked David's imagination and David, in his turn, sparked a whole heap of other guys – just read the list of mighty men and all they did, many things far more amazing than slaying Goliath. Example is like that – like a wildfire. And lets not overlook simple friendship either. In his excellent book 'The Four Loves' C.S. Lewis notes with alarm that the modern world and modern literature ignore this love which – for the ancients – was the highest expression of human love. (e.g. Jonathan and David, Plyades and Orestes, Roland and Oliver) It was what Aristotle called it 'Philia', Cicero; 'Amitas' and it certainly seems to us as the least natural – or the least instinctive – of the loves, which may give us a clue as to why the Greeks set such a value on it. With their stoic view of all things earthy or bodily being corrupt it was only natural that something that seemed so otherworldly and spiritual, should be prized as it was. But our understanding was equally distorted, first under the 18th century Romantic philosophers, who saw it as a 'vegetarian' substitute for the more natural loves. And then again in the modern era after Freud's rantings that 'all friendships were really sexual' – homosexual or otherwise. But when comparing friendship to romantic love, Lewis says that it is lovers who want naked bodies, not friends – what friends want is naked souls – and whereas lovers stand face to face, friends will be side by side, looking out at something else, some other interest. Their friendship is not so much about themselves as some other interest which incidentally is why those that just want friends can never have them – rather like a man cannot have fellow travellers unless he leaves his house! Friendship itself is not the journey, other things are, and these interests can be equally evil as good. For David and Jonathan it was knowing God, for others it might be politics, philosophy, piracy, Porsches, ping pong or play stations. (I think it was done supremely well in the 2010 film *The Damned United*, at the centre of which is the friendship of Brian Clough and Peter Taylor, and also in *The King's Speech* between King George VI and his speech therapist; Lionel Logue) One other interesting point is that a true friendship will relish other people with a similar passion joining the group. That makes it again very opposite to the exclusivity of romantic love. Why is this? Well, it seems that each new member to the friendship will in their turn bring out differing facets of the others. Of course the ultimate expression of this will be heaven itself.

So yes, to go back to my original point, we should not underestimate the power of friendships to change our world, and the world – for that matter. Jonathan caused David to raise his sights not just to endeavours of faith, but also to a life of humility. The giving of Jonathan's armour, clothing and weapons to David, made an impression on him beyond the moment – for him it became a way of life. It is something I have experienced from others too and we should know that our generosity can really shape the people we love.

The Jesuits used to say, 'Give me the boy until he is seven and I will show you the man.' It is a saying with a great deal of truth, though not the whole story. Many have risen above and sunk below their beginnings and we must never discount the grace of God which happens on many occasions to overturn human premise. We have seen a little of David's early life in this chapter, but what he would become was not certain. The historian Plutarch remarked, in his life of Pompey the Great, that early success can intoxicate some men to ruin but to others it is received as a token of their future greatness. For David, exalted at such a tender age, we might have expected to see him a made man from then on, but that was not the path that the Lord had for him. The kind of king God needed David to be, could only be forged in the heat of the wilderness. It is invariably the same for us and will be the subject of the next chapter.

Life Application Devotion

Chapter 8 – Is this the Day to Seek Great Things?

- David, like Jesus, was honed by God in secret. Do you feel like this too sometimes?
- Using your 'sanctified' imagination, write down what God might accomplish through the gifting and ministry he has given you. Dream big but be specific too.
- If God was offering it right now, which would you chose; (a) half the level of fruit given as your last answer but with remuneration and applause from your peers/church/denomination/missionary society etc, or (b) something 'beyond what we can even ask or think' if it came with persecution and total anonymity?
- Prayer: (Start with thanksgiving & praise, particularly for God's thoughts toward, and plans for your life.) 'Oh Lord My Rewarder and Exceeding Great Reward, it is to you and you alone that I now bring all my heart's wrestlings and desires in this difficult area. I openly confess my struggle to you for I believe that you alone have the power to give me my truest heart's desire; that I may serve and honour you without pride or self interest and that you would use this life you have redeemed to accomplish whatever your heart desires.

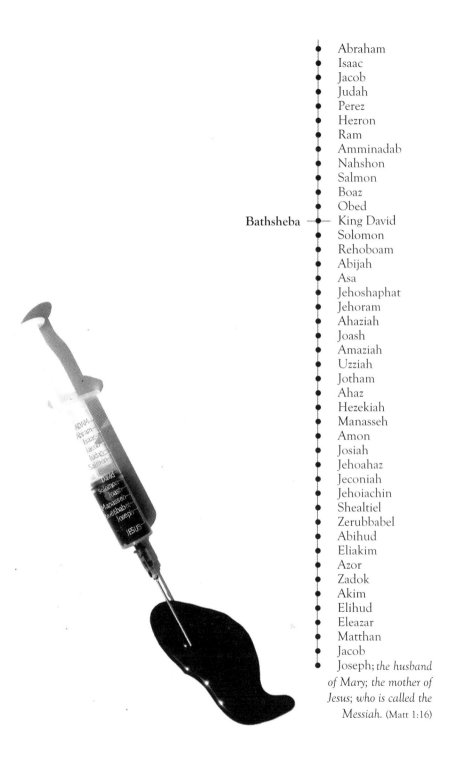

Abraham
Isaac
Jacob
Judah
Perez
Hezron
Ram
Amminadab
Nahshon
Salmon
Boaz
Obed
Bathsheba ——— King David
Solomon
Rehoboam
Abijah
Asa
Jehoshaphat
Jehoram
Ahaziah
Joash
Amaziah
Uzziah
Jotham
Ahaz
Hezekiah
Manasseh
Amon
Josiah
Jehoahaz
Jeconiah
Jehoiachin
Shealtiel
Zerubbabel
Abihud
Eliakim
Azor
Zadok
Akim
Elihud
Eleazar
Matthan
Jacob
Joseph; *the husband of Mary; the mother of Jesus; who is called the Messiah.* (Matt 1:16)

Chapter 9

'Rise a Knight' (Read 1 Sam 18–30 & all of 2 Samuel)

'I used to ask God to help me. Then I asked if I might help him. I ended up by asking him to do his work through me.' Hudson Taylor

There was a smell of burning and then blood curdling shrieks of laughter on the street. I came round from my heavy sleep very quickly and the adrenalin pulsed through my body like liquid ice, 'Ruth, get up, we're on fire.'

The sounds of shouting and laughter faded. I went onto the landing and down the stairs. Funny, I thought, the smell of smoke has faded. There was smoke in the front room but not much, it was only when I opened the front door that I could see the flames licking up the cypress tree and plumes of smoke rising past our bedroom window. The potted tree had died and dried up months ago, and though it went up quickly, it was not big enough to cause any real damage to our first married home.

But the gloss paint never came off the walls.

Cans of the stuff had been thrown over the frontage, and more worrying still were the messages painted on the door and over our car, about what they thought of me and how they were going to kill Ruth. That was about 1998 and we were pioneering a new church in a difficult area. We saw the perpetrators of that particular attack all come to acknowledge Jesus as Lord, but there were plenty of other times when we felt hated and intimidated in those early days. In fact, I bet there are not many church planters who can claim to have been urinated on for the sake of the gospel, but I was. It happened while I was leaving the youth club we rented for the outreaches, a flat-roofed building on which scores of teenagers would jump and shout. The ceiling plaster would fall like confetti as we sang to Jesus. The offending youth responded to the altar call two weeks later and I made him kneel before the Lord, in front of all his peers, to pledge his life to Christ. I figured that he of all people wouldn't claim not to be a sinner; like so many did, I mean, I had the coat to prove it!

Amusing enough I suppose, but it is no joke to live under the constant threat of death – as many believers do. I have only felt a mere tinge of that and I have also alluded to my experiences in Bosnia, but there are others who live with that nearness of violence for many years on end. David was one such man; he said on one occasion, *'there is a step between me and death'* (1 Sam 20:1–3) and it summed up his early life, though he was not speaking about lions, bears or giants, but rather the grinding national slander and character defamation and his endless pursuit by Saul. By the time David was captain of the army, he must have thought his rise to prominence, to fame and power, would come with ease – but, as we know, God had a deeper work to do in David that neither success nor victory could accomplish in his character.

The Honing of David's Gifting
Through Persecution and Suffering

'... they kissed one another and wept until David could pull himself together. Then Jonathan said to David, "Go in peace, because we've sworn in the name of Yahweh saying that He would be like a beacon between us and between our descendants forever..." 1 Samuel 20:41–42

By the time this heart rending scene takes place, it has dawned on David that there is another road that God has chosen for him, a road less travelled; the road known to so many of you no doubt, the road of humiliation and unjust slander. A noxious cocktail of Saul's spiritually induced paranoia, court intrigue and character assassination, will lead David on a gruelling, flesh crushing exile for more years than he could ever imagine at that point. Everything must die. We will look at the facets of his trial below and through it all please hold this in your mind, that you may have a correct story or 'end-point' in your mind – a gift, a ministry, a destiny that you know the Lord has for you but – never presume the journey to that goal will be without pain, not on this earth anyway. I think it was Tozer – thinking of Jacob – who said, 'never trust a man who doesn't walk with a limp.' Jacob, David, Joseph, Moses and Paul are men that were figuratively made to 'limp' through life, that they 'should not trust in themselves but in the power of God.'

Character Assassination

On one or two occasions we can see it is the slander that really gets to David; we see it in his conversations with Saul and in his psalms too. John Wesley once announced that he had been slandered as having committed every sin known to man, apart from being a drunkard. At that very point a woman stood up at the back and shrieked, 'Liar, Wesley, you liar. Everyone knows you sold your soul to the devil for drink', to which he replied (to the Lord and not to her), 'Thank you Lord, my cup is full.' Slander and defamation are very hard to cope with; I know, I have been accused of all sorts – and the only remedy to all this that I can see is to learn from Wesley and the Lord Jesus; to make our plea to God. If we keep our integrity, then the Lord will protect our reputations, pure and simple. Are you so proud that you would be greater than your master?

The Valley of Humiliation

Like Job, David was stripped of everything;

His Wife – Now maybe David later felt he'd been better off without Michal, (as Job might have when she challenged his faith!) but that loss of intimacy for an extended period could arguably have led David to go deeper with God. Remember, some of his best loved psalms come from the wilderness years.

His Friends – Particularly Jonathan but also the network of 'not-so' important friends. Think for one moment if you were cut off from your work colleagues, neighbours, cousins, youth group, postman, aunties, school friends, church friends etc. To have all the many strands that balance and secure your life severed and to know that your friends are also being fed false information about you. I believe this will be a major issue for Christians in the last days, even as it is for many of our suffering brothers and sisters around the world today.

His Home – I may be softer than most but to be away from my home, my bed, my books, guitars, my favourite mug, my favourite pillow even, for any time longer than a week makes me really homesick! It's one thing to say 'I don't sleep well in hotel beds', quite another to sleep in a cave living as a fugitive.

His Family – Due to the rage of Saul, David arranged for his parents to seek asylum under the king of Moab, but we must assume his brothers went on the run with him. Certainly his sister's boys, Joab, Abishai and Asahel, cut their teeth with David in those early years. But I wonder whether David was ever weighed down by the trials he had brought upon his own family. It is one thing to endure hardship, quite another to see those you love uprooted and persecuted for your sake. To see this burden played out in real time' we need look no further than the testimonies of church workers – from over 52 nations on earth where persecution is hottest – where wives must struggle on without husbands, children without mothers or other siblings.

His Work – for a man to lose his job is a devastating blow: David describes himself as a '*dead dog*' and that can be a very succinct way of describing the emotions associated with unemployment. It strikes very deep into the way we are wired, and the indignity of not being able to provide for ourselves or our families can be a major cause of depression. I have been self employed for almost all my adult life; the Lord has often been able to often use lack of work as an avenue for his grace. Not only have these lean times channelled my teaching gift into writing, but they have also caused me to derive my identity and self worth from *who I am* in his world – rather than *what I do* in my world. I am not claiming to have cracked this, but I would encourage those very many people who the Lord is leading through this valley not to despair, for it will yield real fruit for later ministry, if you keep your integrity. In fact we'll see in this chapter how David uses this time to serve and protect others.

Three Lessons From David's Wilderness Years

Authority is God given

David is acutely tested on two occasions to take what God has given him – before the time of his own training is over. Both in the cave and in the camp, David was urged by others to take the crown by murdering Saul, but so tender is David's heart and so yielded is his life, that it says in 1 Samuel 24:5 '*his heart smote him*' – even when he cut off a piece of Saul's garment. If we are to see the fruit David saw we too must submit ourselves to every authority and every situation that God has put over us. James says we are blessed when we '*stay under*' trials. The tempter will use every means possible to draw us out from under this training, but we must resist. God only has one training college – and this is it. There is an authority that is from men – especially in the religious arena – that can be earned by education or 'obtained by stealth', but there is also an authority from God whose affirmation is only given to those he has tried. We must humble ourselves in our service – to the least of the saints and the work of the gospel; if the Lord wishes to do anything more with us, that is his business, not ours. Self promotion and aggrandisement is often a subtle temptation but clearly obnoxious; God help us all to reject every way of Satan.

King work

David does the work of a king because the oil has been poured on his head, rather than because the crown is on it. This is tremendously important and something we should grasp, for we too are the people of tomorrow. A kingdom has been *conferred* upon us and we, as the anointed princes of God are commanded to exercise his delegated power on earth, whether men (or even what men call the established church) acknowledge us or not. God makes us responsible for what he shows us, and the work of his kingdom has little to do with having others serve us – and everything to do with protecting and serving the weak. David does this even when some might have just been licking their wounds. At Adullam, Keilah, Ziklag and Carmel, David is the protection of Israel – while Saul's ministry disintegrates in petty factionalism and self–obsession. In the Keilah incident particularly, David's 'un–merry' men were already too busy being intimidated by Saul to reach out to others. 'We're afraid enough just here in Judah. How much more afraid do you think we'll be if we go against the Philistine army at Keilah?' 1 Sam 23:3 But David knew that his own level of comfort or convenience was no deciding factor in doing the will of God. God simply showed David the need and made him the answer. We sometimes feel like David in that wilderness; our circumstances have almost boxed us totally into an Adullam's cave of dependence on God and then, through facing fear, frustration and distraction – we hear him asking us to expand our ministry, exercise our gifting, be the answer to someone else's prayer, even give some money away! The time will never be perfect; don't procrastinate, push on, push in and do what he has called you to do. 'Go in this thy might,' God said to Gideon and also now to us, in effect it is something like, 'stop moaning, let me make you the solution'.

There was once a teacher in China called Mabel who suffered terribly during the Cultural revolution; her home was taken and she was left to live despised and hated in a garden shed with a sign outside citing her crimes, one of which was giving out bibles and thus misleading people. After a while the isolation and persecution got to her so much that she wanted to end it all. 'Lord, I'm sixty five and I've had a good life but I can't go like this anymore. If you still have work for me and still want me to live,' she said raising a meat cleaver above her wrist, 'then you will have to stop me doing this.' Somehow she never brought that cleaver down and somehow Mabel went on for another eight years, until one day people – including high party officials – started turning up at her shed asking for bibles. She was puzzled and asked an official how he knew to come to her. 'Well, ' he said, 'because for years you had that sign over your house saying that you had given away bibles, I just wondered whether you had any left.' And so using her foreign contacts Mabel became the first conduit for new bibles in China after the Cultural Revolution! She saw the fruit of her labour for her 'King work', but we must admit that just as many do not. Keilah for David might have looked like a bad pay off in earthly terms, but that's not the point – the point is obedience to our calling. God give us grace to stick to it, even when it looks like we are forgotten.

Vengeance is Mine

David has been so faultless over so many trials that it comes as quite a shock to see him arming up to slaughter a whole village over a personal insult. He had been so busy guarding his heart regarding Saul, that Nabal slipped in under the radar. Abigail's timely reminder that '... *the lives of your enemies he will sling out as from the hollow of a sling*' shows the masterful use of a metaphor, calculated to conquer David and help him recover his bearings. 'The sling, the stone, Goliath, the Lord – of course, what on earth am I doing?' We may not have four hundred armed men, but we each have a tongue – and how we speak when tired or hungry does matter to heaven more than we know. I was in a situation last year where a 'Christian' I had been helping stole a lot of money from me and then covered his tracks by slandering my integrity wherever he went. At a low point I was moaning about it, 'I mean, can you actually believe he had the nerve to slag me off like that and say such things after all we did for them?' My friend Paul, who knows me very well, smiled and said, 'Well at least it is not as bad as the truth.' Paul was right, for at the end of the day, we have no reason to be proud; in fact we have very little to defend if we have truly seen the darkness of our hearts. So let's just rejoice that God will still have us, and leave it at that. Let men say what they want, but entrust our integrity to God.

To know God

This might sound strange, but remember where David's best psalms come from – that's right, from those cruel wilderness years. An Islamic convert to Christianity was kept by the Egyptian police for a month inside a dark stone box, five foot cubed. While he suffered in that place he says that he came to an end of himself, saw himself as he really was before a Holy God, and beyond that found a very different Jesus than he knew before. This might sound strange to some, but he explains that the 'filling was so great because I was so empty.' Here then is the key to the wilderness – for David and for us – to bring us to an end of ourselves, that we might be more filled with all his fullness. 'Do not fear the cross,' the Holy Spirit told Richard Wurmbrand soon after his conversion, 'you will find it the greatest of joys.' It was for him even when the Communists came to arrest him, it may be for us too in all we might face with Jesus.

Legends of the Fall

'Nearly all men can stand adversity, but if you want to test a man's character, give him power.' Abraham Lincoln

For all our abilities, we fall – all of us, and David was certainly no exception. Even within the short time that I have been a disciple of Jesus, I've seen many godly men fall through pride and sin, even some close to me. Saul's tragic fall, and the devastating consequences that it would have for his family and his country must have been something that haunted David as a warning written large. I shudder to think of Jonathan dying on Mount Gilboa with his father, and all the other brave men that fell – for one man's disobedience. Saul could never let go of his personal insecurity, a littleness and bitterness of heart, that would eventually infect the whole court and bring destruction to the nation. We all have those Achilles' heels in our flesh; some wounded area that has turned gangrenous. Remember and please, please never ever forget, that you are never more in sympathy with Satan than when you are defending your 'own' corner, your own right to yourself, your own righteousness. Yes, that's right, it will often be over 'good' things that we'll be seduced, if at all. Satan knows better than any that men mistake brass for gold more readily than they do rusty iron! And, as C. S. Lewis reminds us in that excellent book 'The Great Divorce', demons are not made from mice but from Archangels.

Hell's best kept secret even now is that the world is kept thinking that to be in league with Satan is simply to be an occultist. What damage can 100 warlocks do compared to one preacher who preaches 'another' gospel? There is no comparison! Some of Satan's best, most obedient, most fruitful servants have been good, religious people who can be played like puppets because their minds are 'carnal'. Paul says that these people's 'end is destruction' because their real 'god is their own intellect, advancement and personal comfort' and their entire life's focus is on 'earthly things.' (Phil 3:18) Notice that their crimes might seem to us no greater than being a bit too focused on self–realisation and what we wrongly call 'the real world'. Jesus' rebuke to Peter, 'get behind me Satan' was because he had 'in mind the things of men,' and there was no sorcery about it at all, just human sympathy ridden by Hell. Those outwardly moral, evangelical, 'four-square-on-the-Bible' Pharisees had no idea that for the most part they were - in Jesus' words - 'children of the devil', and that the fruit of their evangelistic campaigns made converts that were 'twice the sons of hell' as they were. This is why we so mistake Satan's subtle operation in the world; we see a preacher or a worship leader fall into some major public sin and we think, 'Oh no, now Satan's got him'. But we may be very far from the truth! Satan has probably overplayed his hand and likely begins to regret it! Why? Well, where will that preacher or worship leader go when he has lost all his following, his kudos, his album or book sales? Exactly, nine times out of ten he will throw himself without pretence on the mercy of God and so be lost to the powers of darkness. Satan's real job all along - and please hear this if you hear nothing else - is to *keep his goods in peace*, to make me and you believe that our 'little' sins are really not so sinful after all, that they are excusable even and so with deadened conscience we might serve him unfettered all our days; kept in peace, yes, but for which final destination? We might find out only too late.

'Search me oh my God' cries David in the psalms and well he might for any area left unyielded to the Lord is an area where darkness can have a legal right to grow and multiply strength. The work of rooting out these - what I call - 'thought-ifications'; mental or spiritual strongholds - belongs to the Holy Spirit alone, he reveals them at the right time and we respond in repentance. And it must be repentance friend; I'm sure there is a great many places for spiritual healing but this certainly is not one. Beware of self pity like the plague, it is the best material by which hell builds a prison for us against God's grace. And if he grants you repentance and you seize that, then 'by his stripes' you will be healed body, soul and spirit - praise God!

Through David's spectacular failings and sin - as with our own - we see the immeasurable grace of God shine through in sustained brilliance. For David there were two main areas, the second more serious than the first.

Fear Based Decision Making

'I shall one day perish by the hand of Saul' (1 Sam 27:1) It is little wonder that, through the sheer exhaustion of his trial and the year in, year out grind of his wanderings, David believes and reiterates the voice of the enemy. (Compare this incident with how Elijah was affected by Jezebel's threats, *'Take away my life, Lord.'*) David's decision to seek protection under an enemy king (and a Philistine king at that) would precipitate a life of deceit and difficulty for him,

and almost bring him into a battle against his true king, his best friend, and his countrymen. It is a comfort to me that God's plan can even be fulfilled despite our failure and mistakes. He saved David from real danger in this instance and, though we may never experience the acuteness of David's circumstances, we can certainly have faith in the same gracious God who can save us from our bad decisions.

Becoming Omnipotent

'Ye shall be Gods' was the temptation that 'took out' Adam and Eve; the same hollow promise offered to the men of the Renaissance and Enlightenment eras, and we see it thinly veiled behind every form of subsequent sin. On three very fateful occasions David loses touch with who he is, in relationship to God. Whether distracted, carnal or just plain puffed up with the intoxication of power, David treats those within the orbit of his protection with a distorted omnipotence that eventually brings calamity upon his family and the nation. The first incident involved a walk on the palace roof, historically a very dangerous place for any of us to walk, for was it not here that Nebuchadnezzar would spout all that 'self made man' stuff: 'Is this not *my* kingdom that I've made with *my* power for *my* glory'. We all have our 'palace roof' moments where we substitute the word '*my*' for '*thy*'; so too we see David surveying God's subjects as objects to serve his own pleasure. *'Mine, mine, mine, they all exist to serve me.'*

K. P. Yohannan – a man who with forty years experience and responsible for thousands of missionaries in Asia, said that if a Christian worker falls away, or makes shipwreck of his faith, 99% of the time it will not be big, scarlet sins like adultery but slow, crimson ones like accumulated pride and selfishness. Herein lies David's initial, hidden fall and if you have ever found yourself, as I have, gloating over other Christians or exalting in your gifting, dedication or abilities – take heed, friend, for mischief is at your door.

Why? Because this is pride; that one sin which everyone hates – in others – and which only the Christian ethical system claims is a major problem. Pride led Satan to fall from his exalted position, and he has had little trouble tempting us to copy him since that time. Indeed Christians of another generation called it a Cardinal sin – the word 'cardinal' comes from the Latin for hinge or literally 'pivot'. Should it surprise us that pride seems to have slipped under the radar of modern ethics, and yet be such a big deal to Christians? Perhaps not for this is the very nature of self deception, and yet I have said that we all easily see it in others and despise it too.

C.S. Lewis dedicates a chapter to it in 'Mere Christianity', and says that the more guilty of pride we are the more we will see and hate it in others. Now there's a thing! He says that pride is primarily competitive and though greed might drive you to get a big car or a big house, it is pride – going unnoticed – that will drive you to make sure the house is bigger than your neighbours and the car faster. The irritating guy at work or at the party always trying to top your story or joke is doing so because your pride and his pride are in competition with each other. In fact you are both guilty here. The man or woman who flirts with your spouse does so not so much out of lust – though that may be there too – but so that they may prove themselves better than you. It is my pride in action when I look down on someone else, congratulate myself as being better than them in a certain area. It is my pride that will tear into public figures when I see the news; I want to get them below me, I am better, cleverer, more righteous and more pure. Because of pride I can never really ever be content or happy while there is still someone in the universe richer, cleverer or more beautiful than me.

And this is how pride ultimately comes to exalt itself against God and hence it became the root of so much sin. Of course some sins unite men, but pride – above every other – divides and separates us; friend from friend, sibling from sibling, neighbour from neighbour, son from father, husband from wife, management from workers, nation from nation, men from God. And we must not think that God demands we repent of pride because it offends his dignity – for most of what we call dignity is in reality pride – and he doesn't have a shred of pride, something not easy for us to imagine. His only wish is to see us shed our pompous, barbed-wire costumes, and get wonderfully free of all that ridiculous tyranny. For until we do that we cannot know him – I mean, it is impossible to know him – for how can we look up at him, when we are so used to looking down on everyone all the time? I suggest we start each week repenting of pride, putting it in our diaries even, and asking the Holy Spirit to 'seek and destroy' it. And that probably means 99% of what we call humility too, for as Oswald Chambers remarked long ago, 'conscious humility is the most satanic pride of all.' Never mind the proverbial 'cobwebs in our hearts', let's allow the Holy Spirit to 'kill the spider' and we'll soon see the cobwebs go. The other options are not encouraging; either pride must die or everything else is forfeit.

God has called us, as he did David, to the battlefield and not to the palace roof; if you are walking on one, you are not walking on the other. David must have spent many years regretting the fact he never went to battle that spring, for from that afternoon stroll on the palace roof sprang a whirlwind of family trouble. God help us all.

The second great stage of David's tragic fall involves his son: Absalom: In Deuteronomy 28 we're told that the price of disobedience will be that parents would not be able to enjoy their children, something that we can see being fulfilled as David comforts Tamar, buries Amnon and banishes Absalom. But worse followed the banishment of Absalom: another occasion when we see David exercising an omnipotence of sorts. For this son was not embraced quickly or forgiven fully by the very same David who had experienced so much forgiveness for sins far worse. When the kingdom of God truly comes to us, or anyone, Malachi's prophecy that *'the hearts of the fathers will be turned to the children'* will happen – and also vice versa. But notice it is the fathers who turn first, this did not happen and though we might argue that Absalom was not truly penitent, David was also in error here and would pay for it during the civil war. In our case the command is clear to *'forgive men their trespasses'* and if we decide in a deluded 'omnipotence' to withhold forgiveness then we too will reap the consequences. God forbid that any of us fathers should ever cry, as David did, after a rebellious son, 'Absalom, oh my son Absalom, would that I had died in your place.' These are surely some of the most heart wrenching words found anywhere in all world literature, and mirrored dimly in the film *Gladiator* – where emperor Marcus Aurelius embraces his evil son, Commodus, 'My son, your failing as a son, is my failing as a father.'

God give us wisdom in this area to be fathers worthy of your name.

The third way that David displayed this spirit of 'omnipotence' is during the Census. On the face of it the 'sin of numbering' as it has been called, is worse than the others. David was tempted into self-adulation and independence from the very power that had sustained him from lions, bears, giants and kings. He had the fighting men inventoried, and thereby brought a plague upon the land that left 70,000 dead by the hand of one angel. This has always shocked me, even does now for these are deep waters. Oswald Chambers wisely said that 'sin in man is doing without God' – for here is the kernel of outright rebellion. I need hardly say to sensitive readers that if we take this measure to our lives, our ministries, our church programmes and activities, that it is well possible that greater and graver sins are abounding inside, rather than outside, Christendom's walls. How many of Martha's dishes do we serve him for which he has no appetite? How many times have we cried out to God like Abraham did over our best efforts, 'oh that Ishmael might live before you'? Even now I can scarce think about the books and songs I've written, even this one without a tinge of apprehension. God deliver us all from the sin of independence.

'The King's Great Matter'

This was a euphemism used to describe Henry VIII's difficulty in producing a male heir, but the continuation of any dynasty has always been a major preoccupation of monarchs throughout history. To provide a legitimate heir was a major deal; no heir, no succession, and worse, perhaps civil war, destruction of all that you had built. This is what makes God's promise to David so amazing, *'Your house and your kingdom will endure forever before me; your throne will be established forever.'* 2 Samuel 7:16

Here God is promising David something so staggering that we may quickly skip over the words without letting the ramifications fully hit us in our cosseted twentieth century world. What God tables to David is an unconditional offer; actually even more than an offer, an outright statement of divine intent; that King David's descendants will occupy the throne of the nation forever. Now, this can only be fulfilled in two ways: either his descendants – that rule for their lifetime – will go on reproducing forever, or that one descendant, one of his 'seed' will be an eternal being and therefore rule for his eternal lifetime. This binding agreement made between God and David ranks alongside the other three that he had previously made with Noah, Abraham and the Hebrews at Sinai. But has history proved it true?

King David lived and reigned about 3,000 years ago. His descendants continued to reign over all or part of the land of Israel until the time of the Babylonian conquest, which was about 2,600 years ago. Following the captivity and the Jews' subsequent repatriation, they were ruled variously by Persians, Greeks, Syrians and even a successful Jewish monarchy under the Maccabees – though this freedom-fighting stock was not the pool from which God would draw THE LINE. So, with regard to God's promise to David, there were continuity gaps. This did not mean that God had failed, but rather that the monarchy had yet to come of age and was thus forced under a sort of divine regency until the appointed time of fulfilment. That time was fulfilled with the coming of Jesus. (We will see why when we come to study Zerubbabel.) As a human, he is a descendant of King David. As God, he is eternal. Therefore, he is in a unique position to fulfil the promise made to David.

Who Am I?
David's Prayer

(From 'THE LINE' album, words and music by Henry Brooks)

Who am I that the ark should come to me
Who am I, a total unknown from a poor man's family ... that the
Oil should pass over better men for me ... oh, it's more than I can
Say, too big a thing for words, but Lord have your way

One step away from Death, my life's been on a razor's edge this far ... But you
have been
My fortress, my rock, my shield in my darkest hour and what more can I
Say, now you've promised this throne for all time to come
A descendant of mine, will have it for all time, Lord let your will be done

For I know the plans you have are bigger than all I see right now
So I won't lean on my own understanding today
But I'll trust all you've promised and do what you say
And not forget in the grind, that you want heaven to rule on earth through
my line
So stretch this wineskin Lord and fill it as you will, just let your kingdom
come

I've seen the mighty fall in battle, their shield so vilely cast away
Stronger men than I have fallen in pride, in sin, so this is why I pray
Search my heart oh Lord, seek out every secret and wicked way
Give me a heart that's pure, a heart just like yours, like the one you've shown
to me

So create in me a clean heart like yours, oh Lord ... I swear that
Religion's made me cold and I can't do this on my own,
A right spirit's what I need, it's what I've always known
Oh Lord never let me be, a cause of stumbling to those who will look to me
I want them to see you, in everything I do, that' is why I pray.

My heart still grieves for you my brother, your love has been so very sweet to me
I've not forgot all that you taught me about faith, fear and Giants in your Mishmash victory
And when I swore to you that day, to protect you and your family
I always thought you'd be, right here alongside me, and I'm missing you today

So won't you find me someone that I can love in my brother's name
... I don't care if he
Loves me back or bites the hand that feeds him, abuses my trust, I must love just the same
For the debt I owe, to the one who was willing to give up the throne
It's not much I know but find me someone to love in his name.

Life Application Devotion
Chapter Nine – When you go through the fires, I will be there

- Can you identify with David in this Chapter? If so, list the similar areas of persecution *and temptation* that you have experienced AND where you feel most vulnerable.
- Now prayerfully offer the list to the Holy Spirit for additions and amendments, adding anything he reveals to you.
- Prayer: (Start with thanksgiving & praise, particularly for his strength and faithfulness to you) Oh Lord, My Defence and Deliverer, I bring you this list with a certain knowledge that – as I submit to you – you will not only use even my weakness to manifest your strength, but also use my trials to produce your patient perseverance and character in me. Any thought that stands against this I renounce as a lie. In Christ I am 'more than a conqueror' and I am sure 'that he is able to keep what I have entrusted to him until that day'. I have no desire to be greater than my Master, if they persecuted you Lord then I take every insult as a badge of honour only pleading that I may also share your heart toward my persecutors. Lord, show me creative ways to bless those who have hated me for your sake. (Journal any specific responses to this last request.)

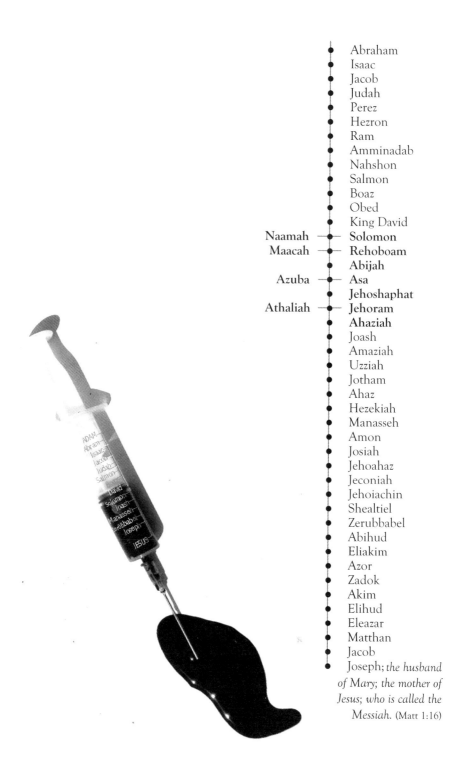

Abraham
Isaac
Jacob
Judah
Perez
Hezron
Ram
Amminadab
Nahshon
Salmon
Boaz
Obed
King David
Naamah — **Solomon**
Maacah — **Rehoboam**
Abijah
Azuba — **Asa**
Jehoshaphat
Athaliah — **Jehoram**
Ahaziah
Joash
Amaziah
Uzziah
Jotham
Ahaz
Hezekiah
Manasseh
Amon
Josiah
Jehoahaz
Jeconiah
Jehoiachin
Shealtiel
Zerubbabel
Abihud
Eliakim
Azor
Zadok
Akim
Elihud
Eleazar
Matthan
Jacob
Joseph; *the husband of Mary; the mother of Jesus; who is called the Messiah.* (Matt 1:16)

Chapter 10

The Legacy of King Solomon (Read 1 Kings & 2 Kings 1–3)

'What we do echoes in eternity' 2000 film, *Gladiator*

It is all too easy in the hustle and bustle of twentieth century life to lose the focus of who we are before God, and of what he has called us to do with our lives. We all possess a peculiarly human frailty that manifests in two equally fruitless ways:

Making a Living and Losing a Life

This is the mental culture of just 'getting by', living without an eternal focus and having little to show for our lives beyond a nice car, a fine home and a gold watch from our employer. Question – Is it possible, friend, that your heart was designed to live for a destiny bigger than this life has to offer? If so, have you found anything bigger and better with which to displace these trinkets? Is it possible that they are all just poor substitutes for real purpose, real joy?

Resignation in the Face of Giants

The second is to see the great evils of our day; injustice in the world; immorality in society; unbelief in the church; and just throw our hands up, cover our eyes, or point our wagging fingers and say, 'This is all so terrible, so shameful, so big, who could do anything to even dint the iceberg?' Perhaps some of you are nodding reluctantly because you have tried reforming the world and got a nasty shock at how difficult it is to change people and systems. Perhaps you have become cold and disillusioned in that area of thinking and feeling, have retreated to nominal church attendance, the school run and nine to five routines. Perhaps you have no time for such grand notions because life's grind and income tax exacts its ounce of flesh from you ... but you still had dreams and perhaps, even now, regrets. For you, my challenge at the outset of this chapter is this; has being swamped by so much negativity shaped you, rather than you being shaped by God?

> *'How can I tell you what it was like to be young; to dream big dreams? And to believe when Alexander looked you in the eye you could do anything. In his presence, by the light of Apollo, we were better than ourselves.'*

Above are the words of Anthony Hopkins playing an even older Ptolemy in the 2004 film, *Alexander*. Men of my grandfather's Chindit regiment would say the same about General Ord Wingate, as one soldier put it, 'For a brief moment in our lives he made us bigger than ourselves.'

If some can claim this of mere men, what can we say of Jesus Christ?

I have seen a certain shadow settle over some middle aged people that I think goes way beyond troublesome teenage children and mortgage payments. I think it is an unnerving and nagging question, not 'Could I have *done* more for Jesus?' but more haunting still, 'Could I have *been* more with Jesus?' My mother-in-law once jested that she would like 'She did what she could' written on her gravestone. Now this might be better than Spike Milligan's, 'I told you I was ill' but personally I would prefer to have an epithet more like Prince Jonathan, 'He hath wrought this day with God.' My intention is certainly not to burden anyone to 'do more for God, the church, the poor, or society' but rather to open your eyes to see that 'you could be more with the Lord'. Have you limited God's power to transform your life? Are you allowing Jesus to be all he is in your life? In short, 'Is it not time for me to have a one man or one woman revival?' The world recently celebrated the bicentenary of the abolition of the slave trade, but few people pointed out it was a 'one man revival' of William Wilberforce that led to such a calling and such a sustained career. Just think – what adventure could await you?

It starts with you and me, always has – always will.

Father and Son Stories

This chapter examines four generations of King David's descendants who forward the *legal* lineage of the Messiah another 136 years closer to Jesus' first coming. I say 'legal' because God has also established another hidden, physical seed line from David and Bathsheba's other son, Nathan. This is the line that would eventually reach Mary; it is recorded in Luke chapter 3 but we do not have the later stories from this lineage in the Bible. If we take God's promise to Abraham being about 1900 BC then we are half way to Jesus. So far we can surmise that this *promise* or *seed* would be the one who would '*crush the serpent's head*' (Gen 3:15) and in whom '*all the nations of the earth will be blessed*'. But we also now know that he would also be a king like David, from David's family and that he would rule forever. Is there anything else we should know about the promised Messiah from our reading of the Bible? Well, yes actually, but only if we allow the Holy Spirit - who breathed these Scriptures and shaped the lives of the Jewish nation - to interpret His own words. And though many things were hid from the Old Testament saints, Ephesians 3v5 says that these things are now 'revealed to us by his holy apostles and prophets by the Holy Spirit.' So it might be an opportune time to use this privileged vantage point of history to list some of those 'revealed' facets of where 'THE LINE' will end;

- He is the eternal Redeemer that will come to earth to reconcile mankind with God (Job 19:25-26)
- Although Satan will try to attack Him, the Messiah will have ultimate victory (Gen. 3:15)
- One day He will rule over everything and all nations will bow down to Him (Is 45:23, Ps 22)
- The Messiah will descend from Abraham (Gen 22:18), Isaac (Gen 26:4), Jacob (Gen 28:14), Judah (Gen 49:10), Jesse (Is 11:1--5) and David (2 Sam 7:11--16).
- He will be born in the city of Bethlehem in the county of Ephrathah (Mic 5:2) when a bright star appears (Num 24:17). It will be a miraculous, virgin birth (Is 7:14)
- The Messiah will be unique, having pre-existed His birth (Mic 5:2).
- He will perform many miracles: calming the sea (Ps 107:29), causing the blind to see, the deaf to hear, the lame to walk, and the mute to talk (Is 35:4-6).
- He will be a great teacher and will use parables (Ps 78:2)
- He will come to save mankind (Is 53:3-9)
- He will become man's sin offering (Is 53:3-9) and present Himself to Jerusalem as both the anointed King (Zech 9:9) and the Passover Lamb (Is 53:3-9).
- This will occur 173,880 days after the decree by Artaxerxes to rebuild both Jerusalem and the temple (Dan 9:20-27). So, in early April, 33 AD, the Messiah will present Himself to a rejoicing Jerusalem riding on a donkey (Zech 9:9).
- But then He will suffer greatly (Is 53:3-9)
- Many will reject Him, including His friends (Is 53:3-9)

- He will be betrayed by a friend (Ps 41:9) for 30 pieces of silver (Zech 11:12,13).
- Later, that money will be thrown on the floor of the temple (Zech 11:12,13) and will eventually go to a potter (Zech 11:12,13).
- At His trial He will not defend Himself. He will say nothing (Is 53:3-9) except as required by law.
- Israel will reject Him (Is 8:14).
- The Messiah will be taken to a mountaintop identified to Abraham as 'the Lord will provide' (Gen 22)
- There He will be crucified with His hands and feet pierced (Ps 22)
- His enemies will encircle Him (Ps 22), mocking Him, and will cast lots for His clothing (Ps 22)
- He will call to God, asking why He was forsaken (Ps 22)
- He will be given gall and wine (Ps 69:20-22)
- He will die with thieves (Is 53:3-9)
- But, unlike the thieves, none of His bones will be broken (Ps 22).
- His heart will fail (Ps 22), as indicated by blood and water spilling out (Ps 22) when He is pierced with a spear (Zech 12:10). He will be buried in a rich man's grave (Is 53:3-9).
- (In three days) He will rise from the dead (Ps 16:10).

Does this remind you of anyone?

This chapter takes fleeting sketches of the reigns of Solomon, Rehoboam, Abijah, Asa and Jehoshaphat, and also the maternal influence of two bad women and one good. These women are mentioned intentionally by the scriptures as a hint to how the vacuum left by paternal compromise and ungodliness was being filled. Sometimes this is not pretty, but it is certainly pretty useful for us. These are very much father and son stories. We all have a family history, we all have our own generational baggage and we all have something to pass on, whether good or bad. The consequences of David's sin and Solomon's compromise are seen for generations. But it does not have to be that way with us, for the same principle works in reverse too. For example, look at the descendants of the 18th century American Preacher, Jonathan Edwards. When the Bible says that 'righteousness exalts a nation' it is not just religious rhetoric, it really is a fact. An investigation was made of 1,394 known descendants of Jonathan Edwards of which 13 became college presidents, 65 college professors, 3 United States senators, 30 judges, 100 lawyers, 60 physicians, 75 army and navy officers, 100 preachers and missionaries, 60 authors of prominence, 1 a vice-president of the United States, 80 became public officials in other capacities, 295 college graduates, among whom were governors of states and ministers to foreign countries. His descendants did not cost the state a single penny. As the good books says, *'The memory of the just is blessed.'* (Proverbs 10:7)

The great Irish politician, Edmund Burke, once said 'People will not look forward to posterity who will not look backward to their ancestors.' He's right of course, if we don't learn the lessons of our spiritual forebears, then we will not be in a position to orientate our priorities and pass on something better to subsequent generations. So let us look back at a few of them – and place ourselves honestly before God, to see whether there is more that we could receive from him to pass on to others.

Solomon

Solomon starts well after a tricky handover, establishes a good domestic political footing and is initially wholehearted in his pursuit of God.

He contracts a political marriage to an Egyptian princess, but that does not at this time seem to be held against him. Then comes the dream at Gibeon, *'What shall I give thee,'* which is about the most searching question you could ever receive from God. What do you want in life? What's your goal, your five-year-plan, your fifty-year-plan, for that matter? It is good to consider these things, but even better when we can respond like Solomon did, *'A wise heart to serve your people.'*

We can learn from God's response, that if we seek first his kingdom and to serve the saints then God will let everything else 'overtake us'. And God really does answer his prayer, to the point where not just the Queen of Sheba, but *'All the kings of the earth sought his wisdom.'*

But what went wrong?

A man I knew once, said of the fall of King Saul, 'Forty years is a long time to be the anointed ruler,' and it is – ample enough time for those weaknesses of character to be manifested. But what was it with Solomon? Was it the love of wealth, the conceit of knowledge, the intoxication of power? No, nothing so obvious. For Solomon it was his 'love' for many foreign women who eventually led him into idolatry. Seven hundred wives and three hundred concubines is a lot by anyone's standard; if only he had had wisdom for himself to know, 'in loving one woman you love all, but to love more than one, you will love none at all'.

This would have serious repercussions for the next generation, indeed for many generations. For one of those women that Solomon fathered children by was Naamah, an Ammonite, a worshipper of Molech. The name of that child was Rehoboam.

Rehoboam

Rehoboam reigned for seventeen years, had eighteen wives, sixty concubines, twenty-six sons and sixty daughters. He was an insecure, foolish man trying to fill his father's massive shoes – substituting youthful ignorance for wisdom, and exchanging slogans for substantial government.

Solomon sowed to the wind, and during the reign of Rehoboam, Israel reaped a whirlwind of idolatry and sexual perversion on a national religious scale. And then there was also national division, a civil war, defeat and humiliation. 1 Kings 14 tells us that the southern kingdom of Judah *'did more evil'* than all their fathers before them, the text also reminds us again about Rehoboam's mother's name, as if to say, 'Here, look at the fruit of this people, mind you, it's no wonder when you consider the root of this man's maternal influence.' When Solomon left a gaping vacuum of godly example for his son, it was filled by his idolatrous wife and so in this case the hand that rocked the cradle, ruled the kingdom's morality. The advice which may be gained from this experience for young people is: be careful who you marry; be careful who you let raise your children. Naamah means 'pleasant' and I do not doubt that Solomon was infatuated by her pleasant figure and her winsome intellect; but to let a Molech worshipper be the mother of a prince in Israel?

I mean, what did he expect?

And it did not stop with her either, for Rehoboam would also marry very badly. Perhaps it was his own mother who chose him Maacah as a wife; perhaps having been subject to an overbearing female influence, he chose someone like her – it does happen that way. One thing is clear, she would rise to be a pernicious, idolatrous influence over the next two generations: her son, Abijah and grandson, Asa. So much so that the Bible records King Asa, not as the son of so'n'so but as the *grandson* of Maacah.

She was one tough lady and the clue to her nature might be in her name which means 'to emasculate'. I meet too many women who love to belittle or emasculate their husbands in front of others; it is a ghastly sight. It turns out that Maacah was the granddaughter of Absalom, the rebellious son of David. The prophet Samuel once told King Saul that *'Rebellion is as the sin of witchcraft'*, and it is horrifying to see the rebellious spirit of Absalom now manifest in the idolatry of his granddaughter. Once again, what the fathers sowed, the nations reaped. Maacah would be a spiritual forerunner of Jezebel who murdered the prophets of God and whose granddaughter Athaliah would seek to exterminate the very line of David. While these women are to be viewed with horror, we must not overlook the devastating cost we also see when men abdicate their God-ordained responsibilities. As Edmund Burke noted, 'All that is necessary for evil to triumph is for good men to do nothing.' Would there have been the rise of Nazism if all the Christian ministers had stood as firm as Pastor Paul Schneider – who they killed by lethal injection? Would we have seen French or Communist revolutions if the church had been living out Jesus' teaching? You rarely have the rise of one without the acquiescence of the other.

Abijah

Maacah and Rehoboam's son reigned for three years; he had fourteen wives, twenty-two sons. We are told that he had a 'divided heart and was not fully devoted to the Lord', using his spare time to make his own idols.

Asa

Asa would rule for forty-one years leaving bitter sweet memories behind him. Asa got rid of his father's idols, deposed his grandmother, Maacah, from being queen mother for making an Asherah pole. He was fully committed to the Lord and, like Nehemiah, built the defences of God's people. In 2 Chronicles 15:9 God says *'I am on your side so long as you are on mine',* and because it becomes evident 'that the Lord is with Asa' many Jews from the rebellious ten northern tribes emigrate south to Judah. They all make a covenant with the Lord on pain of death to seek him only, and Asa wins a landmark victory when they are outnumbered two to one by the one million Libyans and Cushites. This signal victory brings peace for thirty-five years and all looks rosy for the kingdom, though it may not be so inside the royal heart. Asa seems to me to be a bit like Oliver Cromwell, and it is evident that an autocratic deceit grew in Asa as the years rolled on. It is a great shame, and we should not wish to detract from his many achievements, but the scripture is clear and we ought to give this attention. Asa's religious reformation was partially marred by his self reliance and the oppression of some of God's people. (Church leaders, beware how you deal with or even speak about '*your people*', for they are not *your* people at all, they are his and to oppress or bully them is to touch the apple of God's eye. God, give us Jesus' heart and gentleness when we deal with people.) It all started when the king lost his rag with the prophet Hannani who had rebuked him.

Later on when Asa was diseased in his feet, '*He sought the help of doctors but not the Lord.*' Pride comes before a fall and we can so easily become unteachable – particularly men. Abigail Adams was not just the wife but also the mother of an American president and she could see the failing clear enough, saying that we should not 'put unlimited power in the hands of husbands. Remember all men would be tyrants if they could.' The Oracle of Apollo at Delphi – over which, ironically was written the inscription 'know thyself' – told Cicero not to put too much stock in the advice of others but to 'trust in his own genius'. That same flattering spirit still speaks with ease into the hearts of Christians today and we must resist a self sufficiency that cuts us off from receiving criticism or advice. Something that sobered and saddened me last year was hearing that a number of men I know of, who have done great things with God, like Asa did not finish as well as they started. I believe David feared this sort of backsliding having seen what his predecessor had become, and this is probably why the word of the Lord to him at one time was '*I will not take away my mercy from you as I did from Saul*' (2 Sam 7:15). Even so he did become a stumbling block to those around him, and it is a scary thing to see others fall because of your example. Once again Mrs Adams was well near the mark when she said, 'arbitrary power is like most things which are very hard, very liable to be broken.'

What I am, more than what I teach, will be what I pass on to the next generation; for these things are caught more than they are taught.

This is a real challenge to us, to be able to treat those two impostors 'success and failure' with a dispassionate humility, and not lose touch with who we are under God. God help us last out for Jesus, for God resists the proud but gives grace to the humble. We cannot underestimate our ability to deceive ourselves, we need each other. The last sermon I heard from a man who fell in this area was on 'authority and submission', the very areas in which he, himself, later proved to have forsaken for some months.

How scary is that?

And though I'm not suggesting that women are exempt from this sin, I cannot escape that it is one of the biggest challenges to insecurity in the male psyche. In fact I would say most men cannot take criticism; Mark Anthony had Cicero's hands cut off and stuck above the speaker's rostrum as a punishment for criticizing him, such was his vanity. Hitler couldn't even bear any horse in Germany to be called Adolf! Special laws were passed to fine anyone who did not rename their nags. When Mussolini rose to power in Italy he apparently initially wore a black suit and bowler hat until his critics pointed out he looked like the comedian Oliver Hardy. Apparently he was so insecure that thereafter he only appeared in public wearing the military outfit with which we associate him, and he certainly never went to the cinema to see a Laurel and Hardy film either! Given that level of pride and vanity, can you imagine trying to contradict their insane policies? God have mercy on our wives, children and churches to deliver us from being so small as not to be able to accept criticism.

To be specific, are you sure your life is accountable and open to others so that others feel they could speak constructive criticism? When was the last time you asked your spouse, a trusted friend or church elder whether there is anything you are missing? Does your church, your marriage, your family, foster an atmosphere of genuine accountability? And as important: are we shying away from telling someone a considered message that the Lord has given us? If you really love someone and can see a wrong attitude or act (and have prayed about it) it might be that the Lord will use you to remove the odd splinter from their eye. 'Oh but I feel such a hypocrite!' Well okay, many times we only recognize the sin that we know ourselves by experience, so use their failing to bring you to repentance first, but don't forget your obligation to them once the beam is out of your eye. In some cases not to do so will be a sin.

Jehoshaphat

Jehoshaphat was thirty-five when he came to the throne and he reigned for twenty-five years. His mother, Azuba, and her father are both mentioned so we are to assume in this case their combined influence was a very good one. Every giant in history will almost invariably point to a quiet but powerful maternal influence; if you find one that hasn't, then you are looking at the exception not the rule. If you are a mother, don't give up, supposing Mrs (Hudson) Taylor had not been praying on that Saturday afternoon in 1849, where would China be now? For at the very moment she was praying her son was giving his life to Jesus Christ. And what about James Fraser's mother and her ladies' prayer group? Without their intercessory prayer where would the Lisu people be now? And then there is Sally's mother and aunty who laid her as a baby on a church altar offering her to God and covenanted secretly to pray everyday that Sally would one day be a missionary. Sally knew nothing of it until she joined YWAM and later became the wife and helpmate of Floyd McClung, rescuing thousands of young people from drugs and despair.

And then there is that poor mother in India who fasted every Friday for three and a half years praying that one of her six sons might be a missionary. She had seen the others grow up to take secular employment and so she cried out, 'Lord, let just one of them preach.' Was her sacrifice worth it? Well, put it this way, her youngest and most timid son –K. P. Yohannan – founded Gospel for Asia and they now have over 16,500 missionaries and planted more than

29,000 churches in the 10/40 window. So the answer is yes, a mother praying and fasting is a history shaping weapon. Or what about those two women in their eighties on the Isle of Lewis, who seized hold of the verse 'I will pour water on him that is thirsty and floods upon the dry ground' (Is 44:3) and so saw Revival come to the Hebrides.

It might be an appropriate juncture to thank God and also encourage praying grandparents too. My friend Colin still remembers his blind grandmother rocking back and forth in her rocking chair, muttering prayers for him and his siblings all day long. After her lengthy petitions she would conclude, 'and now Lord I need to sleep' and almost instantly be snoring! All her own children went into full time Christian ministry and all her grandchildren believe. Please never accept the lie that your prayers and example will not shape their futures.

Jehoshaphat walked in the footsteps of his father, even rooting out some male shrine prostitutes. There was still a tendency for convenience; DIY religion as people sacrificed on the high places rather than the place that God had designated in Jerusalem. After three years he sent out teaching priests, so again we see this desire to strengthen God's people by the word. His father strengthened physical walls and Jehoshaphat strengthened the spiritual fortresses of God's people with sound teaching. One of the biggest deficits in the church in the UK is a low level understanding of God's word. 'My people perish through lack of knowledge.' There is no substitute for a personal knowledge of God and his word when it comes to avoiding deception. The effect of these Bible teachers in Israel was dramatic; *the fear of the Lord fell on the surrounding lands*. My experience as a pastor leads me to think that many troubles that surround us would be subdued also if we gave proper attention to our understanding of, and obedience to, God's word. I get the feeling that Jehoshaphat inherited a softness from his mother that counterbalanced the unbending hardness of his father's character, but this softness was also open to exploitation as we shall see.

Jehoshaphat's biggest failing was a civil and then a family alliance with Ahab, the wicked king of the northern ten tribes. Jehoshaphat wasn't as 'hard core' as his dad; he may have even struggled to get his dad's affection which might go some way to explain his disastrous ecumenical escapades. He was a guy who loved peace, loved to be loved, and why not? There had been peace since the year of his birth, a hard won peace. But in his desire to be accepted, to heal the breach, he made trade and military treaties with Ahab at the expense of truth and righteousness. Benjamin Franklin said that there was no such thing as a bad peace and though we can applaud the general sentiment, in this case it definitely does not apply.

This is a very delicate issue; we do not want to foster a party spirit, there is too much of that already. And there are such things as secondary issues in Christian theology, and we should not break fellowship with other Christians because they hold a different view about the rapture, theistic evolution or other doctrines however important we may feel they are – and they are! But the wisdom of God is first peaceable, not argumentative and our flesh is only too active sometimes in theological arguments. When the revolutionary ecumenic George Whitfield was asked for an opinion on the hot topic of his day he said, 'I would not pour any more oil on that unhallowed fire.' But, similarly, we have to guard against desiring unity at any price. At the end of the age, Jesus warns us that peace and men's desire for it, will be the precursor to big trouble. In Britain we have allowed the political scientists to tamper with some fundamental laws of civil liberty – due to the perceived threat of terrorism or child abuse – with George Orwell daily looking more like a historian than a prophet.

To Jehoshaphat's credit, he repented when rebuked by a prophet, which is more than his father had done. He sent out a second wave of teachers and he also set up a judiciary in the towns. Like his father he also faced a great national crisis. This time it was annihilation at the hands of a Moab–Ammonite alliance. The fasting and prayer were answered and the people obediently went out against the enemy with the singers in front. God brought a great victory which was the high point of Jehoshaphat's reign – great because God did it alone without any need for Israeli infantry. Towards the end of his life he made great provisions for his children whom he placed apart in their own cities, making sure they had enough earthly wealth. But, as we will see, this was all to no avail, for although he had brought a limited revival, the nation – let alone his own household – was not in order. Sometimes we too can do so much for ourselves and our families in one area, but have it all undone because an obvious gate was left open in another.

The result of Jehoshaphat's open gate is horribly stark. There he was providing a financial future for those dearest to him but he never considered whom he had let marry his oldest son Jehoram. In this chapter I have already said 'be careful who you marry and let raise your children', here at the end we see Jehoshaphat marry his son to Ahab and Jezebel's daughter, Athaliah. The devastating effects of that union would almost destroy the royal line, starting with Jehoram's own brothers, whom he murders after Jehoshaphat's death, an evil act that I have no doubt was encouraged by his evil wife. We will see much more from Athaliah in the next chapter, but the point is clear: we ignore our responsibility to the next generation at our peril.

What We Do in Life …

There is a common thread among most of this very diverse cast of kings and that is they are at their best (and the nation is at its safest) when their own repentance led the nation into a revival. We too are at our best when we stop looking outside at the darkness and start getting real with God. No fronts, façades or banner waving – just yielded hearts, expectant and open. The pioneer missionary to American Indians, David Brainerd, found out early on that it is far too easy and far too comfortable to criticize the low level of Christian experience that others have settled for. When others settle for less we must redouble our own search for the real thing – criticizing them won't help. We're called to light a candle, not curse the darkness. Whether we go all out for personal revival or just go with the standard Christian flow, we should know that the effects will also follow in the next generation. We could easily change that initial *Gladiator* quote to 'what we do in our lives echoes in our posterity'. The best thing we can do for our family, our church, our society and the future generations is have a one man, one woman revival today. God make it so.

One Man Revival
The song of Jehoshaphat
(From 'THE LINE' album, words and music by Henry Brooks)

I look back and see my family dysfunctional
I look out, society's falling apart … I look to
the future, I see the world's a scary, scary place
I look in and see my lukewarm heart

I look back and see the limits of all I've achieved
I look out and it should break my heart
I look up and see a God who is wanting to move
I look in, I know where he should start

I need a One Man Revival, it's got to start with me
I need more than these hands, Lord, I need to use these knees
I need a One Man Revival, it's got to happen to me
 big enough to live for, a king's destiny

I've been cold and cursed the darkness that was around,
I saw those who wouldn't take their part
I tore down, but the idols were soon rebuilt
I passed laws, but didn't change one heart

I made peace with men when I should have fought
and the preachers brought the fear of God
but I know, most sermons are soon forgot so ...
I'll be a message to be read by all

I'll be a One Man Revival, it's what I've come to learn
Set my life on fire, Lord, let them see it burn
I'll be a One Man Revival, it's more than what I say
Let them see your life, Lord, flowing out of me
And when the chips were down,
it was you who came through for me and turned this nation around
When the enemy was at the gates,
I prostrate my life to you and you blew them away

Life Application Devotion

Chapter 10 – Mutual Subjection

- Name the person / people around you to whom you feel yourself accountable.
- Describe *how* and *when* they have spoken into your life regarding something that had to do with your gifting or ministry? How would you sum up their impact on your life and ministry?
- When did you last ask for advice over such things?
- Who around you do you feel looks to you in similar matters?
- And when did God use you to pray for them and/or speak into their lives?
- How long is it since you specifically asked God to be used in such a way?
- Prayer: (Start with thanksgiving & praise, particularly for his guidance and protection, particularly for those people he has used to correct and guide you.) Oh Lord My Shepherd, I thank you for these people that you have placed around me. Help me put aside pride and independence or any thought that tells me I can survive as Christian without such input. Lord give me a heart of wisdom and humility that I may know you and in so doing also know myself. Lord, I openly invite you to send more people into my life if need be that I may know your discipline (discipl*ing*). Father, give me your gracious and courageous heart also that I may have the sensitivity and boldness to be a blessing to others in this way. Is there anyone you wish me to talk to or pray for today?

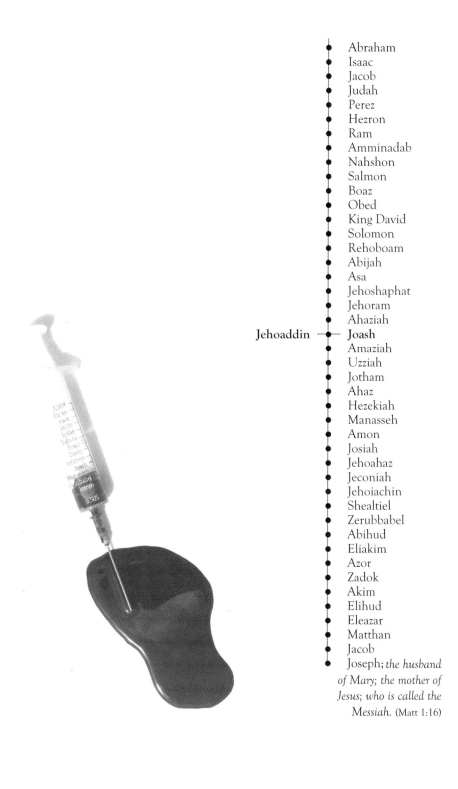

Abraham
Isaac
Jacob
Judah
Perez
Hezron
Ram
Amminadab
Nahshon
Salmon
Boaz
Obed
King David
Solomon
Rehoboam
Abijah
Asa
Jehoshaphat
Jehoram
Ahaziah
Jehoaddin ——•—— **Joash**
Amaziah
Uzziah
Jotham
Ahaz
Hezekiah
Manasseh
Amon
Josiah
Jehoahaz
Jeconiah
Jehoiachin
Shealtiel
Zerubbabel
Abihud
Eliakim
Azor
Zadok
Akim
Elihud
Eleazar
Matthan
Jacob
Joseph; *the husband of Mary; the mother of Jesus; who is called the Messiah.* (Matt 1:16)

Chapter Eleven

The Firebrand (Read 2 Kings 9–12)

'The Lord rebuke thee Satan ...
is this not a brand plucked from the fire' Zech 3:2

Frida witnessed her family being massacred by Hutu men with machetes and was then asked how she wanted to die. She could not afford a bullet, which they offered to sell her, so instead she received what should have been a fatal blow to the head. She was put in a mass grave with her slaughtered family, only to find herself still alive and conscious. She eventually climbed out of the pit covered in filth and blood and later became a Christian. The strap-line to her biography is very apt for our story in this chapter, 'chosen to die, yet destined to live'.

This is the story of an intended genocide, not of the Hutu and Tutsi, but that of the clashing of two lines of Jezebel and David, of two religions and, more importantly, the clashing of two wills; that of God and Satan. God's will being expressed through his promise to Abraham and David; and Satan's will through his desperate attempts to destroy the royal seed that would one day *'crush his head'*. For Satan this is no game, he's playing for his life and to prolong his rebellion. But this story also more subtly reveals – in a way that affects us – the clashing of two ways of life and modes of logic; the one fiercely independent and antagonistic to the creator, the other in submission and harmony with his will. It is the story of what happens when even a good father compromises with the world. Jehoshaphat provided for all his children's financial futures but neglected his number one priority: to train them and protect them from the influence of evil. It is the story of one wicked woman, Athaliah, and one good one, Jehosheba, of corrupted kings and faithful priests; where the compromise of one generation is manifested with shocking cruelty in the next; where what seemed like tolerant, unbigoted religious thinking and reasonable foreign policy brings a blood bath into the royal nursery, threatening to extinguish the very words and promises of God.

The story starts with Jehoshaphat's grandson Ahaziah being murdered by Jehu. Why? Because Jehu was charged by God to destroy the lineage of Ahab. So you're saying that members of God's chosen and anointed line are now being killed in his judgement against the ungodly? Ah, but the lines have now been blurred after grandpa Jehoshaphat married his son to Ahab's daughter Athaliah. So Ahaziah is actually visiting grandma Jezebel and so not only shares her lineage but also her destruction. Scary stuff – Ahaziah dies with the wicked but even worse, his mother Athaliah is now left in charge of the royal nursery. Does she look at her tender grandchildren and feel pity?

The Death of Womanhood – Athaliah

'But when Athaliah the mother of Ahaziah saw that her son was dead, she arose and destroyed all the seed royal of the house of Judah.'
2 Chronicles 22:10

One of the most haunting things I have ever seen on film was Mrs Goebbels quietly killing her six beautiful young children with cyanide capsules in the 2004 film *Downfall*. I could not lose the hideous memory of what I had seen. Why? Because, I figured, it was so anti–everything God had made women to be, literally the ones who give and nurture life. (When God says in Genesis that Eve will be 'the mother of all living' – literally 'breathing', there is a literal application; for the mitochondria – that essential part of each cell that facilitates aerobic action – is given by the females' ovum and not the male sperm.) It is very hard, but not impossible, to override this hard wiring with ideology, political, religious or even feminist ideology at that. The real Mrs Goebbels wrote, 'The world that comes after the Führer and national socialism is not any longer worth living in.' The last survivor of Hitler's bunker, Rochus Misch, gave this eyewitness account of the events to the BBC:

'Straight after Hitler's death, Mrs Goebbels came down to the bunker with her children, She started preparing to kill them. She couldn't have done that above ground – there were other people there who would have stopped her. That's why she came downstairs – because no–one else was allowed in the bunker. She came down on purpose to kill them. The kids were right next to me and behind me. We all knew what was going to happen. It was clear. I saw Hitler's doctor, Dr Stumpfegger give the children something to drink. Some kind of sugary drink. Then Stumpfegger went and helped to kill them. All of us knew what was going on. An hour or two later, Mrs Goebbels came out crying. She sat down at a table and began playing patience. This is exactly how it was.'

Chilling though this is, I think the sheer butchery by Athaliah – for power's sake – seems infinitely worse. Her pernicious influence is first felt at the rise of her thirty-two-year-old husband to the throne, at the death of Jehoshaphat. No doubt as a result of her scheming, all her husband's brothers and near kin are murdered. The Bible writers are very clear to remind us whose daughter this is, for Athaliah is driven by the same demonic forces that controlled her mother. Her name means the 'Lord restrains' and this woman will not stop from destroying the seed royal unless God restrains her. This would appear to be the nearest Satan will come to destroying the royal line promised to David, so it might be well worth us looking at the specific personality of this unclean spirit in Bible history, and also how it affects our lives today.

The Spirit of 'Jezebel'

Of course spirits are not male or female, so when I say 'Jezebel' I am referring to a spiritual power that exerts a particular dark influence in this world.

To see the power of Jezebel's influence we need look no further than one historical manifestation in Athaliah's mother, Jezebel. When this Sidonian princess was wed to King Ahab of Israel her influence caused over ten million Jews to forsake God and bow to Baal. She brought a whole nation, save seven thousand, to their knees before Satan and systematically butchered anyone who submitted to Yahweh. According to Strong's analytical concordance her name is derived from two words which combine to mean; 'island habitation'. This has been taken two ways; in a positive way to mean 'chaste' or – as we may interpret it here – in a negative way; that *she will not cohabit* or at least not unless she can dominate. Though she may pretend submission, it is a guise to gain advantage. We are not talking about total demonic possession but certainly a high degree of oppression in her attitudes, values and thought life. This spirit is the force in our society that drives obsessive sensuality, unbridled witchcraft and much hatred of authority.

You can also see this spirit seek a foothold in men in positions of authority, bending the pastor into an unyielding authoritarian, isolating himself from accountability. Another effect on men is to neuter them into spiritually powerless eunuchs, perhaps trapped in forbidden sexual desire and thereby rendered ineffective. The spirit will, all too easily, latch on to women embittered towards men because of the neglect or abuse of male authority. As Jezebel belittled Ahab and as Herodia belittled Herod, so the spirit can be seen in the wife who cannot dwell contentedly with her husband but must always belittle him in public. The spirit is the turbo that drives mankind's already perverted sensuality. Through the media and fashion world it reprograms women to behave and dress with one objective; 'use every flirtatious glance, every curve, every bit of exposed skin to net and control men, to have them notice you, bow to you.' What a terrible parody of feminine beauty this is; for sure, she was designed to display sheer beauty, but how like Satan to take something God created and then force us to prostitute it for power. A woman's physical beauty is a gift from God for her to give to her husband or husband to be; that is a beautiful and precious gift. If you are tempted to buy clothes that you know will cause other men to look at you, you've got to honestly ask yourself, why am I doing this? Whose influence am I under? The same question can apply to men too, though not usually to the same extent in this area.

Jesus called Satan the 'wicked one'; he uses the Greek word 'Poneros', 'the corrupting one'. This does not just mean Satan is corrupt but that his great pleasure on earth is to corrupt us, that we share in all he has become. I saw a mother interviewed on television who said she had taken her teenage daughter to Ibiza expressly so she could be 'broken in'. This savage initiation, in which her precious child would lose her virginity to a stranger, made the middle aged woman smirk with glee. It reminded me of all those poor Greek girls who would be taken to the temple of Aphrodite to offer their virginity there. In a similar way, Satan's only joy is for us to share in the disintegration of his personality. He is never happier than when causing pain to God and you.

What we call the 'spirit of Jezebel' had a front row seat in a first-century church at Thyatira when Jesus wrote them a letter to expose it. The spirit was manifesting, this time through a woman, 'who called herself a prophetess' and started to mislead men in the congregation by teaching what she called 'the deeper things of God' – basically ritualistic fornication. Jesus says these things are in fact 'the deep things of Satan' (not God) and he was about to bring judgement against her and anyone who carried on submitting to her. This spirit has claimed politician and preacher alike; the sincere man of God who cannot pray because he is Jezebel's slave to pornography and does not know how to break free; the woman who wants to go on for God and yet cannot stop her fantasies about another man in church who is perhaps 'more spiritual' than her husband. This spirit has overseen and powered the separation of many marriages and ministries. Jesus holds responsible the church that tolerated this spirit's defiling influence, but he is gracious too, even forgiving those who have been her slaves. But they must repent. '*Behold, I will cast her into a bed, and them that commit adultery with her into great tribulation, except they repent of their deeds*' (Rev 2:22).

Because this spirit is primarily one that seeks to control others our escape route is through humility and repentance. Tolerance is the primary virtue of all multicultural western societies; political correctness is just one manifestation of this, though Aristotle wisely noted that, 'tolerance and apathy are the last virtues of a dying society'. But it is not a virtue in the kingdom of God. Jesus' withering words to the church at Thyatira, 'You *tolerate* that woman Jezebel to teach and seduce my servants.' We *tolerate* this spirit by allowing Jezebel's influence in our families through what we allow into our home; that is books, magazines, TV, film, internet, even friends. Similarly we tolerate it in our churches by allowing manipulative and domineering people to manoeuvre themselves into positions of authority over us; for Thyatira it was a woman, for us it might be a man, it might be you! And you don't have to be an elder to exercise authority in Jesus' precious church, you just need someone to listen! Beware of the urge, or the person, that leads you to gossip, fault find and lambaste other church members. Repentance means a change of mind, but we must let that be seen in what we do, what we throw out of our wardrobe and what we don't allow to come from our mouths. We must also verbally renounce the spiritual stronghold that this entity has forged in our thought life. To re-*nounce* is to re-speak out our intention, to verbalize our will in accord with Jesus' will; simply put, we must speak the authority of Jesus Christ over this spirit's authority in our lives and families and church. Do not be surprised if you experience intimidation and discouragement – both Elijah and John the Baptist suffered from standing against this spirit – nevertheless we must push through and allow the Lord to have total dominion.

It cannot stand against Jesus.

This spirit was the force behind Athaliah; anti-God, anti the basic instincts of womanhood, anti-God's promise to David's line, basically Anti-Christ. That same force was seen through the control freak Herod when he tried to slaughter the Jewish babies when Jesus finally came. Athaliah sacrifices her own flesh and blood for power and autonomy. She becomes a ghastly aberration of womanhood. It's not so much that all Bible women were chained to the kitchen sinks – just read the Bible version of the virtuous woman in Proverbs 31, a one woman home and business wonder! But equally let's not be duped by the political scientists who, certainly in Britain, have phrased their policies to suggest it is a problem that some women don't give up their children straight away to childcare and go back to work.

Hollywood director Aaron Russo once claimed that Nick Rockefeller had admitted to him that the Rockefeller foundation had bankrolled much of the US feminist movement because they realized that one half of the population was not contributing income tax. A startling thought if true, though it certainly is true that effects of family breakdown since that time have created a tsunami of emotional, social, medical and financial problems greater than any perceived benefit. People never trusted politicians before: we shouldn't start now over something so important. As one British prime minister said, 'It may be the housewife at her kitchen sink and not the gentlemen at Whitehall who know best after all.' It was ever thus! Athaliah sacrificed her share in traditional womanhood to follow the ways of her mother, but thankfully we have another role model in this chapter.

The Promise Keeper – Jehosheba

> 'But when Athaliah the mother of Ahaziah saw that her son was dead, she arose and destroyed all the seed royal of the house of Judah. But Jehosheba the daughter of the king, took Joash the son of Ahaziah, and stole him from among the king's sons that were slain, and put him and his nurse in a bedchamber. So Jehosheba, the daughter of king Jehoram, the wife of Jehoiada the priest, (for she was the sister of Ahaziah,) hid him from Athaliah, so that she slew him not. And he was with them hid in the house of God six years: and Athaliah reigned over the land.'

2 Chronicles 22:10-11

The word Jehosheba means 'Jehovah's promise' and it appears from the text that she must have arrived shortly after the butchery of her nephews and literally plucked twelve-month-old Joash from among the other corpses. How he was missed is a mystery – what is not, is that she risks her own life, and her own retirement, in secreting the child and his nurse to safety. We know that the father was no protection to the child, for he had been 'taken out' by compromise but where was the mother? Dead perhaps, or in hiding for her own life; whatever the reason another woman has to step in and be a mother to this child. She is an encouragement to us to look wider than our immediate household for people to rescue from Jezebel's clutches. I'm sure many women reading this are not insensible to the 'orphan' cries of children and adults who they already know, perhaps in their own street or extended family. Maybe God is already showing you a neighbour, a nephew, a grandchild who needs your prayers and encouragement. It has certainly been a major part of how the Lord has used Ruth and me over the years; our home, and certainly our hearts, are rarely empty of other people's children. Some have grown up and we now only have contact with them through Facebook; others, like a young girl whose father died when she was three, is asleep in the spare room not ten feet from me as I write these words.

But Jehosheba is also something else to us, something even more wonderful and the clue is first in her name 'Jehovah's promise'. Another clue is in the text. By her bravery God uses her to uphold *the promise* Jehovah made to David. Her husband's rallying cry was, '*Behold, the king's son shall reign, as the LORD hath said of the sons of David*' (2 Chron 23:3). Who did God use to make that promise happen? Who was the answer to her own prayers? Who made the will of God and the promise of God come to pass? It was all Jehosheba. When we see how God cannot be thwarted by evil or disaster it should encourage us that even in our lives of trouble, he is still able to steer the ship for us. For example when the bills come in and the bank account is stretched then remember how close it seemed for THE LINE; and remember, God is still on the throne. But beyond that, also see the place where you can be the answer to someone else's need, for this is infinitely more blessed. Jehosheba defied the government and the witch (who incidentally may have been her own mother) in favour of what was right. Jehosheba chose to be a mother to the motherless; someone who gave, not took, life; someone who nurtured life and did not pillage it. The world desperately needs women like this. One of the great tragedies of the twentieth century was that the provision of 'on demand' welfare from an omni-competent state – whilst being a source for much good – inadvertently destroyed the democratic fabric of British civic life and for none more than that of women. Millions of Christian women involved in nursing, teaching, mothers' union, mothers' meetings, Sunday schools, charter schools, ragged schools and a host of other philanthropic works (and I mean a host) were gradually replaced or swallowed up by secular professionals. Sometimes they were replaced by a tenth of the number of state paid practitioners to do the same job; slowly from the late Victorian period onwards to the 1970s women were disinherited from their invaluable role in communities. A very readable and generous history of this subject is given in Frank Prochaska's 'Christianity and Social Services in Modern Britain.' For one thing it kicks in to touch the imposed secular stereotype of hard-nose, tweedy, Victorian, religious do-gooders. In an age when medical science was still primitive there were thousands of women compelled by the love of Christ to minister to the poor in this way; many contracting and dying of the diseases they themselves picked up in the slums. We in the UK we have scoffed at our peril; our current Prime Minister's philanthropic 'Big Society' initiative has proved nigh impossible to get airborne. *He looks for fruit long after the root is severed.* It is incumbent on you ladies out there, particularly those who have not already got their hands full with their own children, to seek the Lord for his opportunities to fulfill a mother-ministry.

Father to the Fatherless – Jehoiada

*'And Joash did that which was right in the sight of the LORD
all the days of Jehoiada the priest.'* 2 Chron 24:2

Even at 100, Jehoiada is willing to be at the centre of what God is doing. That's right Granddads, 100 years old, so no slinking off to the comfy chair with cardigan and slippers; God has only one retirement plan, *'to him who is faithful with little things, greater things will be given'*. God called Abraham and the prophet Joel as old men and we should not be surprised if our most fruitful service in the kingdom is done when our feeble bodies have lost their pride and many of our fleshly strivings have ceased. Deuteronomy 33 15-16 talks about the ancient hills being the most fruitful and bringing forth choicest fruits. Corrie ten Boon's amazing testimony 'The Hiding Place (a book which everyone in the world should read)starts with two 'ordinary' Dutch spinsters in their fifties to whom nothing exceptional ever happened beyond the household routines.

Another example that come to mind is Christian Wolfkes, a poor carpenter living in a remote Romanian village called Noua. His prayer for years had been, 'Dear God, I have only one very great wish which I beseech you to grant me. I long to bring a Jew to Christ before I die….but I am poor and old and sick. I cannot go out looking for a Jew myself and there are no Jews in our village. Please, God, bring a Jew here to our village and I will do my best to bring him to Christ.' Now I bet this 'life-goal' does not appear on most westerners' retirement plans, but in this case God had given the carpenter a particular prayer that he had wanted to answer all along. One day a young, party-going, atheistic Jew – called Richard – was 'sent' by God to the town of Noua to recover from an illness. The carpenter gave Richard his own Bible, and though he fought 'tooth and nail' with the Holy Spirit, soon Richard submitted his life to Jesus. That young man was Richard Wurmbrand and soon his name would be known around the globe. Christian Wolfkes too is known, but mainly in heaven where one day the great books will reveal the true contribution old men and women have made to the advance of the kingdom. I expect to be shocked.

Take for example a little Chinese woman called Ann, she had spent a lifetime caring for her family when they were ill and dying; first her parents, then her four brothers. She was 82 when the last brother lay dying and knowing that Ann would have no support after he died, he told her to lift up a paving slab in the kitchen. She did, and found a stash of gold coins, no doubt left over from her brother's mafia dealings but more than enough to live on. When he died she did not know what to do at first, it being the first time she had ever had time to herself! She wanted to serve the Lord, but the house church had no real use for someone so old, so she decided that she would travel the country on trains and talk about Jesus wherever she went. And she did; for the last five years of her life Ann went on sleeper trains around that vast country gossiping with her fellow passengers about Jesus. Many were high party officials and some threatened her, but she chuckled, 'What are you going to do, jail a helpless, old lady!' She was right of course, the very thing that disqualified her from church ministry – her age – was the very thing Jesus would use. No one knows the number of people Ann witnessed to over those five years, or how many she led to Christ, but a story filtered back recently from a house church leader that will make you smile. While he was visiting a Communist party official – one known to be kind to Christians – the house church leader took a wrong turn on the way to the toilet and found the official's wife reading a Bible in a side room. She told him that a while ago her husband had been on a train and – you've guessed it – a little old lady started to talk to him about Jesus; 'I'm travelling around China telling as many people as I can about Jesus before I die.' The official did not become a Christian, but when he told his wife she was so moved that she got a Bible herself so she could read about this Jesus. So it goes to show that retirement presents some excellent opportunities for mature Christians – look what Ann did, and on Mafia money!

Jehoiada's name means 'the Lord teaches' and this is what he does for Joash, but more than that he becomes a father to him – even choosing Joash's wives. Jehoiada also becomes the impetus behind the restoration of the monarchy, and more importantly, assumes the fatherly responsibility of instructing the young king.

The need for spiritual fathers has never been so great:

- US research (The Barna Group) showed the probability of which family members influence others in becoming Christians. The probability of a child influencing the conversion of a sibling or parent is 3.5%, that probability increases to 17% when the mother is the Christian, but it jumps to a staggering 93% for the father, i.e. a believing father is over 4.5 times more likely to influence his family than his wife – but what if he isn't there?
- 40% of children born in America have no father on the birth certificate
- In the UK 43% of children are now born outside wedlock
- A quarter of all UK children under the age of fourteen are raised in a single parent home
- 50% of today's 16–24 year olds in the UK have had no Christian input beyond what they learned in school
- Is it any wonder that in the last 20 years 49% of previously church-going men under the age of 30 stopped going to church?

Now I know some phenomenal women who do an incredible job bringing up children without a father and I'm not knocking them at all. However, the brute statistics of the direct and observable effects of fatherlessness on the social fabric of western society is only too obvious: increased crime and violence, decreased community ties, a growing 'divorce culture' and cycle of fatherlessness, dependence on state welfare and spiralling health care costs. We see it all around and every time you switch on the news. If you want to understand how western society got into so much mess in such a relatively short period of time, you need to Google things like the 'sexual revolution', or 'the Kinsey report'. It turns out that sexual freedom is anything but free. In a much quicker way the Russian communists tried over months what we have let happen slowly over decades; but they quickly experienced the devastating social effects and overturned their ruling against marriage. It appeared that marriage was not a bourgeois construct invented to keep the proletariat from real freedom and pleasure after all!

But what this all means to us men is that, just like the women (Jehosheba's descendants), we need to be prepared to risk our domestic comforts to rescue (literally give life to) future 'kings'. The world needs new 'Jehoiadas' to father spiritual orphans. Will you do it? Are you open to it? Our homes and our hearts must be open, if the Lord wishes to use us this way. So the responsibility on men is very great indeed, to be men of God; men for God, men who can understand, live and teach the scriptures; men who will not be neutered by Jezebel's luxuries, but will do something to reverse the tide.

And you young dudes reading this, don't think you have to be old, and have a grey beard or something.

When I was in my first church plant assignment I became a surrogate father over and over to boys and girls when I was only in my early twenties. I remember one twelve-year-old boy called Joe whose father was a drunk and his mum a prostitute. He was malnourished, very small and gaunt but used to come round to our place with his sister to do cooking and Bible study. He told me that the only thing that survived their house fire were the words 'Jesus is Lord' that he had written on the wall above his bed. Another boy who used to come round was a lad called Sam, whose father had died when he was two. He was off the rails, and always blowing up at school and getting kicked out. Everyone said he'd go nowhere except jail, but the Lord found him and I have a picture of the day we baptized him. He's now serving with the army all over the world and keeps in touch through Facebook.

The influence of a young married couple can be very effective in this area, and even though having a young family does limit your energy, the main thing has always been to demonstrate the love of a Christian marriage and the tranquillity of a godly home. The New Testament says our homes should be literally 'harbour–*ous*' and when they are, you will find 'orphans' turn up like bees to honey. It was the 'Dilarum House' idea used by Floyd and Sally McClung (lit. House of Peace) in their outreach work to hippies across Europe and Asia; let these guys feel the peace and love of a Christian family. And how was Floyd himself transformed from a very average American evangelical? You guessed it, he was spiritually fathered by an missionary called Pop Jenkins who modelled the crucified life for Floyd, and challenged him to be the same. (You can read McClung's story in 'Living on Hell's doorstep') And though I cannot speak for older men whose children have flown the nest, we can see from men like Jehoida, Pop Jenkins and the Romanian carpenter, there is no reason on God's earth that their ministries as fathers should not be explosive and revolutionary. So never mind the Financial Times, garden slippers and potting sheds, get a denim jacket and start a youth group!

The Firebrand – Joash

I'll never forget the sight of my friend Alistair floating face down in the estuary, going out toward the sea. We had been on a two week expedition to the far northern fjords and mountain wilderness of Iceland, just four miles from the artic circle. We were now wading across a large estuary with heavy packs on our long walk back to civilisation and that is when the unthinkable happened, Alistair stumbled and went down. He was quite small compared to his pack and there was no way he could right himself, so on he went toward the sea. No one was near enough to grab him either. I was still only half way across myself, struggling against the currents, wind and heavy rain. But I will never forget the sight of him, helpless, done for, floating face down, flailing without a hope. No hope that is, until karate black–belt, physics teacher Martin Keen came sprinting down the far bank like some latter day Gotham hero, leaping in after Alistair and pulling him and his pack to the bank. It was a proper movie rescue, just like the time my older brother nearly drowned in a white water canoeing accident. He went down for the third time and was just starting to see his life pass before him – just like people say – when our scout master Gerard pulled him out. He and Alistair, like Joash, know what it is like to be plucked from death at the last minute.

> 'The LORD rebuke thee, O Satan; even the LORD that hath chosen Jerusalem rebuke thee: is not this a brand plucked out of the fire'?
> *Zech 3:2*

As the Lord did to baby Joash on a personal level, so he would do for Israel after the captivity. In the very revealing passage above, the prophet Zachariah uses the imagery of a piece of wood pulled from the flames. God's speciality is running situations that seem to be too close to the wire, humanly speaking. He also specialises in resurrecting situations and people from the ashes of human despair. Joash's life and David's line seems all but done for, but the Lord '*restrains*' Athaliah's evil arm, bringing salvation through his *promise keeper* (Jehosheba) and *teacher* (Jehoida). You may identify with Joash, I know I do on occasions. What made me kneel on that mountainside in Bosnia during the war, and call out for a living God – if he existed? How close was I, three years later, to not going to that Christian meeting when invited? When I look around and see so many, supposedly more earnest people, searching for truth and meaning – and think I found it so easily, it is a miracle. My lifestyle was so steeped in sin at that time it is a wonder God seemed to pluck me out of those flames with such ease – but he did.

But that brings us on to another point: how did surviving affect Joash psychologically?

It is hard for us to imagine what it must have been like to grow up knowing what had happened to your brothers and sisters and that you had somehow escaped. Why me? What is so special about me that they died and I survived? Nick Schluyer and three friends capsized a yacht in the Gulf of Mexico in 2009. He slowly watched his friends die of hypothermia, he himself being saved by a winter coat. He later said, 'I had a secret guilt, particularly at first....it would have been different if I'd been able to save somebody, but to come out of the water on my own, knowing I'd lost three friends, its very hard.' In the same year a teenage girl called Bahai Bakari was with her mother on Yemeni flight 626 when it crashed into the Indian ocean. Much later she recalled the doctor's words 'she said I was the only survivor...I was lucky to have escaped, but that one day, perhaps in ten years I would feel guilty to have survived.' It was this guilt that many in England faced after the great bubonic plague wiped out nearly half the population between 1348-1350. Why had God spared us when everyone we knew, good and bad, had perished so horribly? Psychologists call this 'survivor guilt' and if not processed properly, they say, can lead to depression, apathy and generalized anxiety. But that is not all Joash faced, for all through his tender years he has the mounting expectation that he has been preserved by God, chosen from the unsaved, plucked like a firebrand from the fires of Satan's wrath – to be a king, to rule, to defend others. Such responsibility and knowledge is hard to grasp.

And yet isn't that just like you and me?

You may sometimes – as I do – look back and wonder what a truly awesome thing it is, that by some miracle you were saved, that you saw who Jesus was, even though your friends and family could not. It is at times like these when you may feel a lot more like that little boy Joash, growing up in the safety of God's household while outside the forces of darkness lay waste to your friends' lives and marriages.

Maybe you marvel at such times at the promise from God that you, like little Joash, have been chosen to be made *'unto our God kings and priests: and we shall reign on the earth'* (Rev 5:10); that his intention has always been to share his authority with us. That is to exercise his real authority on *this earth*, during Jesus' 1000 year reign and also in the new universe which he is creating. And what is authority but delegated responsibility? And how is he training us for this? Is it at church? A little maybe, but 95% will be in our jobs, with our families, tidying up toys, washing dishes, doing nappies, submitting to others, letting someone else have their way for a change.

Jezebel and Athaliah have their way of telling you how to have power, but it's all lies, all of it. It is how Satan tried to do it, but failed miserably. Now all he has left is the dubious glory of trying to make it work through others; there is no repentance in him. If you have a strong stomach, watch that film *Downfall* which I mentioned before – you won't find any repentance in Hitler either; the failure was everybody else's fault. When we see people who seize power this way like Sulla, Caesar, Napoleon, Hitler, or whoever, we see those who cannot use it or even keep it. No, for the real authority is given by God to the meek; it is they, not the 'supposed' strong, that will inherit the earth at Jesus' second coming (Matt 5v5). His way is the way of love and service of others, let him fill you with this type of heart attitude, and you may have *'authority over ten cities'* (Luke 19:18) when He returns. These eternal principles are even now under test. If God had destroyed Satan the moment he sinned, he might always after have been accused, 'Ah, but you didn't prove your way of love was the more excellent way.' By the close of history God will have proved it, most supremely in the Cross of our Saviour.

The Gauntlet

The challenge is clear, to the women: are you prepared, having heard this call to close your ears, your hearts and your homes to the life-hating spirit of Jezebel and rather dedicate yourselves to be live-givers, opening your hearts to spiritually and physically fatherless people?

And, you men: are you prepared to allow God to make you spiritual fathers? To forsake the ease and compromise with Jezebel's luxuries and use your brief time on earth to fulfil your destiny as men of God? To use the delegated responsibility that God has given us with gentleness and reverent awe as ones *who must give account,* and remembering the crown of headship we are offered on this earth is a crown of thorns?

And, young people, the saddest part of the story is that Joash was only really faithful to the Lord while his mentor lived; after Jehoiada died he was led astray into idolatry by the princes of Judah. He even killed one of Jehoiada's sons when that son rebuked him in the name of the Lord for backsliding. You, like Joash, are the kings in waiting, plucked by the sheer unmerited favour of God from the deserved flames of judgement: will you remember that your lives have been bought with a terrific price and will you covenant with God to heed his instruction, even when no one is looking over your shoulders? Everything that Christ gives must also be inherited by overcomers. You must *'walk worthy of God, who hath called you unto his kingdom and glory'* (1 Thess 2:12); only then, by lives of humility and love will you indeed be princes with whom he will entrust ten cities when he comes.

The Firebrand

Joash gives thanks to his Aunt, Uncle and the Lord

(From 'THE LINE' album, words and music by Henry Brooks)

I can't exactly say how it happened to me
But they say I was lying among the slain, the day that you found me,
And what can I say to you, for giving back this life to me?
How can I repay all that you did for me that day?

I guess, I never really knew my own Mum and Dad
In a childhood so screwed up, you were the only family that I had
And what can I say to you, you risked all for me?
How can I repay all that you did for me that day?

I feel just like a firebrand tonight
Plucked from the flames of certain death, I was precious in your sight
I want you know this firebrand is burning hot tonight, and just wants to say 'thank you'

I want to thank you both for looking after me
You saw I got my milk and meat and the mentoring that I needed
And what can I say to you, you sustained this life in me
How can I repay all that you've done unto this day ? ... Sometimes I still ...

feel like a firebrand tonight
When the ones I loved died in the dark but I got out all right

What purpose did God have to choose someone too weak to fight? But I want
to say 'Lord, use me'
Now you're telling me that I was born to reign
And what sin and death would sweep away, has been restored again
How can I take it in, the height of my destiny?
How can my life reflect my future not my past? ... Oh Lord please ...

Blow on this firebrand tonight
To light a fire throughout this land, a burning and pure light
I want the world to know to see your love, your glory and your might,

Add kindling to this firebrand–again tonight
Fan flames of royal destiny that once burned so bright
So people drowned in hopelessness will once again unite
Just want to say 'Reign in me'
Just want to say 'Reign in me'

Life Application Devotion

Chapter 11 – On becoming a Spiritual Father or Mother
- Is there anyone outside your immediate family whom you consider as a
  spiritual father or mother? If so list their names and thank God for the
  specific strengths that they bring or have brought to your life.
- Are you seen - even if not verbally expressed – to have or have had this
  ministry to someone else? If yes, then list what it is exactly that they look
  to you for.
- Prayerfully list three ways you could allow the Lord to use you more
  effectively in this role. (This might be anything from 'having more time to
  be available' to 'being more full of the Holy Spirit and fruit of the Spirit.')

Prayer: (Start with thanksgiving & praise, particularly for his perfect
fatherhood) Oh Lord God, Father to the Fatherless, I offer myself and my
home to you and your precious church in this role. By the power of your
Spirit I ask you to open my eyes to see these spiritual orphans you are putting
across my path and my heart toward their needs. Lord please fill me and use
me to be the answer to their needs.

	Abraham
	Isaac
	Jacob
	Judah
	Perez
	Hezron
	Ram
	Amminadab
	Nahshon
	Salmon
	Boaz
	Obed
	King David
	Solomon
	Rehoboam
	Abijah
	Asa
	Jehoshaphat
	Jehoram
	Ahaziah
	Joash
Jerusha	Amaziah
	Uzziah
Abijah	Jotham
Hephziba	Ahaz
Meshullemeth	Hezekiah
Jedidah	Manasseh
Hamutal	Amon
Zebidah	Josiah
	Jehoahaz
	Jeconiah
	Jehoiachin
	Shealtiel
	Zerubbabel
	Abihud
	Eliakim
	Azor
	Zadok
	Akim
	Elihud
	Eleazar
	Matthan
	Jacob

Joseph; *the husband
of Mary; the mother of
Jesus; who is called the
Messiah.* (Matt 1:16)

Chapter 12

The Chief of Sinners (Read 2 Kings 14-23)

'You think you're better than I am? Where we came from, if one did not want to die of poverty, one became a priest or a bandit! You chose your way, I chose mine. Mine was harder. You talk of our mother and father. You remember when you left to become a priest? I stayed behind! I must have been ten, twelve. I don't remember which, but I stayed. I tried, but it was no good. Now I am going to tell you something. You became a priest because you were ... too much of a coward to do what I do!'

Tucco to his brother Pablo in the 1966 film, *The Good, the Bad and the Ugly*

The Good, the Bad and the Godly

'Every fool's got a reason to feel sorry for himself, turn his heart to stone,' so says one of my favourite singers, Bruce Springsteen but I have to admit that I've often more empathy with the prodigals – like Tucco from the quote above – than with a cold moralist whose holiness has all the cleanliness of a fresh-washed corpse at the morgue. In this chapter I will introduce you to sinners who became saints and saints who became sinners. Their testimonies will help us, perhaps save us even; for testimonies are salvation clothed in flesh and blood, everyone has one, you, me, every believer and especially my mates who, back in 2002, I labelled 'The Good, the Bad and the Godly'.

They weren't the average church crowd but I didn't want anything *average* for this mission. We were pioneering a church in a town infamous for high unemployment, social disintegration, drinking and drug abuse – and, of course, that hard-man culture of violence. We had been there for nearly five years and had seen the grim reality of physical, emotional and spiritual poverty first hand. I'd been working on a construction job with Big Dave and when he told me his story, and about his friends, I thought, 'Yeah, these guys are just the sort to get through to the people of this town.'

Big Dave had a broken childhood; perhaps they all did. He'd been a bouncer and debt collector, and was eventually jailed in the UK and Spain for his work in organized crime; he still had shotgun pellets in his brain. Then there was another Dave, again rather big. He had been a Hell's Angel, and one time the most wanted man in the UK. Next was Rick, a big time drug dealer; and then there were the two Allans, one an ex-junkie, the other an ex-witch. We put up our big marquee, stuck up the 'Jesus is Lord' banner, and advertised far and wide that the 'Good, the Bad and the Godly' were coming to town.

Most nights I preached from the parable of the sower and sang Keith Green and Larry Norman songs – though I got choked up a number of times, such was the presence of the Holy Spirit. God was there to do what he does best: save sinners; and when Dave and his mates testified no one was left in any doubt that Jesus can save the worst sinners and turn their lives around. Big Dave is now married, has a Renewal Energy company and is the treasurer for a police crime prevention committee. (You've got to admire God's sense of humour!) Hell's Angel Dave is a web engineer with wife and kids. Ex-drug baron Richard lost his private plane when he was busted by the police, but now flies all over the world teaching missionaries for YWAM. The two Allans are sorted too, basically the gospel 'does what it says on the tin', recycles sinners, stops them perishing, makes them useful again. The gospel has always been good news for big sinners, though it has always been anything but for the people who insisted on doing it themselves. As Jesus prodded such people – with a tone somewhere between irony and rebuke – he had not come for 'righteous' but sinners, not to heal the 'fit' but the sick (Mark 2:17).

What an Awful Lot of Rot

It is plain enough from our vantage point in history that men would go to extraordinary lengths – and I do mean extraordinary – to reject Jesus' simple diagnosis and 'build cisterns of their own'; that is, to find a man made solution. I felt some years ago that the Lord wanted me to study the decline and fall of the Roman empire, and I have read nothing since then that does not confirm to me that we are more like them in their decline than we could ever admit.

*'It is scarcely possible that the eyes of contemporaries should discover ... the latent causes of decay and corruption. This long peace, and the uniform government of the Romans, introduced a **slow and secret poison** into the vitals of the empire. The minds of men were gradually reduced to the same level, the fire of genius was extinguished, and even the military spirit evaporated.'*
Edward Gibbon, *Decline and Fall of the Roman Empire*

'Slow and secret poison,' the poor old Romans hadn't got a clue what was causing the moral rot that weakened the greatest empire ever seen. Most had a sneaking suspicion it had something to do with the 'effeminate' Persians and all their silks, harems and easy living. Livy, who died in AD17 lamented of the 'dark dawning of our modern day when we can neither endure our vices nor face the remedies needed to cure them.' Some, perhaps with only a smidgen more self knowledge, Seneca for example, came gradually to see that 'evil has its seat within us' and that he the great stoic 'was not a tolerable man, let alone a good one'. Others deflected the blame for the decline toward the military and patrician classes whose vices and opulence seemed more than ample to induce the civic anaemia that would eventually render the empire powerless against a more vigorous civilization. But for some – and this seems closer to commentators of the present day – the field of reference was so narrow that almost any contemporary explanation was plausible. For example one writer in 129BC blamed all the troubles on the new 'Via Appia' road system and redistribution of land!

But it is not just western civilization, but mankind in general, that has had problems diagnosing the *sin* we do and the *sinners* we are: in fact they all failed miserably; the Bible alone calls a spade a spade. I have already said that the 'antiquated', 'Victorian' word sin is coming out of the Oxford English Children's dictionary. Before the last century Christianity gave the explanation and remedy for the ills of society but somewhere along the way Feuerbach, Marx and Freud 'helped' us start the twenty-first century with a clean slate, and for the last hundred years people have increasingly looked to their governments and psychiatrists for diagnosis and solutions. It is not just the 30% of today's American women who suffer depression, for now preschool children are the burgeoning market for anti-depressants. Over 6% of them are classed as clinically depressed and the overall growth figure for children increases by 23% per annum. The pharmaceutical companies must be rubbing their hands at such a growth market. It is no different in the UK where we have one of the highest self-harming rates of any European country; where one in ten children are now classed as having mental and emotional disorders and 25% of the adult population will suffer with mental health issues each year. I'm not suggesting that all clinical depression is guilt related, of course it isn't. A believer in my own family suffers with a bipolar disorder and was not our Lord himself said to be 'a man of sorrow and well acquainted with *grief*'? (The word 'grief' here has its root meaning in 'to be worn down' and can equally apply to anxiety as to physical sickness.) But just read those statistics above one more time; the huge percentages involved, and children as well, I mean come on! Surely somewhere along the line someone has got to join the dots and stop inventing more 'isms', pills and government initiatives.

The British government already have 2000 cameras in people's homes to stop people from sinning. At the time of writing the first draft of this manuscript they wanted to place another 20,000 into British homes – but I can guarantee that no politician will ever go back to first principles and deal with the problem at source. Why? Because some of their number have laboured so long to sever the Christian roots under a misguided secularist fanaticism. And now do they wonder why there is no fruit when they inspect the branches? In the UK we have passed laws, on the grounds of race discrimination, that forbid Christians proclaiming that Jesus Christ is the *only* answer for sin. Think of it, the *diagnosis* and the *prognosis* have both been outlawed. Rather reminiscent of the American dietician who banned his clients from eating cottage cheese because, 'well, haven't you noticed, only fat folks eat that stuff?' And so we must be content with every new hair-brained scheme from on high, like 'happiness lessons' for children in primary schools, where they can practise yoga and meditation. Perhaps we should not be overly hard on the great men of our day, that they are so blind to sin's source and cure, for they are in good company, though perhaps more exalted than they merit.

> '*The names of Seneca, of the elder and the younger Pliny, of Tacitus, of Plutarch, of Galen, of the slave Epictetus, and of the emperor Marcus Antoninus, adorn the age in which they flourished, and exalt the dignity of human natures. They filled with glory their respective stations, either in active or contemplative lives; their excellent understandings were improved by study; philosophy had purified their minds from the prejudices of the popular superstition; and their days were spent in the pursuit of truth and the practice of virtue. Yet all these sages (it is no less an object of surprise than of concern)* **overlooked or rejected the perfection of the Christian system.**'
>
> Edward Gibbon, *Decline and Fall of the Roman Empire*

Seeds of Corruption

In this chapter we will look at the lives of three bad kings and five good ones, from Joash to Josiah, and hopefully recover something of our true selves before God – something of a 'sin reality check'. And before you say it, no, I don't like those trendy teachers that make you wallow in the seemingly inescapable 'brokenness of frail humanity', where Mr Urban Keynote Speaker triumphs in his 'guts'n'all' spiritual honesty and says, 'I just can't get off any more on all that glib, "victorious Christian living" jargon. Let's all hold hands and focus on what bad sinners we are and leave the rest to Jesus.' I appreciate the sentiment, but above the noise of all that self-indulgent wound licking I bet it is hard to hear the apostle say, 'I'm not saying that I'm fully getting it or already totally mature, but I'm fleeing in that direction so that I can take hold of the life that Christ Jesus has taken hold of me for.'

When we match our wills to 'flee after' and 'apprehend' what Jesus has stated he will do, his whole resurrection power is on hand to deliver us from our flesh. When Jesus says 'if any man wants to save his life he must lose it', he actually uses the Greek work for destroy. Sometimes repentance and separation from our cultural value system needs to be a whole lot more radical than just saying the sinners' prayer. I'm sure that for some of these things that have a strong hold on us it will feel like cutting off arms and gouging out eyes. But sin is an illusive little gremlin, it morphs, hides and deceives with surprising ease. Part of doing a 'sin reality check' is about correctly identifying exactly where the sneaky little beggar lurks.

One of the great tragedies of the Victorian Christian history is that sin outwitted most of them in the second half of the century. Gradually sin was seen to spring less from the corrupt natures of men, and more from inanimate objects; cards, alcohol, gambling, horse racing etc. Wesley might have seemed almost prophetic to them when he talked of the convert who had been 'starched and ironed before he had been washed'. And so the same generations that witnessed the revivals and missionary 'explosions' were, at the very same time, being sold new lenses to view sin with and before long they plunged headlong into an overemphasis on social action. As one expressed at the time, 'Nowadays Martha has it all her own way.' I read one example of a 'successful meeting' where the minutes recorded many pledges taken and then almost as an afterthought, 'some conversions'. As in the case of Rome, 'The seeds of corruption were sown even in the times of plenty.' Within fifty years 42% of the churchgoing population had stopped going to church. In losing touch with who they were in Adam, Britain lost touch with who they could be, and needed to be, in Christ.

The lesson of history is hideously clear, when the theology of sin was lost in the church – a church too busy trying be relevant to culture, as it happens – the world went looking elsewhere for answers. The raft of ideology that most would just lump together under the heading of 'modernity' – took a long time to take hold, but as the church got trendier or woollier, and the state control of education and social services became absolute, who else could save us? The heirs of the Victorians were not too slow to conclude that the Messiah they sought had relocated from Canterbury to Westminster. As Sir Richard Gregory put it, 'My grandfather preached the gospel of Christ, my father preached the gospel of socialism, I preach the gospel of science'. It was the fulfilment of Chesterton's observation that 'The modern world is full of the old Christian virtues gone mad.'

And what happened to a nation can happen to us individually too, through pride and deception. Remember that next time you find yourself tutting in HMV: that DVD or poster or that computer game may be many things but it, in and of itself, is not 'sinful'. That is simply a wrong use of the word and one, as we have seen, that leads to our deception. The 1904 Welsh Revival flew against this trend and it is interesting to hear Evan Roberts tell his co-workers, 'You need not say anything about the theatre and the public-house. You preach the love of Christ to them, and if his love will not constrain people to lead a better life nothing else will.' Of course there were many others in that day who saw what was happening; how much we need Santiago Cassio's revelation, 'Lord Jesus, you took me from behind myself where I had hidden and placed me before my face and lo I am ugly with sin.' Like I said, sin's a sneaky little beggar. See if you can spot him at work in the next few descendants in the Line.

Stories of Purity, Pride and Then Perversion

Wiser in Their Own Eyes – Amaziah to Uzziah

King Amaziah follows his father Joash (mentioned in the last chapter) to the grave; both were assassinated, which was previously unheard of in Judah. The indignity of being murdered was divine payback; in Joash's case for his cousin; in Amaziah's for idolatry. Next comes King Uzziah who is very like his great, great, great grandfather Asa; a bit of a Cromwellian-type, hardcore, military autocrat. Interestingly all the above are recorded as 'good' kings, but each one fell in the same area: they would not stand being corrected by those God sent. (Men be warned!) Uzziah became famous for siege engines and a long history of reform and conquest. He reigned for fifty-two years, and did such a great job as a gifted military leader that he thought he'd turn his 'can-do' aptitude to the old-fashioned temple worship. Who knows, perhaps Uzziah wanted to be head of church and state; he wouldn't be the first or last. It is not unlike the stories of Henry II and Henry VIII who in their day were withstood by Thomas Becket, Thomas More and John Fisher – all of whom died for it. In King Uzziah's case God struck him with leprosy before he could punish the brave priests who withstood him. God give us teachable and humble hearts; there is great protection there. Sin is always 'crouching at the door'; we need each other, as pride invariably comes before a fall.

Cultural Relevance – Jotham to Ahaz

King Jotham assumed a regency in place of his leprous father. He was a good king and 2 Chronicles 27:6 records that he '*became mighty, because he prepared his ways before the LORD his God*'. His son, Ahaz was not so prudent. He was like someone who accrues gambling debts because he's greedy, but then goes to a loan shark for help. It was unfortunate for him and the nation that the priests of his day didn't stand up to him, as they did to his leprous grandfather. Without a godly support network the King descended into a paganised form of Judaism, even to the point of sacrificing his own son. It was this same King Ahaz who took a fancy for a rather trendy Syrian altar that he had seen on a state visit. He had his own fancy replica of it installed in God's temple. Ahaz also meddled in temple affairs; reordering the worship; insisting they use his new altar for sacrifice (and the old one for his own private use). The world has so many ways of persuading us to modernize our creed or contemporize our worship, but we should remember that progression in the real world is rarely *uni–linear*. What I mean, is that usually there is a straw that breaks the camel's back; there is a turn of the screw that breaks the thread, some progressions that undo the whole, at least in the real material world. In the areas of socialist history or science's rewriting of its own 'glorious ascendance' we are asked to believe – as with evolution – that everything goes on and on and on, and up and up and up.

I have seen such naivety, even in Christian sub–culture, where substance is sacrificed to the cult of Relevance. But the things which are eternal are, by their nature, eternally relevant and of such things the Christian must deal. A new 'Philistine cart' might look great, contemporary even, and it might be what everyone else is using – but let's not replace substance with packaging when it comes to worshipping God (2 Sam 6). Read Exodus 20:25, he will never share his glory with our flesh, and nor will he receive glory from our flesh – it simply has never been like that. If we don't bring him our hearts, he simply won't turn up and we'll be left singing and harmonizing with each other – sounding great – but that's all.

Unfortunately for Ahaz and Israel it didn't stop with that fancy pagan altar, it never does with us either; for once we surrender the simplicity of 'spirit and truth' worship to copy those Philistine or Syrian ways, there will be more incursions. In Judah's case Ahaz let the visiting Syrian king make his pagan offerings in the Jerusalem temple. I will refrain from ranting at this point about the abominations of the interfaith movement and even some of the dangers of an unguarded ecumenism, but will merely point out that this was major triumph for Satan, who has always desired to be worshipped in God's temple (something he did again under Antiochus Ephiphanes and will do under Anti-Christ). And there is an application for us in all this: for as the new temples of the Lord we can allow ourselves to serve Satan by sins great and small (Read 1 Cor 6:15). If we bow to peer pressure and invite these pagan kings to have use of *our* temple we must not be surprised if they want to pollute our worship and service to a holy God.

How Art Thou Fallen? – Hezekiah

King Hezekiah succeeded his disastrous father but thanks to the godly influence of his mother Abigail and her father Zechariah, he was saved from repeating his father's stupidity. Once again, it is not possible to stress more firmly that – even with an apostate father – a mother's prayers and a grandfather's example are powerful, history-shaping weapons. My friend Dave started to backslide as a teen and his mother often told him, 'You can waste your time if you want but I've prayed that you will one day serve Jesus and that's what will happen.' And it did.

Perhaps Hezekiah's revulsion for the interfaith mess left by his father was also enforced by the knowledge that his older brother had been sacrificed to Satan. It was on his watch that God killed 185,000 proud Assyrians in one night with one angel (apparently some of their skulls are still in the British Museum). But once again where trial and persecution could not corrupt this godly man, pride did. It is easy to point the finger at Hezekiah but remember, he'd come through some hard times; credit where credit is due, he was a good king. But equally we must not overlook what he displayed to the Babylonian envoys; not just the palace and temple treasures but the kind of material pride we might also see in self-made men. He had achieved success in his ministry, but had forgotten it was all a gift. I often have to remind myself (actually it is more often my wife who reminds me) not to keep spouting all the wonderful things the Lord is doing through us. Sometimes it may be blowing his trumpet, but most times it is blowing our own.

Tellingly, all this happened in the extra fifteen years of life that he was given by God, beyond his appointed time. It is perhaps a shame that Hezekiah was not more like Queen Elizabeth I who said, in her famous Golden Speech, that she did not 'desire to live longer days than I may see your prosperity and that is my only desire'. Easy to say when you are young with years in front of you, but what about when the time finally draws near? Even Queen Elizabeth resisted death in the end, sitting on some cushions for days with one finger in her mouth. When Robert Cecil pleaded with her that she 'must go to bed' she replied, 'Must is not a word to use to princes little man, little man. If your late father were here he would never have dared to utter such a word.' It was her final illness and you can almost feel the bitterness of death in her rebuke. Another great prince, the Roman Emperor Severus – who died at York – summed up the stripping finality of it all, 'I have been everything and everything is nothing'. Our own Dr Samuel Johnson said, 'no man can face death without uneasy apprehension', though the atheist Bertrand Russell said he felt that he could. Whether he did or not we cannot know though Rousseau said of men like that, 'he who pretends to face death without fear is a liar'. Why? Because as W. B. Yeats saw, neither 'dread nor hope attend a dying animal,' but 'a man awaits his end dreading and hoping all.' Everything hinges on the next step that you are about to make, a step that approaches as on a conveyor belt which you cannot stop. Before your eyes pass everything you have done or not done, so many things that you would change or undo or redo before meeting your judge. Because, as Epicurus remarked, 'what men fear is not that death is annihilation, but that it is not!'"

Even one of the Enlightenment's great sons Thomas Paine buckled in that hour, 'I would give worlds, if I had them, that 'The Age of Reason' had never been published. Oh God, save me for I am on the edge of hell alone.'

And I think we can all feel great sympathy here for Hezekiah when he pleads with God for a bit longer. And though you do not perhaps feel it now friend, one day you too might wish to have a million pounds to buy just one more year, just one more day even. But for Hezekiah it would have been better still if he had submitted this desire to God – for sometimes He gives us what we crave even when we are prone to abuse it. The extra fifteen year gift caused pride and ingratitude (2 Chron 32:25), the latter being harder to understand than the former. For under his reign he had seen heaven fight for him, had been blessed with the prophetic ministry of Isaiah, he'd heard the prophecy (and possibly seen) the *virgin conceive and bear a son* (Isaiah 7:14), entire planetary bodies move for his benefit, and now he is granted life beyond his time; was it any wonder that his heart was lifted up? We get puffed up if someone says we preached a half decent sermon; he had people coming from all over the nation with gifts after 'he' had saved them from the Assyrians. But the growth of this pride was not the major outcome of this fifteen years; a baby was. For it was also within this extra time that Manasseh was born.

The Making of a Monster – Manasseh

Why didn't Hezekiah chose one of his older sons to rule? Had they become dissolute through the contradictory paternal example, or was this son of his old age, this earnest and intelligent twelve year old, such a prodigy that the crown should pass to him? Manasseh means 'to cause to forget', an interesting choice. Joseph (who gave his son the same name) wanted to forget his family's failings; what was Hezekiah hoping to forget? His previous parental failure perhaps? I have been told that if a parent displays religious hypocrisy or grotesque character flaws, it will produce a wholesale disgust and rebellion against those standards in their children. The responsibility for us to model, and not merely preach, the born again servant life, is tremendous. Children are not as easily fooled as we think.

Now it is all too easy to see a villain, a Hitler, and say, 'well that's them, they're monsters', without taking the trouble to know them or ourselves. It is because we are so conditioned by things like the Bond movies to think that evil is something else, something that bald, scar faced men with white, furry cats do in secret hideouts surrounded by evil henchmen. But when we look at Manasseh, butcher and villain though he may be, it is also very obvious that he started out with creative, religious zeal. It seems the spur of it all was that he thought his father's religion was oppressively narrow minded and puritanical. It was not progressive or inclusive to meet the needs of a modern world. Manasseh is not recorded initially as a licentious man with animal passions, but rather a guy who was seriously into religion. He wasn't one for chucking out Jehovah worship, but he certainly wasn't going to impose his religion on other ethnic groups either. No, for that was the old way; what he wanted was – what we have come to call – a post–modern multicultural society of harmony and peace between the diverse elements. No longer 'our truth is the only truth', now it was, 'each has his own truth and we must have dialogue between religions'. First Manasseh started rebuilding the very shrines his dad had destroyed outside the city, but then of course, he thought, 'wait a minute, what kind of hypocrite am I? If these religions are as equally valid as ours then we need to represent it inside the city and where better than the temple! Of course those stuffy, bigoted priests won't want change, when do they ever? But we've got to drag this archaic system into the modern world, all this monotheistic, racist hogwash, looking down on everyone else's religion. It's bad enough we displaced these people in the first place, at least we can honour their ethnic roots.'

Of course it is nothing new to us in Britain, in fact it is nothing new full stop, as Gibbon again reminds us; 'The various modes of worship, which prevailed in the Roman world, were all considered by the people, as equally true; by the philosopher, as equally false; and by the magistrate, as equally useful.' In Europe what the political scientists call multiculturalism is *useful* for simple fiscal reasons: we have an irrecoverable cultural fatigue. Europe's fertility rate is 1.6, the population is shrinking at a compound rate, and but for the (mainly Islamic) immigration, none of us would be having our welfare or pensions. So multiculturalism for them is simply a necessary tool for survival. But this was not the case for Manasseh – in which way he was more honest. For he was an ideologue; that is he actually believed in his chosen *ideal* and also had the power to experiment on a massive scale. And in his case the new cultural mode of expression in Israel was not nice at all.

> '*And he did that which was evil in the sight of the LORD, after the abominations of the heathen, whom the LORD cast out before the children of Israel. For he built up again the high places which Hezekiah his father had destroyed; and he reared up altars for Baal, and made a grove, as did Ahab king of Israel; and worshipped all the host of heaven, and served them. And he built altars in the house of the LORD, of which the LORD said, In Jerusalem will I put my name. And he built altars for all the host of heaven in the two courts of the house of the LORD. And he made his son pass through the fire, and observed times, and used enchantments, and dealt with familiar spirits and wizards: he wrought much wickedness in the sight of the LORD, to provoke him to anger. And he set a graven image of the grove that he had made in the house, of which the LORD said to David, and to Solomon his son, In this house, and in Jerusalem, which I have chosen out of all tribes of Israel, will I put my name for ever.*' 2 Chronicles 33:2-7

Yes, Manasseh is no mere talker; soon he was proving his religious devotion with the ultimate price, sacrificing his own son to the satanic idol Molech in the fire. Over a fifty-five year reign his idealistic religious fervour descends into despotism and suppression; it says that he fills Jerusalem with innocent blood. It was the same in the demise of the Roman Empire when the 'government appeared every day less formidable to its enemies, more odious and oppressive to its subjects'. And it is exactly what C.S. Lewis says is, by necessity, the outcome of all moral relativists like Manasseh; in the end, value judgements will only be made by that which never claimed to be objective in the first place – arbitrary and brute instinct. Perhaps you never thought it would end there, well it must. If you have a spare hour, read Lewis' *The Abolition of Man* lectures – they will blow your mind. The Bible records that Manasseh led the people to sin more than the pagans God had removed from the land originally. As a punishment God sends the Assyrians under King Esarhaddon to capture Manasseh and that's when you think, 'Ah, at last he got his payback, now he can fester and die slowly and good riddance.' But wait, what is this we read in Chronicles 33:12-13?

> '*And when he was in affliction, he besought the LORD his God, and humbled himself greatly before the God of his fathers, And prayed unto him: and he was entreated of him, and heard his supplication, and brought him again to Jerusalem into his kingdom. Then Manasseh knew that the LORD he was God.*' Chron 33:12-13

Amazing though it would seem to us *righteous* persons, God accepts Manasseh's prayer. According to external sources, it was Manasseh who had the prophet Isaiah put inside a hollow trunk of a tree for high treason – i.e. speaking out against the king's idolatry – and was sawn in two. I often wonder whether Manasseh ever heard Isaiah preach about the depths of God's forgiveness, and whether that is something that came to him in that prison cell. As ever, God is 'all or nothing', and his offer made by Isaiah holds true even for the chief of sinners,

> '*Come now, and let us reason together, saith the LORD: though your sins be as scarlet, they shall be as white as snow; though they be red like crimson, they shall be as wool.*' Isa 1:18

His spell in prison, and his deliverance, established one thing for Manasseh; 'the Lord he was God', basically no other God was able to help him in time of trouble. Like the woman who had spent all she had, Manasseh found that the hems of Jehovah's garments were better than all the other supposed doctors. Many have come to Jesus that way too, not just for the scarlet sins everyone can see, but the deep crimson sin that runs to the depth of our very natures. He is restored, and does his level best to get Judah to serve the Lord only; he builds up the defences, cleans out the temple and starts proper temple worship. He works hard when he gets the crown back, but all of the reforms and repentance cannot achieve two things. Firstly, to remove the coming judgement for what Manasseh had done. '*I will make them an object of horror among all the kingdoms of the earth because of Manasseh, the son of Hezekiah, the king of Judah, for what he did in Jerusalem*' (Jer 15: 4). And second, it was not enough to save his idolatrous son Amon who went back to his father's old ways when he died. Amon managed to find idols his father had actually made. These he worshipped before he was finally assassinated.

But that is not the end, for before he died, I fancy Manasseh was able to spend time with his grandson. With this six year old he would talk and pray. Because she gets a mention I believe the boy's mother, Adayah, encouraged the grandfather, particularly when she saw her own husband proving to be such a bad role model. Whatever the truth of this assumption, that boy would grow up to be one of the most tender and best kings the nation ever had, perhaps second only to David, and after him the rest would be wicked men. The name of this great king was, of course, Josiah.

> '*This is a faithful saying, and worthy of all acceptation, that Christ Jesus came into the world to save sinners; of whom I am chief. Howbeit for this cause I obtained mercy, that in me first Jesus Christ might shew forth all longsuffering, for a pattern to them which should hereafter believe on him to life everlasting. Now unto the King eternal, immortal, invisible, the only wise God, be honour and glory for ever and ever. Amen.*' 1 Tim 1:15–17

Chief of Sinners

(Manasseh sings to his grandson Josiah)

(From 'THE LINE' album, words and music by Henry Brooks)

Hey Josiah, come and sit here on my knee
Your Grandpa's old but I've got so much to say
Missed this chance with your Dad and it breaks my heart
Says I sold out and gone traditional at last
But if he'd seen where my broad way led me to
All the pain, that I put this family through I feel like

The chief of sinners, that's from only what I've seen
But God saw this heart of darkness, fathomed all that was unclean
For I wasted my whole life on these new age old age lies
But in prison they did not help me, then I realized

It was you, all along, it was you, my father's God
What had seemed a narrow way to me, was just a path more seldom trod
But I'll never understand your grace and mercy, Lord
That you'd take me back at this late hour, even after all I've done

Hey Josiah, come and sit here on my knee
Your Grandpa's dying but he's got so much to see
Missed my chance, to live for him when I was young
So seek the Lord and don't you do the things I've done
And maybe sinners (who are desperate) many years from now
Will hear of me (take heart) and repent, when they hear just how, God saved
This chief of sinners, when I'd nothing left of mine
Except filthy rags and chains and all the carnage left behind
But I swapped this life so scarlet for garments white as snow
And those hidden crimson stains of guilt will forever be unknown

It was you, all along, it was you, my father's God
What this fool thought too narrow was a path so seldom trod
And I'm ever in your debt my father God
You raised my head at this late hour, even after all I've done

Hey Josiah, come cuddle up here and pray with me
Sacrificed my own kids for my career and ministry
Now they're lost and it's only me and you

This old man has faith to see all that the Lord will do
And maybe you, will be the one to turn them round
Long after these weary bones lie in the ground

So I trust you to God's cleansing in his pure and holy fire
To do what my hands could not, but what my heart desires,
Lord, use this precious life to rescue this nation from the liar
That the narrow way, will go on 'till one day you'll send Messiah
Yes fulfil your promise Lord through Isaiah and Jeremiah
And gives us hearts of flesh on the day you send Messiah

Life Application Devotion
Chapter 12 – Bringing Our Past to Him

- Are there any sins from your pre-Christian days (or even current strongholds) that you find hard to forget? If so, spend some time thanking God for the blood of Jesus Christ that cleanses all sin, confessing aloud, 'If we confess our sin he is faithful to forgive our sins and cleanse us from all unrighteousness' (1 John 1:9)

- Some Christians carry a general guilt, not for specific sins committed B.C., but because of wasted years, ruined relationships and lost opportunities that can never come again. Can you identify with this?

- If you have answered yes then you will identify with Paul when he called himself 'the chief of sinners' (1 Tim 1:15) and the 'least of all saints' (Eph 3:8) for he carried memories of the blood of Christian Martyrs in his mind. But he also said, in the same verse that, 'he was not behind the least of the apostles', 'perfect' (Phil 3.15), 'blameless' (1 Thes. 2:10) and that when he visited the Roman church he would come 'in the fullness of the blessing of the Gospel of Christ.' (Rom. 15:29)

- The point here is that when we come to Christ, we can only offer our sin and sinful past; indeed it is only *such* things that he accepts in any case. Thereafter we cannot lay claim to any part of our past as a right any more than we can deserve what we exchanged for it; redemption by the blood of Jesus. He may use our past – as he did Paul's as a witness for his saving power – and he has certainly promised to 'work all things together for good', but that essentially is not our business; we are slaves bought for a price, our only concern now is that, by repentance and obedience, 'the life of Jesus might be manifest in our mortal flesh' (2 Cor 14:11)

- Prayer: (Start with thanksgiving & praise, particularly for his sinless life, perfect sacrifice and power–giving resurrection.) Oh Sovereign Lord, God in whom all time exists and who has known me before ever I was conceived, I bring you my past today and give it to you. I renounce any rights I have to wallow in its guilt as much as I renounce any claims I have to a righteousness outside of Christ. If there is anything you want me to do to make amends in certain areas then Lord I trust you to reveal it to me and confirm that through those you have placed around me. Help me live in the fullness of this new life that you have given me.

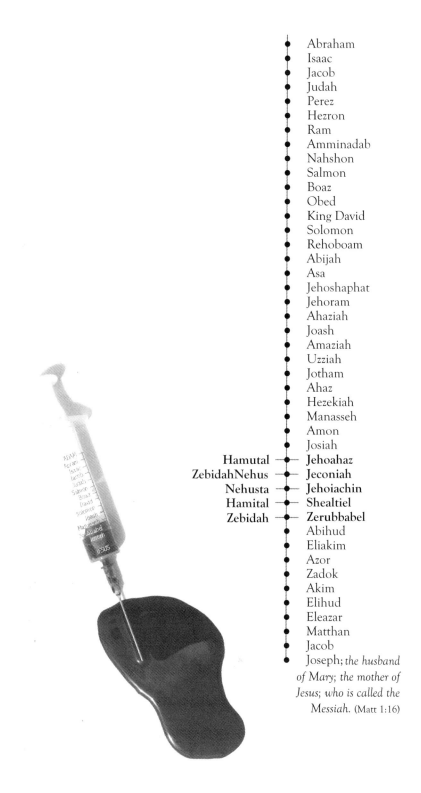

Abraham
Isaac
Jacob
Judah
Perez
Hezron
Ram
Amminadab
Nahshon
Salmon
Boaz
Obed
King David
Solomon
Rehoboam
Abijah
Asa
Jehoshaphat
Jehoram
Ahaziah
Joash
Amaziah
Uzziah
Jotham
Ahaz
Hezekiah
Manasseh
Amon
Josiah

Hamutal	—	Jehoahaz
ZebidahNehus	—	Jeconiah
Nehusta	—	Jehoiachin
Hamital	—	Shealtiel
Zebidah	—	Zerubbabel

Abihud
Eliakim
Azor
Zadok
Akim
Elihud
Eleazar
Matthan
Jacob
Joseph; *the husband
of Mary; the mother of
Jesus; who is called the
Messiah.* (Matt 1:16)

Chapter 13

Midlife Crisis (Read 2 Kings 24&25, Ezra 1-5, Haggai 2 & Zech 4)

'God isn't looking for people of great faith,
but for individuals ready to follow him.' Hudson Taylor

The Magnificent Seven

These seven young bucks were the crème de la crème of British society. They were Cambridge educated; lived in big country houses with rolling parklands; one a baronet, one a world famous sportsman. Each could have looked forward to a life of cocktail parties, dances, polo, croquet and evenings at the opera. They need not have worked if they did not wish it, for they were from the landed classes, the old families. Their lives were every boy's dream, and every girl's too; they could do whatever, and marry whoever they liked – the world was their oyster. They might have basked in the full light of civilization's glory for they were on the top rung of the most progressive industrial society on earth. They were born into it, they were born for it, groomed and preened for it – an empire that was one of the greatest the world had ever seen, on which the sun never set.

But like fools they turned their backs on it all, every last stinking drop of it. The sun never set on it because it had never risen.

For them it was James Hudson Taylor's testimony that broke up the party; they heard his call for China and they said yes.

How could they not? How could we not, when today five out of six people today are unbelievers, having no hope unless missionaries go to them and plant a church? Besides, Taylor himself had a way of phrasing things, 'The Great Commission is not an option to be considered; it is a command to be obeyed.' And Taylor was not an armchair pioneer; even if you have never read another biography you really should read his. 'If I had 1,000 lives,' he said, 'I'd give them all for China'. Words that make me weep every time I read them; boy, did he know how to give the one he had – and so did they. The renowned cricketer was Charles T. Studd, whose family, friends and country were aghast that he threw away his sporting future to go and live like a savage; 'what a shocking waste'. But after his little brother George was taken ill Charles said, 'What is all the fame and flattery worth ... when a man comes to face eternity?... I know that cricket would not last, and honour would not last, and nothing in this world would last, but it was worth while living for the world to come.' And so he did; further offending the pious pretensions of his critics by encouraging a counter-cultural youth movement, whose attitude to worldly success and riches was summed up in the initials D.C.D, 'Don't Care a Damn'. You can imagine how that went down in late Victorian England; amongst the cult of empire, progress and reform, it would sound almost treasonous. In fact he would be barred from most churches today, F.R.O.G. (Fully reliant on God) and W.W.J.D. (What would Jesus do?) are about as revolutionary as we get! But they had found the real pearl of great price and they, as Jesus advised, had 'destroyed' their lives - as far as this world's measure is concerned - to find it. The Cambridge Seven, as they became known, toured the universities and towns of England. Even the story of their departure became an international best seller, inspiring not just British men and women to answer the call but also many Americans.

Their further exploits are the stuff of legends.

The Pampered Prince

There is a close match for the Cambridge Seven in the Bible. It is not a story that is widely preached but its leading hero was in an identical situation to them and Zerubbabel made the same choices. His name means 'son of Babylon' because that is where he was born. It is in the times of the exile when Manasseh's and all of Judah's sins had led to a wholesale kidnap and deportation of the nation. The words of the prophets came true; even Moses had foreseen it, and now here they were, hundreds of miles from Jerusalem and seemingly a million miles from the purposes of God. It wasn't his fault that his family had been such a bunch of screw-ups, (no more than it is ours), but he grew up in a vastly different world than his great, great grandfather Josiah for he grew up as a captive prince in Babylon.

That Great City

Babylon is *the* thing in the modern world at that time; the irresistible force of history, the empire that will outlast all others (or so it seems), as far as anyone knows, they will go on to conquer the Greeks and beyond until all the known world will rest under the city's administration, the government of which will have no end.

To live there was to be at the very centre of the empire's purpose, the centre of world events, the centre of world history. To many, the memory of King David and Solomon's quaint, little empire on the other side of the river was a tale to tell children. You might have been considered a first class lunatic if you still clung to the promises God made to David and Abraham, that their lineage would one day rule the world. The very notion of an empire where God ruled the earth forever through his chosen lineage, the 'seed' from David, may have seemed now to be beyond myth or fairytale. I would guess that too the majority that these things must now be treated as 'symbolic and allegorical', for now Babylon was the master of all she surveyed, Marduk (their god) the great creator and king of the universe, who had given victory and dominion to Nebuchadnezzar. All other gods and ideologies must either abide peacefully under her wing as overlord or be crushed under her feet. Pliny says, 'It was the greatest city the sun ever shone upon.' Another Roman historian called Strabo said, 'Its walls, 300 feet high and 75 feet wide, enclosed an area of 225 square miles. Its temples, palaces, fortresses, brazen gates, quays, artificial mountains and lakes, made it one of the Seven Wonders of the World.'

Robert Koldeway confirmed all this in his fourteen-year dig at the turn of the century; a 14 mile outer section of wall, 136.5 feet thick; masses of gates and towers, the best being the southern Ishtar gate (now in Berlin); two enormous ziggurats on the right and left as you go in;, the temple of Marduk on the right, the famed tower of Babel on the left. Further on he discovered the hanging gardens of Babylon (a mountain-like zoo that Nebuchadnezzar had built for his Persian wife, but where he himself would be an inmate for seven years until he acknowledged the God of Daniel to be supreme). And though the Jews traded, they could not sing again; even though the Babylonian court desired to assimilate their music into their own repertoires, still the Jews could not sing. For that generation had seen such unspeakable atrocities done to their families in war that they hung their instruments up on the trees near that great river and wept (Psalm 137). Each time they tried to remember Zion, all they could see was their sons, daughters, grandsons and granddaughters, as babies having their brains dashed against the city wall by the invading forces. They were broken, for there is no calamity like the one you know you have brought upon your own family. They had become more vile in the eyes of their God than the nations he had helped them eject in the first place.

Bonny Princes

The calamity and spiritual desolation of the nation can be epitomized in the lives of two men, brothers and princes, of the house of Judah. For do not forget, if the captivity was a national catastrophe for Israel, it was ten times greater a calamity and tragedy for the royal house of Judah, who had led the people into idolatry, rebellion and bloodshed. The first brother I have alluded to above, is Zerubbabel 'the son of Babylon', the other is Shimei. They were not kept in a dungeon, but rather like the Saudi princes you see in their flash cars, these brothers and their families were financed by the royal treasury, part of the largess of the king's bounty. And so here they were; pretend princes suckled by a wicked, pagan empire; lackeys and trophies to Babylon's proud conquest. I wonder whether they believed the stories about Daniel, Shadrach, Meshach and Abednego? I would imagine they had met these venerable old men in person - why not? Certainly Daniel was still alive. Had they heard his stories, read his prophecies? Had these inspired them to be more than just paper princes, desire more than just synthetic freedoms?

Maybe, maybe not; but one scroll which they must have read (as it was available to Ezra) contained Jeremiah's prophecies, for he had sent these as letters to Babylon. Why is this significant? Well, because in Jeremiah 22:24–30 it clearly spells out God's punishment on their family due to their grandfather's sin, *'for no man of his seed shall prosper, sitting upon the throne of David, and ruling any more in Judah'*. Basically, one thing was for certain, no matter what dreams they cherished about their futures they would never again wear a crown in Israel.

I think we could draw a striking parallel to the royal house of Stuart and the sad demise of James II's son and grandson. This summer I was four inches away from a lock of Bonny Prince Charlie's hair. He was the grandson of James II. I also saw a real letter written by his own hand to the Clan lords inviting them to Glenfinnan for the raising of the Stuart Standard on the 19th June 1745. But the great tragedy for Charles Edward was not the want of arms or personal valour, but that when that he reached Derby, he and his generals all knew that the English people, and even many of his native Scots, did not wish to own the Bonny Prince as king. And considering his family's track record you cannot blame them. Like Bonny Prince Charlie, Zerubbabel and Shimei had been born in exile, possibly even imprisoned for the first years of their lives. Their grandfather was the very same King Jeconiah who had finally lost the throne, and like Bonny Prince Charlie, Zerubbabel and Shimei's own father wasn't up to much either. But unlike the Bonny Prince – who ended his days as a washed–up drunk in Rome – these two would not be so self seeking and vainglorious as to lead the people they professed to love into a needless and bloody civil war, for at least Shimei and Zerubbabel knew that *their* exile was a punishment from God.

I think these brothers were where many of us are today; we're born again into the royal house and yet we are not experiencing the fullness and authority of our birthright. We are commissioned to be fruitful by an all-providing God and yet somehow become sterile eunuchs to our careers and our desire for luxury. Sometimes Deborah's taunt from Judges 5 comes hard upon us, for we are all too tempted to be like Reuben, Dan, Gilead and Asher; when the call for battle is sounded.

> 'And the princes of Issachar were with Deborah and Barak: They went on foot into the valley. Reuben's warriors did a lot of thinking about it but eventually remained to skulk among the sheepfolds....the men of Gilead stayed beyond Jordan (because it was too far to come), and why did Dan cower in ships pretending it was business as usual? Asher was hanging out by the sea, lying on the beach!. Whereas the warriors of Zebulun and Naphtali laid their lives on the line in the battle'   exerts from Judges 5 v15–18

The meanings of these brothers' names are also significant to us, for they help us identify our own dilemma in a modern age. Shimei means 'fame' or 'to be noticed' and this certainly describes the driving motivation for most of us, to be significant and honoured by our peers. As I have already said Zerubbabel means 'son of Babylon', and we can surely identify here. Yes, we may be called and renamed as citizens of heaven, kings and priests in an eternal empire of an almighty God, sons even of the highest God; but how our earthly sonship is also felt at every waking hour. How keen the adversary is to remind us of our carnality and worldly temptations: 'Sons of God! Hah! If ever there was a worldling it is you, you think more about fancy houses and cars and foreign holidays than ever you do about spiritual things; you're a hypocrite and a liar.' The question is, would Zerubbabel conform to the name his family and culture had given him? Would this son of Babylon ever stand up and look for something more? Of course the question hits us with equal power. Now maybe these guys just ambled along enjoying city life and a bit of mild celebrity status in the most cosmopolitan city on the globe, where there were doubtless career opportunities in the multicultural court. Maybe, maybe not; for if they had any ambitions beyond the party culture, they kept them well hidden, that is until the day everything in their world was turned upside down. A royal decree from the new king would divide the family and even the brothers in two.

The Magnificent Decision

> 'Now in the first year of Cyrus king of Persia, that the word of the
> LORD by the mouth of Jeremiah might be fulfilled, the LORD stirred
> up the spirit of Cyrus king of Persia, that he made a proclamation
> throughout all his kingdom, and put it also in writing, saying, Thus
> saith Cyrus king of Persia, The LORD God of heaven hath given me
> all the kingdoms of the earth; and he hath charged me to build him a
> house at Jerusalem, which is in Judah. Who is there among you of all
> his people? his God be with him, and let him go up to Jerusalem, which
> is in Judah, and build the house of the LORD God of Israel, (he is the
> God,) which is in Jerusalem.' Ezra 1:1-3

Zerubbabel's dilemma and decision was aptly framed by Jo Strummer from the
Clash, 'Should I stay or should I go?'
What would you do if you were them; seriously?
Give it all up, however shallow and phoney it may be, to go and live in a burnt
out rubble mound? To down-grade your lifestyle and standard of living to go
to a place where God has expressly sworn that neither you nor your children
will ever rule as kings? To expose your wife and children to all that
uncertainty, danger, disease, and discomfort? And for what? A city that many
said would never be blessed by God again, even if someone was so mad as to
go all the way back and try to rebuild it.

Would you go? Risk it all to go back west? Does it sound familiar?

Yes, of course it does, Abraham, Rebekah, Rachel, Leah and even Ruth, all
made the decision to take their lives in their hands and go west with God.
And when push comes to shove, for every one who'll go with God there will
always be a thousand who'll stay in easy street, content in suburbia. Abraham
and Sarah went, Nahor did the sensible thing and stayed behind; Lot went,
his cousins stayed behind; Rebekah went, her brother Laban stayed behind;
Ruth went, Orphah stayed. And so too in this case; Shimei stayed in Babylon
but his brother Zerubbabel, however useless he felt, however hopeless he felt
the cause and his place in it, went for the good of his people.

And the ones who go travelling with God, stay in his story; the ones who stay
put, don't.

I could quite imagine that Shimei was more intelligent, gifted, and even more
religious than his brother, but simply put, like the two sons in Jesus' parable,
it's the ones who go in obedience that matter. Remember what Gladys
Aylward said, 'I wasn't God's first choice for what I've done for China … I

don't know who it was ... It must have been a man ... a well-educated man. I don't know what happened. Perhaps he died. Perhaps he wasn't willing ... and God looked down ... and saw Gladys Aylward ... And God said – "Well, she's willing." '

What about us, what might it take to rouse us to live beyond a Christianized version of what our neighbours live for? Hey, my life's not so bad here, you say, but that's the whole point, in Babylon as in the Matrix, they want you to feel like you still have it all. Ezra saw through the *Matrix* and said that life on that side of the river was still slavery.

Would a man love his chains though they be of gold?

Will we need a big life-shaking event before we realize that real life is happening now and this is not a dress rehearsal? I wonder what Zerubbabel would say to us today? Probably the same as another rich kid called Francis Xavier who gave up his castle and privileged lifestyle to be a Catholic missionary to Asia. He sent word back to Europe, 'Tell the students to give up their small ambitions and come eastward to preach the gospel of Christ.'

The Magnificent Adventure

In the 1960 film, *The Magnificent Seven*, Steve McQueen's character looks out across the plains and mocks, 'Riding out there in all that dust and heat ... what a chucklehead.' To which Yul Brynner replies, 'Yep. Not smart like us.' I bet there were plenty of armchair sages who watched the Cambridge Seven depart for China who said similar things. And I also bet there were plenty of Jews in Babylon who did too. But once again history would not belong to those timid souls, but to the men and women who travelled with Jehovah, either to the rubble of Jerusalem or the rice fields of China.

C.T. Studd famously said, 'Some want to live within the sound of church or chapel bell; I want to run a rescue shop within a yard of hell'; and I think that was Zerubbabel's heart too. It is a heart that shares in the mission and anguish of God, and in this Zerubbabel is much like Nehemiah, Cyrus' Jewish cup bearer, who also gave up the easy court life to follow God west. These men had every conceivable reason to stay for there was much good they could do in the east, much influence for good they could exert in government circles. They were in effect like Richard Stearns, a corporate CEO with a call of God to use his gifts in a different arena. Richard is now the president of World Vision which has 40,000 staff in 100 different countries. His award winning bio-story *The Whole in our Gospel* (though overstating one aspect of Jesus' commission) became a best seller in 2010 causing many Christians to think and act more deeply about Jesus call to minister to the poor. Zerubbabel took the plunge, so did Nehemiah, so did Richard; they decided to let God's agenda – God's anguished heart, impact theirs. Perhaps you will too. It might well be that God has called you to be a Daniel where you are in your situation; no one is despising that. But then again you might be reading this and feeling a twinge that you were actually made and trained by God for something else, something beyond Babylon, somewhere out there in the danger and the rubble. You will know if it is you, because you will be insanely jealous of the great missionaries you read about, terrified witless if God ever called you to something like that, but also dissatisfied deep down with your career and Christian experience. If that is you friend then you need to start praying and fasting – there is not a moment to lose. Whether Jesus sends you to tramps in your city, the old folks' homes in your own neighbourhood, or the Auca Indians it is really not your business to do any more than say 'even so Lord, let your will be done.'

If you can truly say this, and follow through, then you will join a very great company of pilgrims. Zerubbabel did too for he did not travel alone. First there were the 'magnificent' nine elders who went with him and then the other 42,360 whom Ezra says had *their hearts stirred by God'* (Ezra 1v5). But as with so much of the real Christian ministry there was no crown for Zerubbabel, just the job description, 'governor'. I think this point is more important now than ever, when it is possible to have stardom inside the church. Rather than being counter–culture the church has created a ghastly subculture; scorned by heaven and unbelieving men alike. As a writer and musician I feel this temptation perhaps more than most, but have found real help in Jeremiah 45v5. Here God sends Jeremiah to speak to his friend with the message that – because of the urgency of the hour – it was certainly not the time to seek 'great things' for himself, and also that – as a reward for his faithfulness – he would have his life spared. It was not the time to 'seek great things', because their culture – like ours – was on the brink of judgement and destruction. Ezekiel 33v9 says pretty much the same thing and we pastors, worship leaders and writers need to take heed; the hour is very late for western civilisation, and we must resist every urge for personal glory on earth. There will be no, 'well done good and *famous* servant' on that great day; brothers and sisters the temptation here is almost insurmountable without constant prayer and grace. In this Zerubbabel is a good mentor.

The journey itself must have seemed epic enough; they retraced the Journey of Abraham, Rebecca and Jacob around the fertile crescent for eight hundred miles. They spent the first seven months getting their houses and farms established, and afterwards gathered as one man to start worship. Kingdom work is always 'within a yard of hell' and their mission was no exception. They were already experiencing Satanically inspired oppression (manifested through the hostility of their neighbours), but it did not intimidate them from celebrating the feast of Tabernacles (significantly the one feast that looks forward to the coming king).

The temple at this time was just an altar on a pile of rubble – no temple foundations even, but they worshipped and offered sacrifices. Perhaps you are reading this now, and you too feel that your life, your family, your business is no more than a pile of rubble. I know this advice will seem trite in your current pain, but please clear some of that rubble away and erect an altar of praise as Zerubbabel did. When Richard Wurmbrand was first jailed by the Communists in Romania, he felt challenged by the verse where Jesus said that when we are slandered and persecuted we should *'rejoice and leap for joy, for great is your reward.'* Richard, emaciated half to death as he was, did just this in solitary confinement and soon started to feel the benefits. In fact a guard, thinking he was starting to go mad, brought him more food! But back to the building of this altar in Jerusalem remember it is the altar that makes the temple. That is why the date of that first sacrifice was carefully recorded because it would be crucial to Daniel's predictions of Jesus' first coming and death.

After this great start they contacted the builder's merchants down at Tyre and Sidon, set up an account and have cedar logs delivered. But then something happened; the building work stopped before even the foundations were laid. Part of my professional life has been spent managing construction sites, not an easy business at the best of times, and not something that comes naturally to me. Phrases like contract management, construction design, management regulations, site health and safety protocol, critical path analysis and project deadlines all bring me out in cold sweats in the small hours of the night. When you take your designs and apply them to the real world of unreasonable suppliers and unreliable contractors, anything and everything can go wrong. I remember one park I was building where I was responsible for the health and safety of over fifty contractors, and one of them disregarded site protocol and used his JCB to rip up a gas main. The police sectioned off the neighbourhood and miraculously no one was killed. I know what it is like to have funding pulled or restricted, to have clients freak out and lose it in front of public officials, to have friends injured, vandals joy-ride site machinery, to have 'no win, no fee' solicitors hound you, to have government authorities stop work; in fact I've even been physically assaulted and had my life threatened in the process of trying to get parks and houses built. I've also seen months of work disappear because of one night's vandalism. Anyone can dream, draw plans and make construction schedules; I once prepared an urban planning strategy for a government agency, complete with a ten year funding strategy. The grand vision for the river corridor of retail, industrial and residential developments, parks, bridges, museums and playgrounds has so far not gone further than my fancy document. Most of my work these days revolves around clicking and typing on a computer; and if this is you too, then make no mistake, there is a vast difference between planning, typing and clicking – and actually building something, in this physical, fallen world.

Zerubbabel's experience would be no different, and after a good start, there was a sixteen month delay when nothing happened. Satan's mode of attack had shifted from the dragon to the serpent; but what exactly could it be that would take these – the elite, committed, Holy Ghost-fired, purpose-driven saints – from doing the will of God?

Was it fear, oppression or a financial shortfall? A plague or sickness perhaps? Did their overlords in Babylon over-tax them to the point that they had no time for the Lord's work? Were they just too busy trying to get by that their chief ministry on earth had to take a back seat? I hear that all the time – so was that it? I wish it were any of those but shamefully it was not. Wow, must be a major league sin; pornography, no, video games? No Surely not soap operas or 'X Factor' and 'Big Brother'? Worry? Vice? Bitterness? None of these; have you guessed yet? You should have, because it is the number one distraction that has the whole world consumed almost all their adult lives, as on a treadmill; that most can only achieve at retirement age. Any offers? For surely it is as deadly as it is ancient, if it can incapacitate God's people and render them too busy for obedience. It is not apparent from Ezra's account – written seventy odd years later – for he simply says, they were ready to build and a year and half later they started. You have to go to the prophet Haggai to find out why they wasted eighteen months.

> *'Is it time for you, O ye, to dwell in your cedar panelled houses, and this house lie waste?'* (Haggai 1:4)

In their case it was a craze for cedar panelled houses; for us it may be a similar obsession with houses; whether it be a little cottage in the country or a bigger, penthouse flat on the waterfront. It's not that God didn't want them to have nice houses; he'd given them seven months to get straight, but when this began to take over their lives it was time to send in the prophets – to whom, fortunately, on this occasion they responded. It was now that the neighbours (whom we would later call Samaritans), who basically had been settled in the land for seventy plus years, were not chuffed that the Jews had turned up to re-occupy the land since the Cyrus 'declaration' (a strange prefigurement of the Balfour declaration in modern times.) They are initially menacing, but when the Jews get their act together by laying the foundation and shouting a great shout, these guys turn up on Zerubbabel's doorstep,

> '... Let us build with you: for we seek your God, as ye do ...' Ezra 4:-2

Now we've already seen that God isn't a racist and that he's accepted Gentiles into his army (Uriah the Hittite), his nation (Caleb), and even into the royal lineage (Ruth the asylum seeker and Rahab the prostitute), but this was something different. These guys were adversaries (literally 'Satans'), they were just there to cause trouble. It might surprise us that Satan would bother with this tactic, but I can assure you from long and painful experience, one carnal 'so-called believer' can destroy a Christian fellowship from the inside, through gossip and squabbling, more easily than a thousand praying witches and warlocks. Or at least he or she can wear out the oversight and members to a point where they lose focus on what they are supposed to be doing in the first place. Zerubbabel sees through the ploy and shows them the door, and it is only after this that we see their true colours.

> 'Ye have nothing to do with us to build an house unto our God; but we ourselves together will build unto the LORD God of Israel, as king Cyrus the king of Persia hath commanded us. Then the people of the land weakened the hands of the people of Judah, and troubled them in building.' Ezra 4:-3-4

These adversaries kept up their opposition all through the reigns of Cyrus, then Ahasuerus (the one married to Esther) and finally in Artaxerxes' reign, got the 'king of kings' in Babylon to halt the work by a royal decree. The little men triumphantly presented their court order and their weapons and made Zerubbabel stop. The delay was so serious and long that he now started to feel that he would never see the end of it. At times he felt weak and afraid, that the job was just too daunting for him; so much so that the prophets would come again with the encouragement to 'be strong and build for God is on **your** side'. Like Timothy, and many of us, the need to 'fan the flames' of the gifting we have, is all too necessary when we feel the task is too great. Hudson Taylor's encouragement to our inadequacy, is that 'God uses men who are weak and feeble enough to lean on him.' In fact Taylor once credited his fruitfulness to his inadequacy, 'I am weaker than most men and find I have to pray about things that most men wouldn't have to pray about.' (If you read no other biography then please read the 'Biography of James Hudson Taylor' by Howard Taylor and Mrs Howard Taylor.)

Zechariah's prophetic encouragement to Zerubbabel has been widely used to encourage us all with the mountains we face.

'This is the word of the LORD unto Zerubbabel, saying, Not by might, nor by power, but by my spirit, saith the LORD of hosts. Who art thou, O great mountain? before Zerubbabel thou shalt become a plain: and he shall bring forth the headstone thereof with shoutings, crying, Grace, grace unto it. Moreover the word of the LORD came unto me, saying, The hands of Zerubbabel have laid the foundation of this house; his hands shall also finish it; and thou shalt know that the LORD of hosts hath sent me unto you.' Zec 4:6-9

God help us become encouragers that lift up the *'weak hands and trembling knees'* of those around us. Truly great men and women are great because of the effect they have on others. The actor and director Orson Welles – a man who said he could remember every encouraging word spoken to him – was deeply impacted when he saw General Marshall leave the hub of a party to talk to a young soldier who had accidentally stepped into the room by accident. Rather than ignore or chide the lad, the General spent ten minutes encouraging him on a sofa in the corner of the room. If we are too busy for this sort of ministry then frankly we are too busy. The ministry of Jesus was to be a 'light to those who sit in great darkness', that is those who have ceased to stand, but sit in the darkness of despair and depression. It must be our ministry too. That promise about the headstone has been taken by some to mean that the spirit of God would mightily come upon Zerubbabel and, like Samson, he would receive strength to manually put the final, massive stone in place. I wouldn't make a doctrine of it, but I confess I like that thought; really like it.

The Magnificent Rebellion

I also really like the way the Lord recalls Zerubbabel and his people to work even though they haven't received any go ahead from the government (Ezra Ch 5). Sometimes you just have to obey God and not men, but it could be a costly rebellion for Zerubbabel, as he was the man in charge. They start to rebuild without 'planning permission' and it isn't long before the 'building inspector' and 'enforcement officers' turn up. After an exchange of correspondence and a search of the historical records, Zerubbabel gets not only a retrospective consent but also a generous government subsidy.

But even then, this did not make Zerubbabel sit back and hire project managers, for one of Zechariah's revelations was that heaven itself rejoiced to have him actually on site with a spirit level. A curious observation you might think, but it is a profound one. When I project manage a park or an engineering operation for a client the buck stops with me: I'm the one on site making sure every contractor is building his stuff straight, (i.e. building it to last). I'm checking the angles of embankments, the depth of concrete, the health of the plant stock or root balls of imported trees, the quality of the workmanship etc. If the work is not up to the job and I sign it off, it's me the client will be suing and rightly so. In fact he can sue me even decades after the job is finished and everyone's walked away with their money. Zerubbabel's client – the Lord – is always on site (the type of client that every sloppy project manager dreads), and God sees what maybe no one else sees: how much care Zerubbabel is putting into the detail (and therefore longevity) of the project. God loves people like that but let's be honest, when most of Christian work is hidden from public applause, it is a major temptation to cut corners; a quick prayer, a sloppy sermon, a rushed Sunday school lesson. At the time when I first drafted this manuscript, I had written six books with none published, but with the sure call of God to keep at it. Often we must sow in faith, but let us sow good seed; let us see it all for what it really is – eternally important.

If his diligence was widely known can you think of a more powerful encouragement to the other workers – 'even the royal family are mucking in, so it must be important'? One thing I love about Winston Churchill was his enlisting in the Grenadier Guards after the Dardanelles debacle. The former cabinet minister headed to the mud, blood, shells, mustard gas, rats and lice of the trenches, as little above a private soldier. By all accounts (not just his own) Churchill was an extreme success – and his men loved and admired him. Churchill was very hands-on, personally courageous, unconventional, sociable, nothing was too much trouble for the former cabinet minister – he trained his men thoroughly and even used humour to chivvy them along when they were depressed and exhausted.

God give us such a heart to be what our generation needs.

When the temple was finally completed the problems did not stop there, for some people complained that what God was doing was just too small. The temple was pitifully small compared to what Solomon had built and the old men cried when they saw it (Ezra 3v2). I knew a dear, old, Pentecostal lady who would forever be going on about how great things were, under the wonderful Carters and Jeffries brothers. I knew another older guy who never stopped brow beating me with the great puritan and reform theologians. In neither case were they trying to attain anything pure or powerful like their heroes, but rather using them to berate those who were trying to head that way. We may never raise the dead – but whatever we may be, let us be it by the grace of God, to the glory of God, without regret or compromise. It is too easy to pour cold water on godly endeavour; I have received at least ten times the discouragement from Christians as I have encouragement. Fortunately the encouragement has come from people who know what they are talking about, which made it easier to disregard the rest. And so too Haggai brings Zerubbabel what he needs. God says, in effect 'Don't worry about the size that you see with your eyes, for this temple will be filled with a glory that will outshine even Solomon's temple.'

Now we know exactly what to look for when God's glory or 'outshining' appears, for it came down and rested on the tabernacle in the wilderness and also when Solomon prayed at the dedication of the first temple. The glory was like a thick cloud of awesome brilliance that would descend. So, according to Haggai, we should be expecting something significantly more spectacular than this glory cloud to come on Zerubbabel's temple. But at the dedication of this temple, all that happened was a general experience of joy. So what happened – was it all just talk? Religious soap? The answer is, of course, that Haggai did not specify when: but we know of a day when the glory of God actually walked into that temple with human feet. Malachi saw it in vision too:

> '... and the Lord, whom ye seek, shall suddenly come to his temple, even the messenger of the covenant, whom ye delight in: behold, he shall come, saith the LORD of hosts. But who may abide the day of his coming? and who shall stand when he appeareth? For he is like a refiner's fire, and like fullers' soap: And he shall sit as a refiner and purifier of silver ...' Mal 3:1-3

Yes, that's right, Jesus is the glory of God and it was not just his wisdom that was greater than Solomon's but also his physical presence was greater than that shekinah cloud that descended on his temple. It certainly helps make sense of John's talk of the light shining in the darkness.

> 'That was the true Light (literally: real light), which lighteth every man that cometh into the world. He was in the world, and the world was made by him, and the world knew him not. He came unto his own, and his own received him not. But as many as received him, to them gave he power to become the sons of God, even to them that believe on his name: Which were born, not of blood, nor of the will of the flesh, nor of the will of man, but of God. And the Word was made flesh, and dwelt among us, (and we beheld his glory, the glory as of the only begotten of the Father,) full of grace and truth.' John 1:9-14

But, you might say, didn't Jesus come to Herod's temple? Partly true, but remember, Herod's temple would actually not be fully completed for years after Jesus was there and also remember that it was the same altar, and it is the altar that makes the temple.

The Magnificent Promise

To me, the personal story of Zerubbabel's troubles and winning through, is at the centre of Israel's national re-emergence.

Like so many before, Zerubbabel left the comforts of the east and threw in his lot with the pilgrim people of God. He played the best role he could in an imperfect situation. In choosing a different path to his brother, the path of difficulty and obscurity with God's people, Zerubbabel is not only rewarded by being the great x10 grandfather of Joseph, the legal father of Jesus, but also something more. You will remember that

prophecy from Jeremiah, that his grandfather's family would never rule; well, in that same prophecy God speaks of *his very own* signet ring, saying that *'even though Jeconiah ... wear the signet ring upon my right hand, yet would I pull it off and chuck it away'*. The signet ring was the symbol of delegated authority; for example, in the book of Esther, Haman brags that the King has given his signet ring to him, that is he is trusted with the ultimate executive power.

This prophecy and the humble position in which Zerubbabel finds himself must have been a daily reminder of all that his family had lost and all he could never be. And that is why it is all the more powerful when God makes a promise, as it is as personal to him as it is unique in history. Have you ever wondered what your job will be when Jesus returns to this planet? We know our nine-to-five lives are the testing ground for our future employment in the kingdom, but exactly what that will be is unknown to everyone. Everyone, that is except Zerubbabel:

> 'In that day, (the day after God has shaken the heavens and the earth) says the Lord of heaven's armies, I will take thee, Oh Zerubbabel, my servant, ... and I will give you my signet ring: for I have tested you ...'
> Haggai 2:23

My prayer for you and me is that we would have such a testimony and such a reward. Friend, you may be tried like Zerubbabel, and life may appear like mountains on every side, but remember Job - who testified that even when no one else could see his heart, that, God *'knoweth the way that I take and when he hath tried me, I shall come forth as gold'*. God knew the hard road Zerubbabel travelled, and knows yours too; take courage and don't back down. Not ever. Everything Zerubbabel did was just training; like Churchill in the trenches, it was the preparation for something bigger in the future. For him, and for us, destiny will not wait for a convenient time when we have all the answers; in fact Churchill once said, 'The chain of destiny can only be grasped one link at a time.' Zerubbabel seized the one link he saw, and lived his life to be something precious in the hand of God; in the end he will be more than ever he dreamed. I wonder what *link* you are looking at right now? I would plead with you to take hold of it and let the adventure begin.

Nicolas Zinzendorf was a man who reminds me of Zerubbabel. He was a wealthy aristocrat muddling along until he too got a powerful call from God. The call came while he was looking at Domenico Fetti's painting 'Ecce Homo' depicting Christ with thorns pressed down upon his head and blood flowing freely. The artist's challenge was inscribed underneath, 'I have done this for you, what have you done for me?' It was a life changing moment; as Nicolas said, 'I have loved him for a long time. But I have never actually done anything for him. From now on I will do whatever he leads me to.' Like Zerubbabel, Nicolas took the plunge for Jesus; he built a town for exiled Moravian Christians, many of whom became the first foreign missionaries. When they went to the West Indies, it was not for religious freedom, but to preach Christ where his name was not known. Two of those dear brothers, men in their twenties with their lives in front of them, actually sold themselves into slavery because it was the only means by which they could reach the plantation slaves in the West Indies. Their friends and families came to wave them off for the last time from Copenhagen, and as the ship departed the two men raised their hands to heaven saying, *'may the Lamb that was slain receive the reward of his suffering.'* Nicolas would eventually go too, though only a third of those missionaries would survive more than a few years. And in effect, this was the challenge that Zerubbabel felt in Babylon – the call that Nicolas felt in front of that painting – that those two men and many like them answered with their very life blood. It is the same challenge that you and I face too. Or do we have just enough religion to keep us out of hell and let us enjoy the delights of Babylon? If so, we need to seriously question whether we've understood the first thing about the real state of our souls, the nature of sin, true repentance, and why Jesus went to the cross. Zerubbabel went, but Shimei stayed; and for every twenty people reading this book, I know that there will be only one or two who do the same, who will put their rights, their careers, their retirement, even their man–made ideas of Christian ministry, on the altar for the glory of Jesus Christ.

I pray that it is you, friend; I pray that it is me. God help us all.

Midlife Crisis
Zerubbabel's last night in Babylon

(From 'THE LINE' album, words and music by Henry Brooks)

It was a hot on the strip in Babylon that night,
The girls all looked so pretty in the desert evening light
And the boys were all dressed to party as they passed me by,
They knew that I wasn't going this time but they couldn't get just why

Because I was done with that and in the morning I'd be gone,
A man needs more than that to build his life upon,
I want to be more than this, more than what life's made me,
I want to be wholly his, something useful in God's hand

Well my family's just a big bunch of screw ups if the truth were known
The illusion that we had it together, as tragic as the way we lost the throne
But in Babylon they want you to feel like you still got it all
Paper princes and synthetic freedoms we got, and no purpose in life at all

Because I'm done with that and in the morning I was gone,
A man needs so much more to place his future on,
I want to be more than this, more than who they've named me,
I want to be wholly his, something precious in God's hand

Well of all the people brother, I was thinking you'd be coming too
Since we were kids we always did stuff together, both me and you ... But I guess all that
Luxury, security and kudos were so hard to turn down ... I'm 42 next week,
Not getting any younger, that's why I'm blowing this town ... But I tell you ...

I'm done with that now though I never saw you again,
But I chose this road less travelled to build my hopes upon,
Lord make me more than this, more than cash and bricks and mortar,
I want to be wholly yours, something special in his hand
They need to see more than this, do my wife and kids and family
To see me wholly his, something useful in his hand

And though it's been no bed of roses here, you can be sure
But his promise still holds true for me and all his ways still pure
And to be part of this beats anything they had back home

It's like I spent a lifetime searching for ... the purpose I now know ... cos

And the big shock was still to come, on the day you spoke to me,
You peeled back the veil and showed me all my life had been
Made me more than I'd dreamed, lit up a nation by my life,
You made me wholly yours, a signet ring your hand

Life Application Devotion
Chapter 13 – Building a Temple for God

- Zerubbabel won favour with God not just for his decision to return to build the temple but also in the diligent way he executed that task. Comparing yourself to him (a scale from 1–10), how dedicated and meticulous are you in 'building' (a) yourself and (b) your local church into *'a place where God can live through his Spirit'* (Eph 2:22). You should have two separate scores.
- If there is a great gulf between these scores then ask the Lord to show you how they could be higher and also nearer together. (How can I better treat my body and his body (the church) and how can I manifest a greater measure of his spirit with the time, gifting and faith he has given me.) Journal these responses adding practical notes afterwards.
- Ask a trusted friend, spouse or prayer partner to score you too and ask them if they have any godly advice to the above question.
- Prayer: (Start with thanksgiving & praise for God's immeasurable kindness in choosing and using you.) My King and Redeemer, it is my heart's desire to be the best temple possible for you to live in and through which to manifest yourself to those around me. I repent of anything; good or bad (name specifics here) that keeps me from submitting my body as a living sacrifice to you and for your church (Rom 12:1). Please show me now if there is anything else you wish to change. I thank you for hearing this prayer, Lord please give me your heart for your precious people. Show me how I can better serve them and build them up. Amen.

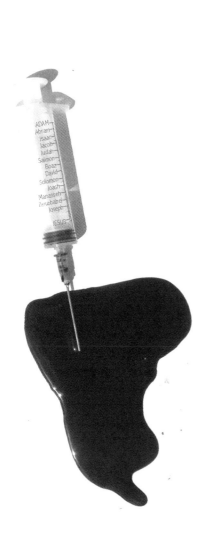

Abraham
Isaac
Jacob
Judah
Perez
Hezron
Ram
Amminadab
Nahshon
Salmon
Boaz
Obed
King David
Solomon
Rehoboam
Abijah
Asa
Jehoshaphat
Jehoram
Ahaziah
Joash
Amaziah
Uzziah
Jotham
Ahaz
Hezekiah
Manasseh
Amon
Josiah
Jehoahaz
Jeconiah
Jehoiachin
Shealtiel
Zerubbabel
Abihud
Eliakim
Azor
Zadok
Akim
Elihud
Eleazar
Matthan
Jacob

Mary —•— Joseph; *the husband
of Mary; the mother of
Jesus; who is called the
Messiah.* (Matt 1:16)

Chapter 14

The Reproach of Christ

'Preferring to be persecuted with the people of God, rather than enjoy the benefits of sin for a short time; assessing ostracism for Christ greater riches than all the treasure troves in Egypt: for he was looking far forward to the final payout.' Heb 11:25-26

By this chapter we have travelled the length of the Old Testament arriving at that point in history when 'the time' really 'had fully come'; the time – as we saw in the last chapter – when a greater glory than had descended on Solomon's temple would enter Zerubabel's.

We've travelled from Mesopotamia to Canaan, Canaan to Egypt, Egypt to Canaan, Canaan to Babylon and back again. It has taken over a period of 2000 years to reach the point in history when all things are now ready. And now, at the end, or rather the beginning, God brings two members of David's descendants – one Joseph, a descendant of his son Nathan; and one Mary, a descendant of Solomon – to be the parents (or foster parent in Joseph's case) of his own Son. God promised David that he would raise up *seed* from David's own body, and that it would be this single descendant who would be *'the one who will build a house for my Name,'* and that God would *'establish the throne of his kingdom forever'* (2 Sam 7:12-13).

Solomon was only a foreshadowing of this promise, but by no means its fulfilment; of course he could never reign forever, for one thing. In this chapter I want to tease out the chronology of Jesus' birth, which reveals that the family did not initially return to Nazareth after the census and birth; why not? We will also examine the character traits of Joseph and Mary and learn what we can from them. And there is plenty – on both sides of this (probably) teenaged couple – as they do, like so many we have seen before in this story, esteem, *'the reproach of Christ greater riches than the treasures in Egypt.'* In their case they would actually see him, *'the root growing up out of dry ground'* right there in Bethlehem, Egypt and Nazareth. What an immense privilege to be chosen. What did they do so right to be used in such a tremendous way? We'll find out in this chapter, and more than that, we'll also see the cost associated with preparing your life to be used by God.

But first some familiar scriptures from Matthew and Luke to get us started:

> '*This is how the birth of Jesus Christ came about: His mother Mary was pledged to be married to Joseph, but before they came together, she was found to be with child through the Holy Spirit. Because Joseph her husband was a righteous man and did not want to expose her to public disgrace, he had in mind to divorce her quietly. After he had considered this, an angel of the Lord appeared to him in a dream and said, "Joseph son of David, do not be afraid to take Mary home as your wife, because what is conceived in her is from the Holy Spirit. She will give birth to a son, and you are to give him the name Jesus, because he will save his people from their sins." All this took place to fulfil what the Lord had said through the prophet: "The virgin will be with child and will give birth to a son, and they will call him Immanuel"* – *which means, "God with us." When Joseph woke up, he did what the angel of the Lord had commanded him and took Mary home as his wife. But he had no union with her until she gave birth to a son. And he gave him the name Jesus*'.
> Matthew 1:18–25

> '*In those days Caesar Augustus issued a decree that a census should be taken of the entire Roman world. (This was the first census that took place while Quirinius was governor of Syria.) And everyone went to his own town to register. So Joseph also went up from the town of Nazareth in Galilee to Judea, to Bethlehem the town of David, because he belonged to the house and line of David. He went there to register with Mary, who was pledged to be married to him and was expecting a child. While they were there, the time came for the baby to be born, and she gave birth to her firstborn, a son. She wrapped him in cloths and placed him in a manger, because there was no room for them in the inn.*'
> Luke 2:1–7

The Setting

When we come to look at Joseph and Mary, we come to look at two exceptional people. God would not let just anyone raise his Son. They were most probably what we would call 'teenagers'. Girls were married off shortly after puberty; we could speculate that Joseph may have been a tad older because he has a trade. The concept of the 'teenager' is a creation of the modern age and I would recommend the '*Do Hard Things*' book by the Harris brothers, if you are a teenager or want to inspire one. Those guys have formed a whole ministry around a 'Teenage Rebelution against Low Expectations' and they have really hit the spot for their generation.

We start in Nazareth but Joseph had likely been born in Bethlehem, sixty-five miles to the south. His family are thought to have moved to Nazareth sometime during his youth, perhaps so their construction business would prosper nearer to the new town, Decapolis, which was being built. It is here Joseph meets Mary, and where the marriage is arranged. Engagement in those days was a binding contract, nearly as binding as marriage is in our day, indeed perhaps more so. That is why Joseph is called Mary's 'husband' (and Mary is called his 'wife'), even before their marriage was consummated (Matthew 1:19-20). An engagement was so binding that it could only be dissolved by divorce. And so these two young people were living in Nazareth, a conservative religious town, perhaps not unlike Salem, Massachusetts where, under the stifling oppression of religious blindness, men and women were executed for supposed witchcraft. When you read accounts of those trials you can get a feel for how controlling a tight knit, religious community can be, and the pressure it can bring to bear on those who find themselves on the wrong side of the line. As Wesley reminds us, even Christian communities can be 'as orthodox as the devil and just as wicked'.

Mary – A Model of Godly Womanhood

Mary was Already Seeking God's Favour

And the angel said unto her, Fear not, Mary: for thou hast found favour with God (Luke 1:30). It is true that we can find favour with God (the Greek here is 'charis', sometimes translated as 'grace') just because of his unmerited kindness, but in Mary's case it is implied elsewhere that there was something about Mary's life and heart that allowed God to make her the one, the most blessed of all women ever born. Let us look at some of these things and see if we can benefit from them.

A Shoot Out of Dry Ground

Nazareth was located along the main highway that was travelled by caravans going from Damascus to the Mediterranean sea ports. Some young girls courted affairs with merchants as they travelled the main road through Nazareth. They fixed ribbons in their hair and flirted with wealthy men. In this way Nazareth was a religious community under attack in a war of cultures, the old patriarchal Jewish religion versus the modern, cosmopolitan Roman empire. When you are under occupation it must have been hard to keep telling the children, 'Ah yes, but these Gentile dogs are all just scum that Messiah will sweep away when he comes, so don't you learn their ways or you will share their fate.' To which they must have asked, or at least thought, 'But Dad, why do you keep paying them then?' Of course Judaism looked impotent under that sort of tyranny and I am sure there were many quislings like Zacchaeus and Matthew who switched allegiance. But not so the community, who would increasingly turn in on itself, devoid of any power other than criticizing the Romans and each other. It might remind you of some churches, and it is certainly a hard place to grow up with any empowerment and vision.

The Fount of Liberty

But amazingly it is exactly this fount of liberty that Mary has in abundance. She is not just physically pure; there is a responsive vitality to her submission, that reveals a heart that has not been polluted by the peer culture of the town. Where does this come from? Well we must give some credit to her parents, for we assume she grew up in her parents' home. Their job as 'gatekeepers' must have been well done indeed. Not just – in doing as Song of Songs 8:8 suggests – *building a wall around her* to protect her chastity but also in protecting her from the cold moralism that would later be used as the very rod to bruise her and her son. But I also think there is something greater about her upbringing, that is only apparent later on when Mary is about three months pregnant and visiting her cousin Elizabeth. I think we have another Naomi/Ruth relationship here, and certainly their prophetic gifts seem to spark each other up as they encourage each other in God.

Elizabeth either must have known that God was doing something wonderful in her cousin's life, or else she was just the sort of person you would turn to for shelter and advice in a difficult situation; either way their relationship is very precious. God help us stick around people who spark us up in the right way, iron does sharpen iron, but it works both ways: our friends really are like the buttons on an elevator, either taking us up or down. It may seem harsh to say it, but there may be some people who influence you that have been brought into your life by the enemy. On the flip side, God has put us in church families, which you might find a mixed blessing on occasions, but I would encourage you to let God use them in your life. It is his standard way, and who knows, that person who rubs you up the wrong way now, might one day provide the spark that ignites your gifting and ministry into a new realm.

Mary's Scripture Challenge

But what is most impressive to me is that Mary was a girl who knew the scriptures and this perhaps is the clue to her being freer than others, to be used by God.

It was the same for Timothy who *'from a child'* had *'known the holy scriptures'* (Tim 3:15). How do I know? Well, in Luke 1:46–55, we hear a song which burst forth from Mary's heart. The entire song occupies ten verses, and in the song Mary quoted from at least five Old Testament books, including the Psalms, Samuel, Isaiah, Micah, and Exodus. Every phrase of Mary's prophecy is filled with quotes from the scriptures. Of course just having access to the Bible is no guarantee of anything, but history shows only too clearly that the nations with populations who read a Bible in their own language shot ahead of those who didn't. Henry VIII had the national fleet on constant patrol to stop Tyndale's bibles coming to these shores, but he failed and his people gained a great treasure and by them so did the world. These men, with minds set free from the tyranny of manmade religion liberated vast swathes of men's thinking, not just in religion but in science and politics too. A brief comparison between their nations, and similar ones without a Bible reading public, will show darkness, oppression and poverty. I salute Mary's parents for a job well done, but none more so than introducing her to the words of life, for there is no other power I know that could give a girl such a heart as she had. The Bible can be read by most in 77 hours – and there is no high speed download for the ISDN generation. If we wish our usefulness or gifting to grow, we must plough deep into the Word. If you find this hard may I suggest you start to pray for a deeper hunger and see what the Lord does.

Mary's Discretion

One last thing that we might say about Mary is that she possessed the unusual ability of being able to keep things to herself. This precisely is what we did not see in Hezekiah in those last disastrous years of his life. After the visit of the shepherds, or the Magi two years later, she could (as all proud mothers are apt to do about their children) have bragged to her neighbours, and said, 'Why even angels sang on the night when my baby was born.' Like Jesus on the cross, Mary never answered her persecutors – who in Nazareth will have been many – by casting her 'pearls before swine'. 'You just wait until he's king of Israel, and then you'll pay.' Although Mary knew that all this was true, she did not say a word. Luke says, 'But Mary treasured all these words and pondered them in her heart' (Luke 2:19). Again after the episode at the age of twelve, when Jesus amazed the teachers of the law by his questions and answers, Mary could have boasted again and said, 'My boy really wowed the big hitters in Jerusalem you know, oh yes, he went down a storm with the theologians.' But instead, Luke says she 'kept all these sayings in her heart' (Luke 2:51). Twice in the second chapter Luke says that Mary possessed the ability of keeping things to herself. I am preaching hard to myself here, for we too should *'study to be quiet'* (1 Thess 4:11) and be *'slow to speak'* (James 1:19), for *'in a multitude of words, there wanteth not sin'* (Prov 10:19). And boy do I know it!

Joseph – A Model Servant and Husband

Bear One Another's Burdens

Mary only spends the first three months of that pregnancy with Elizabeth, and the day came when Mary walked back the sixty or so miles to Nazareth with a growing baby in her bulging tummy, and a growing anticipation in her heart of all that lay before her. Her journey would be one of supreme joy, tempered with the pain of ostracism and hatred. These could lead to her being stoned to death for fornication. As she approached the bottom of the hill and looked up at her home town, was she thinking about the stigma she must now share with her predecessors, Rahab and Ruth? And was the great question that occupied her rocky ascent, 'I wonder whether Joseph will share this trial with me, like Salmon and Boaz did for Rahab and Ruth? Oh Lord God I hope so, I do pray so, for I do not think I can face this all on my own.' Some things seem only just bearable if they can be faced with someone else, someone who understands, and is in it with you. I have been through some times in my life that seem even now to have been intolerable but for my wife, and all the grace God brought to me through her. Would Mary have to survive Nazareth alone, like her son would have to one day? It was a crushing isolation we have already studied in Psalm 69, but would Mary have to face this too?

To Look on Tempests

'Then Joseph her husband, being a just man, and not willing to make her a public example, was minded to put her away privily. But while he thought on these things, behold, the angel of the Lord appeared unto him in a dream, saying, Joseph, thou son of David, fear not to take unto thee Mary thy wife: for that which is conceived in her is of the Holy Ghost. And she shall bring forth a son, and thou shalt call his name JESUS: for he shall save his people from their sins. Now all this was done, that it might be fulfilled which was spoken of the Lord by the prophet, saying, Behold, a virgin shall be with child, and shall bring

forth a son, and they shall call his name Emmanuel, which being interpreted is, God with us. Then Joseph being raised from sleep did as the angel of the Lord had bidden him, and took unto him his wife: And knew her not till she had brought forth her firstborn son: and he called his name JESUS.' Matthew 1:19-25

Joseph says 'yes' to God, knowing what it will mean for him, for like Jean Valjean in *Les Miserables,* he will now share his wife's stigma. Small villages don't forget, but Joseph valued his obedience to the word of God more highly than the social riches of Nazareth. He would now be a laughing stock there but Mary will watch him silently bear it all for his love of *the Lord and her,* exquisitely modelling Shakespeare's sonnet on the nature of true love, 'Love is not love which alters when it alteration finds ... O no! it is an ever-fixed mark that looks on tempests and is never shaken ... Love alters not with his brief hours and weeks, but bears it out even to the edge of doom.' I said above 'his love for *the Lord* and her' because Joseph would need more than romantic love to see him through those difficult years. And – as C.S. Lewis reminds us in *The Four Loves* – that is not to underestimate or down value the powers of Eros – which are considerable. Consider if you will for a moment; romantic love's power to enable a lover to fulfil the whole law toward just one person, turning the most self-seeking individual, even if it is just briefly, into a veritable saint! Part of Eros' glory is that it will lead a man and woman to the altar of commitment, but as any married couple can testify, much more is needed to see the marriage through. If you are young, and recently smitten in love, I daresay you will disagree, for indeed 'Eros speaks like a god,' and at various times in history has been taken to be one. Eros' voice – those feelings and overwhelming impulses of the soul – will feel totally objective, indeed almost outside this world. From the medieval Courtly Love movement right through to Meat Loaf's great romantic ballads, we are invited to idolise – not the beloved, though that can happen too – but romantic love itself; to make an absolute out of it. But we are fools to look for absolutes in the flesh; for when these things seem most divine, it is then they are most susceptible to the demonic. (As Lewis also said in 'The Great Divorce'; it is from 'archangels, not mice that demons are made'.) In history, Eros has been a force for evil as well as good. It has caused many to sacrifice other duties, other good things, and even other loves for its sake – even leaving the lover who spurns family, friends and the duties of society with a righteous sense of merit in the sacrifice. Indeed Eros, unsupplemented by the other loves, can easily chain two tormentors together in a long and hateful marriage, both wanting love from the other and neither being able to give it; both determining to be free but allowing no freedom to the other.

In the end Eros is seen to need help to even survive, or be the thing it once was. The Scottish missionary Temple Gairdner penned it well before his marriage, (Ruth and I borrowed it as a reading in ours too), *"That I may come near to her, draw me nearer to thee than to her; that I may know her, make me to know thee more than her; that I may love her with the perfect love of a perfectly whole heart, cause me to love thee more than her most of all. Amen. Amen. That nothing may be between me and her, be thou between us, every moment. That we may be constantly together, draw us into separate loneliness with thyself, And when we meet breast to breast, my God, let it be on thine own. Amen. Amen."*

And when we, like Joseph and Gairdner have reined-in romantic love to where it can flourish, we will see it as the nearest love that we have to 'Love' himself. (i.e. God) That is to say, Eros becomes the best picture given to men and women of how God *does* feel for us, how we *should* feel towards him and how we *will* feel one day toward everyone else. That is no light thing is it? But to recapture the main point here; as for Joseph, for you and I to last out for our loved ones, in all that will come upon us, we must not commit that sin of making secondary things into primary things; it is a sure way to lose both.

Another Country

Joseph is a man who 'dwells with his spouse with consideration' (I Peter 3:7) and on being summoned to Bethlehem for the census, he does not leave her at home to suffer the slanders of misjudging neighbours, but takes her with him and treats her very gently in her time of need. Joseph is also an obedient citizen in submitting to the census, which many saw as an infringement of the civil liberties of their nationhood. Long gone are the days of Abraham where a man could wander the earth; now passports and taxes were the order of the day, the world had become small. Sounds strangely contemporary, doesn't it? Joseph stood up for Mary and the Lord, but he did not give his life for mere nationalism. In the film, *The English Patient*, the dying Katherine, whose lover is caught between the Allies and the Germans, writes about, 'Where the real countries are. Not boundaries drawn on maps with the names of powerful men. I know you'll come, carry me out to the Palace of Winds. That's what I've wanted: to walk in such a place with you. With friends, on an earth without maps.' In a like manner we must all check that our thinking reflects that of Abraham who went looking for an 'enduring city'. I think on the whole that European readers have had their nationalist zeal slowly ground out of them by two world wars and sixty years of political conditioning; the same might not be said for those in America. There is danger here for us; many young men who could have been Jesus' most ardent disciples chose to be nationalist zealots instead, and we must not make the same mistake.

There is nothing wrong with a right 'love of country' and though it has become a 'demon' in recent history, it can similarly be a safeguard against other errors. (This will be explored in part of 'First Contact', the sequel of this book.) God has come to *save* and call you *not* out of your nation but out of this world's god-rejecting ethos. That *calling out* will seem more acute as times reach the end, but for now our dual citizenship must be expressed in 'obeying every ordinance of man' unless it directly violates our conscience.

Although the scriptures give us only a few glimpses of Joseph, they tell us he was a kind man and a loving father. Perhaps no greater compliment can be paid to him than that of Jesus himself, who when he gave mankind a better conception of the love and character of God, used the term *Father* to express our creator's loving relationship towards us. Even though Joseph fathered a number of sons and daughters by Mary (Mark 6:3), his 'adopted' son was always cherished, loved and disciplined (literally discipled) with the true love of a father. Those other sons were present at Pentecost so we must assume that post-resurrection they would go on to be members in the early church and certainly James was later an elder, letter writer and martyr. (Many also credit the author of Jude's letter as being the half-brother of Jesus too.)

All this we must partly credit to Joseph and Mary's combined parenting. When I daily see the shrapnel caused by fatherlessness or warped fatherhood, I can think of no better accolade for Joseph than to have his adopted son who, even despite being a refugee in Egypt and all that unsettled time, should grow to understand God in this way. Here is a challenge for the men, a real challenge, to model the same love and paternal stability so that our children can accept that revelation without lifelong difficulty.

Home for Christmas

A surface reading of the gospels might make you think that Jesus went back to Nazareth after that episode with Simeon and Anna at the temple. It does say in Luke that after this he went back to Nazareth. This is not untrue but it is not the whole truth. For example, if you were told that I had married Ruth and went to live at a mountain ranch in the Lake District, that would be true though we also lived in Maryport for nine years first. Joseph actually took Mary and Jesus back to Bethlehem for possibly as long as two years after the Simeon incident, before being warned to escape to Egypt. That is why Herod had boys under the age of two executed in keeping with the time when the star first appeared. The wise men were sent to Bethlehem and there they saw an infant (Greek: Paidion); it was only the shepherds that had seen the baby (Greek: Brefos).

This leaves us with the question, why didn't they go home?

And again I think we can see the largeness and tenderness of Joseph's heart towards his young wife and child, for we must assume he would not expose her to ostracism just for the sake of his career. It must have seemed very right to have their first real home in the town of Bethlehem where Salmon and Rahab first settled, where Ruth and Boaz were so happy. Jesus probably learned to walk on the same stones that they and David trod all those years before. Perhaps they lived in the same house that David or Boaz had known; perhaps Zachariah and Elizabeth brought their little Johnny round to visit. There is so much we shall not know until that great day one thing we can say, however is that whatever respite they knew in Bethlehem, it would be short lived. Not only would they become refugees but also they would never be able to go back to Bethlehem, even though they both wanted to. They were heading that way but an angel appeared to redirect them back north, north to the hard faces, north to the cold stares. It was not what Joseph wanted for Jesus, but it was what his real Father wanted – that Jesus would come through all of that untainted, a true Nazarene. Nathaniel asks the question, can anything good come from Nazareth? And you might look at the harshness of your situation, or childhood, and ask the same thing. The answer is yes, yes, yes of course it can. Joseph came out of Nazareth, Mary did, Jesus' brother James did, and look what treasure God refined in there in his own Son, the perfect, spotless sacrifice.

Friend, you are not forgotten, your life can be glorious if you submit it to him. Going back there for Joseph and Mary, was as the Valley of Humiliation was to Christian in *Pilgrim's Progress*; and when the Lord leads us to the 'Nazareths' of our trials, let our hearts echo Bunyan's character, 'Rejoice not against me, O mine enemy: when I fall, I shall arise; when I sit in darkness, the LORD shall be a light unto me.' (Micah 7:8).

Apollyon may be all over you and think he will destroy you in your Nazareth but know this, it is here that angels will fight for you; it is here that the prince of that heavenly city will be 'your shield and your exceeding great reward'. The only danger for pilgrims is that fear may make them flee and so expose their backs. For Christian had no armour for his back, and neither do we, according to Ephesians 6, so never retreat or surrender to this pressure; the promise is to those who overcome, like Joseph and Mary. The will of God was done, not in spite of, but because of them. Cometh the hour, cometh the man and woman after God's own heart; may it be so for us too, for this is not the end of our story, just the beginning of the greatest story ever told and – as they say, the rest is history.

Song of the Quiet Man

Joseph's song to Mary before they leave for Egypt

(From 'THE LINE' album, words and music by Henry Brooks)

It gets me in my guts when I remember
those things they said to you, no right to crush your heart
People we loved, who'd known us since we were born
wouldn't hear us out, all closed the door ...

But I tell you right now, that I'm going nowhere, going to stand by you,
for what the Lord has said, I'm sure that he will do
though sticks and stones may hurt, more than I'll ever show,
I will be strong when it's like you and me against the world

I've loved you Mary since I can remember,
just so pretty with your hair like that and those eyes just for me
we'd planned this home of ours since we were kids,
but the Lord had other plans for us and I would not have missed this for the
world

And I would not have missed you, to see your childhood's prayer,
to have God's will be done to see his hand laid bare
Just so humbled to be yours, to share this trial with you,
my dearest, precious girl and me against the world

Well I'd always said this thing we got's a one off,
now look at our baby boy cutting his first teeth
Zach and Liz brought little Johnny round just the other day,
think he'll be walking soon then there'll be no stopping him, puts me in mind

of all that's been said about these boys of ours,
that they belong to God, are raised up for this hour
And we'll have to let them go, to find their destiny,
to do the will of God when it's him and them against the world

I couldn't take you back to Nazareth, not after what you've been through
But in this town where Ruth and Boaz reaped all that Rahab had sowed
it seems right to be here though my wage can't afford,
all that I'd want for you but Jesus, he makes up for it all

and I wouldn't have the world for this happiness I know
the day he called me Abba, the day that my tears flowed
God entrusted him to us, who's more precious than gold,
frankincense and myrrh or anything in this rotten world

And now the angel says we got to split this town, no settled place to for our
tired heads, no peace for these weary bones
so like tramps to Egypt and don't know if we're coming back,
on the run once more, it's him and us against the world

(Musical epilogue to match the initial song about Abraham and Sarah)

So pack the bags, I'll take him in my arms, well get out on the trail tonight
trade what we cannot keep for what we cannot earn, we've got nothing to lose
but our pride
I don't know all that he wants from me and you, but it's to another country
we're to go
so come my love and kneel with me and let's pledge ourselves to him that
we've begun to see and say
we'll follow this God cos see what he's like, prove every word he says is true
we'll follow him though our flesh is crying out to stop and the voice in our
heads says it doesn't look good
though the family says we're crazy, our neighbours say we're cursed, let's
follow him and soon we will see, that somewhere on this road to our
promised land, we hold the one who'll set this whole world free.

Life Application Devotion

Chapter 14 – Into the War Zone

- In this last devotional we leave Joseph, Mary and Jesus, as God directed them back to the last place they would have chosen; Nazareth.
- Where is your 'Nazareth'; the place where you face slander and ostracism for Christ's sake, that place or situation you fear and from which you recoil?
- List your specific feelings and fears about this.
- Would you be willing to live or minister there if Christ called you to?

Prayer: (Start with thanksgiving & praise to God for his son's incarnation and great love for this world.) My Merciful Saviour, what can I say to you; you who left the security and comfort of heaven to rescue sinners like me and even wash the feet of those who would betray you? Lord forgive any hardness, fear or anxiety I have allowed to take root in my life. I confess that the safest, most blessed place for me to be is exactly where you call me. Where you guide, you provide and as I step out all my needs; spiritual, emotional and financial will be met according to your riches. If that is to the valley of humiliation then Lord I know that I will walk a well trodden path in company with you, only let my lips never renounce what my heart now affirms; that 'the Lord is my shepherd, I shall not be in want'. Lord is there *anywhere* you want me to go? Is there *anyone* you want me to love today? Only give the command and I will obey.

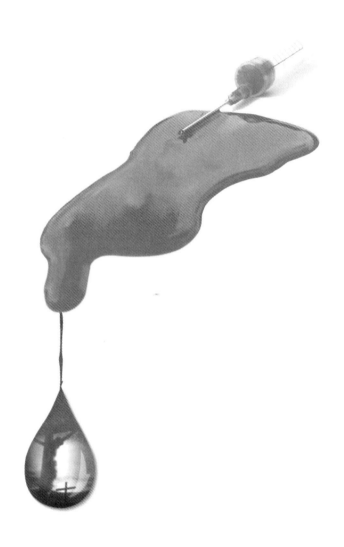

Conclusion

A Brief Lesson in Road Construction

> 'As it is written in the book of the words of Isaiah the prophet, the voice of one crying in the wilderness, "Grade a road for the Master, make sure the surface is well compacted and straight. Fill in your low points and cut down your high; straighten your crooked bits, and level out any rough bits and potholes; Only then will all your family and society be able to gape at God's rescue plan in action".' Luke 3:4-6

At the time of writing I am the landscape consultant for perhaps one of the largest leisure developments in the UK. Quite frankly it scares the life out of me but the Lord seems to delight in dangling me in situations far beyond my comfort zone. I, in turn, try to bounce the favour by passing as much stress and decision making back into his court, none more so than when it comes to the client meetings we've been having this year. It was the morning of one such meeting this summer when I prayed, 'Okay Lord, you know I'm meeting these big wigs from London this afternoon, I've designed a great road system making economic use of the existing contours but I just feel I need something that would really wow them, can you help?'

The project is one vast holiday village with 450 lodges, lakes, a leisure centre and sports facilities. I had designed two very neat one-way systems with subsidiary feeder roads. These feeders were about 70% of all the roads and they were for slower traffic to get people to their lodges. The Lord gave me the idea, 'Hey, why not make them Macadamised gravel roads? But of course, why didn't I think of it before; they're easier on the eye, easier on the feet and most importantly, they are a fraction of the cost. In one swoop I could save the client nearly a million pounds, they're gonna love me!'

So I turned up with my laptop at the hotel where the directors were staying and gave them a lecture on the history of road building and how knowing it, could save them buckets of cash. 'You see the French used to dig down really deep and pile loads of rocks into the base of the road to give it stability,' I announced to the project team that afternoon, as we sat around a low table at a nearby hotel. They looked up, eyes showing their something between alarm and bemusement at this impromptu history lesson. I faltered for a moment but then pressed on, 'but then this thrifty Scottish dude came along (called John MacAdam) and said, "Wait a minute, why all this waste in excavation and new stone? I've found that so long as you can make the earth dry, like in summertime, you can have a stable road surface for a fraction of the cost." Now, the way MacAdam kept the ground under the road dry was to seal the top with small stones and dust. This was fine until motor cars were invented and their speed whipped away the dust seal. That was when they changed the sealing agent from dust to tar, hence Tarmac or Tarmacadam.' Now they looked impressed and so I hit them with the big one, 'Basically gents, most of the roads on our site are for very slow moving vehicles, they don't need to be tar-macadamised, we can save a hundred times my fee by just using a sealed gravel system.'

Their faces broke out into broad grins and they ordered me a drink, we were on.

In fact the Lord helped me wow them at another meeting by further introducing them to ground stabilization technology (yes, I know it sounds riveting but bear with me). With this system all you have to do is strip the topsoil and grade the surface to how you want your road. Then you send this big machine along it and, hey presto, it churns up the subsoil, mixes cement into it and then compacts it all in one motion. No excavation, no storage of subsoil, no bringing in thousands of tonnes of aggregate, for £5.20 per square metre you get a construction traffic base which can then be dressed with Tarmac or gravel later on when you're finished. This represented a further 60% saving on costs for the client, who I hope remembers this when I come to bill him.

The reason I mention all this road construction is because for ourselves and for our generation we are the ones who 'prepare a way for the Lord'. That might sound a bit 'Armenianist' or man-centred to some but if we take the scriptures at their literal meaning then we see the onus is on us, i.e. this is something we *do* and not just talk about.

The western Christian church has, by and large, produced a rutted road upon which the word of God has come to its twentieth-century culture. It is rutted and potholed for want of a proper seal. The waters of humanism and worldliness have so soaked the structure that it can hardly bear the vehicles of personal change, let alone support the heavy traffic of national revival. The radical work of draining those influence from our minds, families and churches has been a subtext in this book (so have some examples of how to 're-engineer a sufficient road seal' that can repel future water).

Some remedies mentioned might seem extreme, or just 'over the top', though if you have read this far, then I guess that you might be the sort of serious person who is willing to reconsider your life, your family, your children's education, your future and pray for a right understanding – a true frame of reference – solely aligned on the words of God. I may be wrong or imbalanced on some of these issues, perhaps even not radical enough. Please don't make me the measure of anything, that would be idolatrous, check out the scriptures and be fully persuaded by God yourself; it is to him you must answer. The need for radical holiness has never been greater and the occasion never more acute.

The generation that will face the great tribulation may not be far away. If the church does not produce Christians who see what we call *civilization* for what it is – the way Abraham and Zerubbabel saw it – then how will they have the backbone to face the fiery trials of those times? What we have talked of in sweeping spiritual generalities – indeed what we have seen in the lead characters of this book, and the choices they made – will come upon that whole generation with cruel and crushing certainty. Upon what will they base their certainty when they can no longer go to the supermarket, the bank, the school; when they cannot own a house, a car, watch 'X Factor', cannot educate their own children; even worship their own God? It will be the dividing point of church history – to most church people ' receiving the mark of the beast' will seem like common sense; 'how else can we be safe?' they would say. But even though choosing to be part of that financial system may look reasonable, normal, practical, it will cost them their salvation (see Rev 14:9–10). That is why I say it is the dividing point for there will be no going back at that point; you're either in or out.

Thinking of the day when he will come to execute vengeance on western, indeed all antichrist civilization, Jesus asked, 'Will the son of man find faith on the earth?' (Luke 18:8) Indeed will he be able to tell the difference between the world and us, the other godless world systems and our 'ministries'? Handel's Hallelujah Chorus is taken from Revelation – at the moment the world stock exchange collapses! Can we say at that point that we will be cheering then? It is a sobering thought and there is much to do.

The call of Jesus in Revelation 3:20 is to each member of the local church, *'if any man hear my voice, and open the door, I will come in to him, and will sup with him, and he with me.'* My encouragement to you is not to waste too much energy trying to reform churches or denominations; many have tried and failed. I am not saying particularly that you should change your church even, as much as *change* yourself in it – or more accurately, allow God to change you. There may be some reading who need to achieve some sort of 'exodus' from their situation, as we have seen in this book. John Wesley was one such man, but he would eventually have the wisdom to challenge individual men to 'get on fire and men will come and watch you burn'.

This has really been the thrust of all I have written, to tempt you to the precipice of an adventure with Yahweh, to truly follow the Lord Jesus Christ; to have a one man, one woman revival yourself. It's no good whining about all that's wrong in your church or in your nation; that is too obvious, too easy and besides, everyone else is already doing that. What the world is looking for, what it needs more than the next Aston Martin or teen idol, is to see you and me full of the Holy Spirit and living fully both in, and for, the heavenly civilization that will replace this one.

The call to you and me is to be the 'any man' who hears his voice and to offer ourselves as living sacrifices to him. I do not say we can do this all at once, and I certainly don't want to lay a religious burden on you, friend, but please pray and fast about what you have read – and allow the Holy Spirit to give voice to the yearning in your heart that hungers for more.

Days before this book went to press, I was chatting outside church with an older gentleman (about something quite unrelated to this book) when he started to tell me what he had discovered in Matthews's genealogy of the Messiah. (I was all ears!) 'It says that there should be three lots of fourteen generations and yet there is *only thirteen* in the last set – there should be one more generation after Jesus!' Suddenly it all slotted into place – 'God's big story and our place in it' – wasn't just a catchy strap–line for the book, it really was what God wanted to say all along. And I knew where the supporting scripture was too: '*he will see <u>his offspring</u> and prolong his days, and the will of the LORD will prosper in his hand. After he has suffered, he will see the light of life and be satisfied; by his knowledge <u>my righteous servant will justify many</u>, and he will bear their iniquities*' (Is 53:10–11) That's right friend, *we* are that missing fourteenth generation in THE LINE; the spiritual offspring of Jesus, purchased by his blood and *born again* into the family of God. What can we say to such a truth? Well, if it echoes the sentiment with which we started this book (the cry within the heart of D.L. Moody) then so much the better.

> '*The world has yet to see what God can do with a man fully consecrated to him. By God's help, I aim to be that man.*'

Amen and Amen

Other Books by this Author:

The Will Houston Mysteries *published by* PiQUANT editions

'..an inspirational story..'
Bear Grylls

'...How refreshing to find a good wholesome story.... set in Cumbria.'
Hunter Davies

- The Shoulders of Giants (Dec 2010)
- The Old School Secrets (Oct 2011)
- The Cradle Snatchers (2012)
- The Student Jihad (2013?)

COMING SOON from PRAVDA

PRESS

REVOLUTIONARY BOOKS

Become a Facebook fan of 'Henry Brooks' for further updates or visit our website www.Giant-Shoulders.com/*Pravda*

First Contact with companion Album (2013)
Written as the sequel & natural extension of THE LINE; this book charts the encounters of those who were *'eye witnesses of His Majesty'* in the 1st century A.D. What did it mean for those men and women who finally stood before the Creator God? And what can it mean for us in the 21st century when we see what they saw?

John Mark (2012)
Chariot races, mortal combat and daring escapes are all part of this 1st century A.D. epic; (a romantic adventure very much in 'the Robe' and 'Ben Hur' genre). For now you can live and feel the New Testament years through the eyes of the Gospel writer: John Mark; following him, Paul, Barnabas through many adventures in Alexandria, Jerusalem, Ephesus and Rome.

'he will see <u>his offspring</u> and prolong his days,
and the will of the LORD will prosper in his hand.
After he has suffered, he will see the light of life
and be satisfied; by his knowledge
<u>my righteous servant will justify many</u>,
and he will bear their iniquities'

(Is 53:10–11)

Notes

Notes